高等院校实验教学示范中心实验教材

生物化学实验技术

双语版，第2版

主　编　王含彦　陈建业

副主编　易　芳　杨映雪　宋永砚　郭冬梅

编　委（按姓氏汉语拼音排序）

陈　竞　陈建业　陈瑾歆　郭冬梅

蒋　振　任勇刚　宋永砚　汤建才

唐　珍　王含彦　杨映雪　易　芳

张蜀敏　张秀云

科学出版社

北　京

内 容 简 介

《生物化学实验技术》（双语版，第 2 版）为满足普通高等院校生物化学实验教学和双语教学的需要编写而成。全书分为四章，选编了 25 个实验。前三章从基础实验技术到综合性实验，内容覆盖了当前生物化学研究中常用的方法和技术，使学生能得到较为系统的训练。第四章设计性实验部分，旨在培养学生的科研思维和应用所学技术开展科学研究的能力。

本教材适用于普通高校生物化学实验教学，可供生命科学、医药卫生相关专业的教师参考。

图书在版编目（CIP）数据

生物化学实验技术：双语版：汉英对照 /王含彦，陈建业主编. —2 版. —北京：科学出版社，2022. 1

高等院校实验教学示范中心实验教材

ISBN 978-7-03-067946-8

Ⅰ.①生… Ⅱ.①王… ②陈… Ⅲ.①生物化学-实验-医学院校-教材-汉、英 Ⅳ.①Q5-33

中国版本图书馆 CIP 数据核字（2021）第 007261 号

责任编辑：朱 华 / 责任校对：宁辉彩
责任印制：赵 博 / 封面设计：陈 敬

科学出版社 出版
北京东黄城根北街 16 号
邮政编码: 100717
http://www.sciencep.com
保定市中画美凯印刷有限公司印刷
科学出版社发行 各地新华书店经销
*
2015 年 6 月第 一 版 开本：787×1092 1/16
2022 年 1 月第 二 版 印张：10 1/2
2025 年 1 月第十一次印刷 字数：249 000

定价：45.00 元

（如有印装质量问题，我社负责调换）

前　言

21世纪是生命科学的世纪，生物化学是生命科学领域中最核心的基础学科和最活跃的研究领域之一。随着生物化学实验方法和技术的不断发展和完善，生物化学在生命科学的各个学科和领域中得到了迅速而广泛的应用。特别是在医学领域中，生物化学和在其基础上发展起来的分子生物学方法和技术已经成为揭示疾病本质、服务疾病诊断和治疗的崭新手段，对基础医学研究和临床诊断治疗都产生了深远影响。

医学生物化学实验主要是以生命科学问题为导向、以实验方法和研究内容为主线，在分子水平上通过科学实验手段来探讨人体正常生理状态下的代谢规律与疾病状态下发生的异常变化，从而为疾病的预防、治疗和预后提供科学的依据和指导。为适应基础医学教学改革的需要，本教材在继承生物化学实验核心内容的基础上，更加强调学科间的交叉融合，更加重视新技术的应用，更加注重对学生创新能力的培养。其目的是在对学生进行系统、规范的医学生物化学实验技能训练的同时，强调对学生动手能力、科研素质、探索精神和创新能力的培养，为学生提供一个理论联系实际、大胆实践操作和积极思考的舞台，使学生通过实验的锻炼，掌握医学生物化学实验的基本原理、基本方法和技术，增强科学思维、创新意识、独立思考、综合分析和解决问题的能力。

本教材分为四章。第一章为生物化学常规技术训练，主要介绍生物化学实验常用的四大技术——离心技术、分光光度法、电泳技术和层析技术，为学生进行具体的实验操作提供基本的技术支撑。第二章为基础性实验，主要包括3个蛋白质实验、4个酶实验、2个核酸实验和2个代谢性实验，以帮助学生加深对生物化学基础理论和核心内容的理解。第三章为综合性实验，共计8个实验，涉及蛋白质、核酸的分离、纯化与鉴定，以及物质代谢与调节，重点培养学生对所学理论知识和多种实验技能的综合运用能力、独立使用能力以及综合分析和解决问题的能力。第四章为2个设计性实验，着重培养学生的科研思维、创新意识与科研能力。最后附上生物化学实验基本知识，介绍实验室的一些基本的安全常识与防护知识要点，使学生养成良好的从事实验工作和科学研究的基本规范。本教材使用中英两种文字编写，有利于提高教师的双语教学水平和学生的英语水平，同时亦可作为留学生的生物化学实验教材，提高教师指导留学生实验的教学水平。

本教材编写人员均为教学、科研的一线教师，他们长期从事生物化学的理论和实验教学，本教材是他们多年教学实践经验的总结和心得体会，殷切希望同行专家和学生在教材使用过程中对本教材提出宝贵意见，以便不断地完善内容，提高本教材的质量和水平。

《生物化学实验技术》（双语版）编委会

2018年10月于四川南充

目　　录

第一章　生物化学常规技术训练

实验 1　蛋白质的沉淀和分离——离心技术

【实验目的】

1. 掌握离心分离的原理及操作程序。
2. 熟悉普通离心机的安装调试、安全使用和日常保全。
3. 了解普通离心机主机的基本构件和工作原理。

【实验原理】

蛋白质溶液加入有机溶剂如乙醇，则蛋白质会沉淀析出，因为有机溶剂可使蛋白质胶体颗粒脱去水化膜。溶液中若加入少量中性盐如 Na_2SO_4，则沉淀更加迅速。

【器材与试剂】

1. 器材

（1）低速离心机。

（2）离心管、药匙、刻度移液管。

2. 试剂

（1）蛋白质溶液：称取牛血清白蛋白 0.5g，溶于 100mL 蒸馏水，配成 5mg/mL 的蛋白质溶液。

（2）95%乙醇。

（3）Na_2SO_4 粉末。

【实验操作】

1. 取一支离心管，加入 1mL 蛋白质溶液，再加入少量 Na_2SO_4 粉末，摇动使溶解。
2. 向离心管缓慢加入 2mL 95%乙醇，剧烈振荡，观察有无沉淀析出，之后 4000r/min 离心 5min，使蛋白质迅速沉淀并收集沉淀蛋白质。

【思考题】

1. 影响离心效率的因素有哪些？
2. 普通离心机的主要应用范围有哪些？

离心技术训练

一、离心机的基本原理

1. 离心力及其作用　离心技术是分离核酸和蛋白质等生物大分子最常用的方法之一。

当悬浮液绕轴旋转时，悬浮中的微粒就同时受到离心力和介质浮力的双向作用，微粒的运动轨迹取决于所受合力的方向。根据物理学原理推导可知：

$$F_{合}=F_{离}-F_{介}=V\times\rho\times4\pi^2N^2r/3600-V\times\sigma\times4\pi^2N^2r/3600=4\pi^2N^2r/3600\times V\times(\rho-\sigma)$$

式中，$F_{合}$表示微粒所受合力；$F_{离}$表示微粒所受离心力；$F_{介}$表示微粒所受的介质浮力；V表示微粒的体积；N表示每分钟的转数；r表示微粒至转轴的距离；ρ与σ分别表示微粒与其介质的密度。显然，当$\rho=\sigma$时，$F_{合}=0$，微粒受力平衡，故将维持距转轴恒定的距离转动，也就不可能被分离开；当$\rho<\sigma$时，$F_{合}<0$，微粒主要受向心力作用，故而将向转轴方向移动，直至浮到介质表面；当$\rho>\sigma$时，$F_{合}>0$，微粒主要受离心力作用而向远离转轴方向移动，直至沉淀到容器底部。因此，$\rho>\sigma$是微粒从悬浮液中进行离心分离的基本条件。使用普通离心机的根本目的就在于使这样的微粒从悬浮液中分离出来。

从理论上讲，凡是能通过离心分离的微粒在悬浮液静置时，受重力与浮力的共同作用也能自动沉降而得以分离，只是分离所需时间较长，效果较差，沉降本领较弱。一般常用相对离心力（RCF）的大小来表示离心分离的本领强弱。

$$\text{RCF}=F_{合}/F'_{合}$$

$$F'_{合}=V\times\rho\times g-V\times\sigma\times g=V\times(\rho-\sigma)\times g$$

$$\text{RCF}=4\pi^2N^2r/3600g$$

式中，$F_{合}$表示悬浮微粒在离心分离时所受的合力；$F'_{合}$表示悬浮微粒在静置分离时所受的合力；g表示重力加速度。

只要调节N或/和r就可影响RCF的值，从而改变其离心分离本领。

2. 离心力与作用时间的积累效应 微粒在悬浮液中被分离的速度快慢除与转动的转数大小有关外，还与离心时间长短有关，即离心力作用于微粒上具有时间积累效应。

由此可见，对同一悬浮液可以在较低转速、较长时间得到与较高转速、较短时间相同的分离效果。但是，若转速相差太大，则会受扩散作用影响而使较低转速离心的分离效果下降。

二、离心机的组成

根据具体的实验要求选择水平式离心机或斜角式离心机。普通离心机分水平式和斜角式两种。实验室常用的离心机主要由离心机盖、离心腔及套筒、显示表盘及调节按钮、电源和平衡附件等部分组成。其中，以下三个部分涉及安全问题，需要特别注意。

1. 离心套筒 检查离心套筒内是否有橡皮缓冲胶垫，胶垫上若附着碎玻璃等杂物应清除。

2. 电源 电源应选择与离心机使用说明书相吻合的电源，电源插座必须有地线以保证离心安全。若实验室没有合适的电源，则应重新安装电源线，电源插座应靠近离心机以方便操作。

3. 平衡附件

（1）天平：普通离心机离心以前，需将转子上的负载平衡。

（2）烧杯与滴管：烧瓶用来盛配平液，滴管用来吸配平液进行配平。

三、离 心 操 作

离心之前应检查离心机安放是否平稳，转轴是否牢固，润滑是否良好，套筒内有无异物，离心机盖能否锁紧等。完成以上准备工作后，应先让离心机进行空载运转，观察空载运转情况是否正常，在无异常时方可进行离心。

（1）调平称量天平。将置于离心机对称位置上的离心套筒、离心管及内盛物配平，相差不超过 0.1g。

（2）将平衡好的离心套筒放于离心机对称位置。

（3）检查离心机是否安放平稳。

（4）关上离心机盖，锁牢。

（5）插上电源插头，打开离心机开关。

（6）调节离心转速和时间。

（7）离心完毕，关离心机，拔下电源插头，任离心机自停。

（8）待离心机完全停止转动后，打开机盖，取出离心管。

（9）清洁离心套筒、离心管及离心腔，关盖。

四、注 意 事 项

（1）离心前必须将放置于对称位置上的离心套筒、离心管及离心液进行精确平衡，重量差不超过 0.1g。对于高速和超速离心机，不仅要求重量平衡，而且要求配平液的密度与离心液的密度相等，以达到力矩平衡。

（2）离心机安放要求水平、稳固，转轴润滑良好。

（3）离心管盛液不宜超过 3/4。

（4）离心机盖应盖紧、锁牢。离心完毕应关离心机、拔掉电源插头任机自停，严禁用手助停，以免伤人损机，使沉淀泛起。

（5）注意离心机的保养。离心机使用完毕，擦净离心腔、套筒及机座。经常做好离心机的防潮、防过冷、防过热、防腐蚀药品污染。

（6）离心过程若发现异常情况应立即拔下电源插头，然后再进行检查。如听到碎玻璃渣声响，可能是试管被打碎，应重新更换试管。

（唐　珍　陈建业）

Chapter I Routine Technical Training in Biochemistry

Experiment 1 Precipitation and Separation of Proteins —Operation of Centrifugation

【Purposes】

1. To master the basic principle and operational procedures of centrifugal separation.
2. To understand the installation and debugging, safe use and daily preservation of the ordinary centrifuge.
3. To know the basic components and working principle of the ordinary centrifuge.

【Principles】

Proteins do not dissolve in some organic solvents, so proteins can be precipitated if the organic solvent (such as alcohol) reaches a certain concentration. Organic solvents decrease protein stability by the dehydration of protein colloidal particles in water solution. Precipitation will be quicker and more complete when a small amount of neutral salts (such as Na_2SO_4) is also added to the solution.

【Apparatus and Reagents】

1. Apparatus

(1) Low-speed centrifuge.

(2) Centrifugal tube, medicine spoon and measuring pipet.

2. Reagents

(1) Protein solution: Dissolve 0.5g standard bovine serum albumin (BSA) in 100mL dH_2O to get a 5mg/mL protein solution.

(2) 95% ethanol.

(3) Na_2SO_4 powder.

【Procedures】

(1) Add 1mL protein solution in a centrifugal tube, then add a small amount of Na_2SO_4 powder and shake it to dissolve.

(2) Then add 2mL 95% ethanol slowly, shake it violently, and observe whether there is precipitate formed. Centrifugate the solution at 4,000r/min for 5min and collect the precipitate.

【Questions】

1. List the factors that affect centrifugation efficiency.
2. What are the main applications of ordinary centrifuges?

Introduction of Centrifugation

Ⅰ. Principles of the centrifuge

1. Centrifugal force and its function Centrifugation is one of the preferred methods for separating various biomacromolecules, such as nucleic acids and proteins. When the suspension rotates around the centrifuge axis, the suspended particles will be affected by the centrifugal force and medium buoyancy at the same time. The movement trajectory of the suspended particles depends on the direction of the resultant force. According to the principle of physics, it leads to the following physical formula:

$$F_R=F_C-F_M=V\rho\times 4\pi^2N^2r/3,600-V\sigma\times 4\pi^2N^2r/3,600=4\pi^2N^2r/3,600\times V(\rho-\sigma)$$

where F_R represents the resultant force; F_C represents the centrifugal force; F_M represents the medium buoyancy; V represents the particle volume; N represents the rotation number per minute; r represents the distance from the particles to the axis; ρ and σ represent the particle density and the medium density respectively.

Obviously, it can be concluded as follows from the above formula. First, when $\rho=\sigma$ and $F_R=0$, all kinds of forces loading on the particles are balanced, the particles will maintain a fixed distance and a constant speed rotating around the centrifuge axis and can not be separated. Second, when $\rho<\sigma$ and $F_R<0$, the particles are mainly subjected by the effect of centrifugal force and will move in the direction of centrifuge axis until they float to the medium surface. Third, when $\rho>\sigma$ and $F_R>0$, the particles are mainly subjected by the effect of centrifugal force and will move away from the direction of the centrifuge axis until they precipitate to the bottom of the centrifuge tube. Therefore, $\rho>\sigma$ is the basic condition of the centrifugal separation particles from suspension. The main purpose of using the ordinary centrifuge is to separate such particles from the suspension.

Theoretically, all the particles that can be separated by the centrifugal method, can also be separated by gravity automatically under the action of gravity and buoyancy together, but it results in more time and poor efficiency. The relative centrifugal force (RCF) is commonly used to represent the centrifugal separation ability.

$$\text{RCF}=F_R/F'_R$$

$$F'_R=V\rho\times g-V\sigma\times g=V\times g\times(\rho-\sigma)$$

$$\text{RCF}=4\pi^2N^2r/3,600g$$

where F_R represents the resultant force when the suspended particles are separated by the centrifuge; F'_R represents the resultant force when the suspended particles are separated by standing; g represents gravitational acceleration. The RCF value can be affected by the regulation of N and/or r, which result in the change of the centrifugal separation ability.

2. Accumulation effects of the centrifugal force and the time The separation speed of suspended particles in the suspension is not only related to the rotating number but also to the centrifugation time. That is to say, there are some time accumulation effects of the centrifugal force on the suspended particles. The same separation efficiency can be achieved by the centrifuge at a higher speed for a shorter period of time or a lower speed for a longer period of time. But if the rotating speed is too slow, the diffusion will weaken the separation efficiency.

Ⅱ. Components of the centrifuge

There are various centrifuges for the separation of different particles. For example, a horizontal or angle centrifuge is selected according to the experimental requirements. All the centrifuges consist of centrifugal lids, centrifugal chambers and bushes, display panels and adjustable buttons, centrifugal power supplies and appendixes for balance, etc. Among them, the following three parts involve security issues, which need special attention.

1. Centrifugal bushes Centrifugal bushes should be checked to make sure the rubber cushions are inside. If there are broken glasses or other debris inside the bush, they should be cleared completely.

2. Centrifugal power supplies Power supplies should be selected and used according to the instruction of the centrifuge. The socket must have power grounding for safety. The power line should be installed if no proper power is available in the lab, and the socket should be installed near the centrifuge in order to operate easily.

3. Appendixes for balance

(1) Balance: The load on the rotor is needed to balance before centrifuge.

(2) Beaker and dropper: The beaker is used for holding the balance solution, and the dropper is used to keep balance.

Ⅲ. Operation of the centrifuge

Before centrifuging, examine the centrifuge and the following staff: the stability of the centrifuge, the firmness and lubrication of the shaft, the absence of foreign matters inside the bushes, the lock of the centrifugal lid. After the examination, do a test run and observe the centrifuge without samples, and the centrifugation is carried out if everything is normal.

(1) Balance: After the balance is balanced, put the centrifugal bush and centrifugal tubes with samples at the symmetrical positions. The weight difference between the two opposite centrifugal tubes should not exceed 0.1g.

(2) Put the balanced centrifugal bush at the symmetrical positions of the centrifuge.

(3) Check the stability of the centrifuge.

(4) Close and lock the centrifugal lid tightly.

(5) Insert the power plug and turn on the switch.

(6) Set up the speed and time of the centrifugation.

(7) When the centrifugation is finished, shut down the centrifuge, take off the power plug and let the centrifuge stop automatically.

(8) When the centrifuge is stopped completely, open the lid and take out the tubes.

(9) Clean the centrifugal bush, tubes and the chamber, and close the lid finally.

Ⅳ. Notes

(1) The centrifugal bush, tubes and solutions at the symmetrical positions must be balanced accurately. The weight difference between the two opposite centrifugal tubes should not exceed 0.1g. For the high-speed centrifuge and the ultracentrifuge, not only the weight but also the density of the samples should be similar in order to achieve the balance of the moment of force.

(2) The centrifuge should be placed horizontally and stably, and the shaft should run smoothly with good lubricating property.

(3) The solution in centrifugal tubes should be less than three quarters of the full volume.

(4) The centrifugal lid should be closed and locked tightly. When the centrifugation is finished, turn off the centrifuge, unplug the power, and let it stop automatically. It is prohibited to stop the machine by hand, which may cause accidents and stir the precipitates.

(5) Pay attention to the maintenance of the centrifuge. After use, clear the chamber, sleeves and engine base. Keep the centrifuge from moisture, extreme temperature and corrosive solution.

(6) Unplug the power immediately if there is an abnormal situation in the process of the centrifugation. Check again to figure out the problem. For example, the tube may be broken if a glass sound is heard. In this condition, the tube should be replaced.

(Tang Zhen, Chen Jianye)

实验 2　硫酸铜的浓度测定——分光光度法

【实验目的】

1. 掌握 721A 型分光光度计的使用方法。
2. 熟悉朗伯-比尔定律及其计算公式的推导和应用。
3. 了解 721A 型分光光度计的构造和工作原理。

【实验原理】

光的本质是电磁波。不同的光有不同的波长。肉眼可见的彩色光称为可见光，波长范围在 400～750nm，小于 400nm 的光线为紫外光，大于 750nm 的光线为红外光。

同一物质对不同波长的光吸收能力不同，不同物质对同一波长的光吸收能力也不同，这称为物质对光的选择性吸收。所以物质呈现出的颜色正是它对光选择性吸收所产生的人的视觉反应。有色物质溶液颜色的深浅与溶液浓度有关，浓度越大，颜色越深，即物质吸收的光越多。若定量分析，溶液浓度与吸光度之间的关系可用朗伯-比尔定律来描述：

若保持特定入射光（即特定波长 λ），则

$$A=\varepsilon Cl$$

式中，A 表示吸光度；ε 表示摩尔吸光系数；C 表示溶液浓度；l 表示溶液层厚度。此公式说明：当一束单色光通过含有吸光物质的均匀透明的溶液时，溶液的吸光度与溶液浓度及溶液层厚度呈正比。这正是分光光度法对物质进行定量分析的理论基础。

【器材与试剂】

1. 器材

（1）拭镜纸和滤纸。

（2）721A 型分光光度计和吸收池（1cm 厚）。

（3）试管和试管架。

（4）刻度移液管。

2. 试剂

（1）蒸馏水。

（2）标准液 s（5% $CuSO_4$）：称取 50g $CuSO_4$ 溶解于 1000mL 蒸馏水中，室温保存。

（3）待测液 u：未知浓度的 x% $CuSO_4$。

【实验操作】

1. 标准曲线法

1）绘制标准曲线

（1）6 支试管，按表 2-1 操作。

表 2-1 $CuSO_4$溶液的标准曲线制作

试剂	试管					
	1	2	3	4	5	6
5% $CuSO_4$/mL	0.0	1.0	2.0	3.0	4.0	5.0
dH_2O/mL	6.0	5.0	4.0	3.0	2.0	1.0
浓度/%						
吸光度						

（2）计算出各管溶液浓度，填入表中。

（3）混匀各管样品，以 1 号管作为空白对照，在 721A 型分光光度计上于波长 650nm 处，测各管吸光度，重复测两次，取平均值，记入表 2-1 中。

（4）以浓度为横坐标，吸光度为纵坐标，绘制标准曲线。

2）测定样品：在波长 650nm 处测待测 $CuSO_4$液的吸光度，重复测两次，取平均值，并从标准曲线上查出浓度。

2. 标准对照法

1）测量：在波长 650nm 处，测标准溶液 5% $CuSO_4$的吸光度 A_s和待测液 x% $CuSO_4$的吸光度 A_u。

2）计算：根据朗伯-比尔定律，可得标准液 $A_s=\varepsilon C_s L$，待测液 $A_u=\varepsilon C_u L$，故 $C_u=(A_u/A_s)\times C_s$。

【思考题】

比较标准曲线法和标准对照法的实验结果，分析两种方法产生误差的原因及误差减小方法。

分光光度法简介

一、基 本 原 理

当一束平行的单色光通过某种物质的溶液时，由于部分光被吸收，透过溶液的光强度减弱。若设入射光强度为 I_0，吸收光强度为 I_a，透射光强度为 I_t，则

$$I_0=I_a+I_t$$

而且溶液对光的吸收与溶液的浓度和通过溶液层的厚度都有关，科学家朗伯（J. H. Lambert）和比尔（A. Beer）分别研究了吸光度与两者的关系。

1. 朗伯定律 朗伯于 1760 年研究了单色光的吸收强度与溶液层厚度的定量关系。

$$I = I_0 e^{-k_1 l} \tag{2-1}$$

式中，I 为透射光强度；I_0 为入射光强度；l 为溶液厚度；e 为自然对数；k_1 为消光系数。此式说明单色光通过溶液时，其光强度随吸光介质的厚度 l 增长而呈指数减少。

2. 比尔定律 比尔于 1852 年研究了单色光的吸收强度与溶液浓度的定量关系。

$$I = I_0 e^{-k_2 C} \tag{2-2}$$

式中，k_2 为消光系数；C 为溶液浓度。此式说明单色光通过溶液时，光强度随溶液浓度 C

的增加而呈指数减少。

将上述两个定律合并起来，即得到朗伯-比尔定律

$$\frac{I}{I_0}=\mathrm{e}^{-\varepsilon Cl} \tag{2-3}$$

式中，ε 是摩尔吸光系数，是每种吸收物质在特定波长和特定溶剂中的特征，波长和溶剂改变时，ε 随之改变。比率 I/I_0 是透光率（transmittance，T），通常以百分率表示。所以

$$T=\frac{I}{I_0}=\mathrm{e}^{-\varepsilon Cl}$$

取对数，$-\lg T=-\lg\frac{I}{I_0}=\varepsilon Cl$

透光率 T 的负对数为吸光度，则

$$A=\varepsilon Cl \tag{2-4}$$

说明溶液对光的吸光度只与溶液的浓度和溶液层的厚度有关，或者说吸光度与浓度呈正比。因此若能测得标准品与待测品的吸光度，就可以通过标准曲线法或者标准对照法测定未知溶液的浓度。

二、分光光度计的基本结构

测定不同的光谱有不同的分光光度计，但是各类分光光度计都包括五个基本组成部分：光源、单色器、吸收池、检测系统和数字显示器/仪表（图 2-1）。

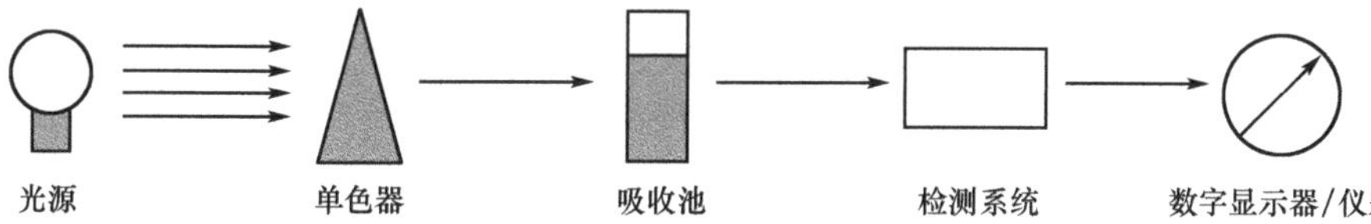

图 2-1　分光光度计的基本构造

1. 光源　在样品分析所要求的波长范围内，光源必须要能发射出稳定的、具有足够光能的光。通常使用钨灯和氘灯两种光源，前者适于 400～900nm 的光谱分析，后者适于 200～400nm 的光谱分析。即在可见光区、近紫外光区和近红外光区常用钨灯，在紫外光区常用氘灯。

通常，用紫外光源测定无色物质称为紫外分光光度法，用可见光光源测定有色物质称为可见分光光度法。

2. 单色器　由很多棱镜或反射光栅、狭缝、聚焦镜、准直镜等排列而成，以选择理想波长的光，并将其引导入样品槽和检测器。棱镜通常由玻璃、石英等制成。玻璃棱镜可用于 350～2000nm 波长范围，石英棱镜可用的波长范围为 185～4000nm。紫外-可见分光光度计使用石英棱镜。棱镜的缺点在于色散率随波长变化，得到的光谱呈非均匀排列，而且传递光的效率较低；光栅的分辨率在整个光谱范围内是均匀的，使用起来更为方便（图 2-2）。因此，现代紫外-可见分光光度计上多采用光栅单色器。

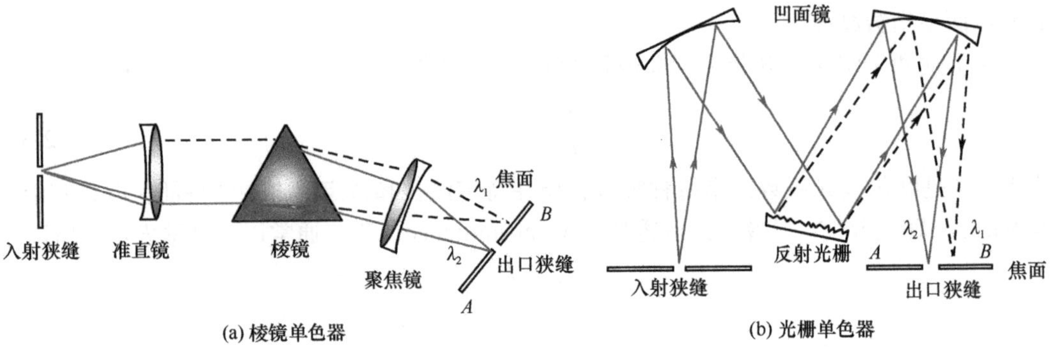

图 2-2　单色器的基本结构

3. 吸收池　吸收池用于盛放分析样品，一般有玻璃和石英材料两种。石英池适于可见和紫外光区，玻璃池只能用于可见光区。为减少光的反射损失，吸收池的光学面必须完全垂直于光束方向。

在高精度分析测定中（紫外区尤其重要），吸收池要挑选配对，因为吸收池材料本身的吸光特征及池的光程长度的精度等对分析结果都有影响。因此吸收池的光学表面必须受到保护，不能用手指或糙物接触和擦拭光学表面，使用后，用蒸馏水彻底清洗。

4. 检测系统　此系统检测单色光透过样品溶液后的光强度变化，并将光能转变为电能，其结果用电流计测定，通过显示屏显示出来。

5. 数字显示器/仪表　来自检测器的数据由读出设备显示，如数字显示器或仪表。

三、分光光度计的操作

以 721A 型分光光度计为例介绍其操作方法：

（1）仪器应放在坚固平稳的工作台上，室内保持干燥，无强光射入。

（2）仪器未接电源前，电表指针必须置于“0”刻度线，否则需要旋动电表上的校正螺丝加以调节。

（3）在进行测定前，先将仪器电源开关接通，打开吸收池暗箱盖，预热 15min 以上，选择需用的波长，调节电位器，使电表指针指“0”，然后盖上吸收池暗箱盖，将吸收池放在蒸馏水校正位置，调节使电表指针处于 100%。

（4）重复上述步骤 3 次，然后进行测定工作。

（5）轻轻拉动吸收池座架拉杆，使有色溶液进入光路，此时表头指针所示为该有色溶液的吸光度。

（6）测量完毕，关闭开关，拔下电源插头，将吸收池取出洗净，放回原处，盖好吸收池暗箱盖，罩好仪器。

四、注 意 事 项

（1）仪器须安放在稳固的工作台上，不能随意搬动。严防震动、潮湿和强光直射。

（2）盛装比色液时，约达吸收池 2/3 的体积，不宜过多或过少。若不慎使溶液溅出，吸收池表面须用拭镜纸擦干，以防溶液腐蚀机械。

（3）不可用手或粗糙的物品摩擦吸收池的透光面。

（4）吸收池用后应立即用蒸馏水冲洗干净，若不能洗净，用 5%中性皂溶液或洗衣粉溶液浸泡，也可用新鲜配制的重铬酸钾洗液短时间浸泡，然后用水冲洗干净，倒置晾干。

（5）必须使用匹配的吸收池。

（6）试管或试剂不得放置于仪器上，以防腐蚀仪器。

（7）测定溶液浓度的光密度值宜在 0.1～1.0。如光密度不在 0.1～1.0，可调节溶液浓度，适当稀释或浓缩。

（8）连续工作的时间不宜过长，以防光电管疲乏。每次读完一组样品后，立即打开暗箱盖。

（9）仪器连续使用不应超过 2h，必要时休息 0.5h 再用。

（10）测定未知溶液时，应先作吸收光谱曲线，再选择最大吸收峰的波长作为测定波长。

（11）721A 型分光光度计的放大器暗盒及单色器箱处放有两个硅胶筒，检测室内放硅胶袋，应经常检查，发现硅胶变色，应更换新硅胶或烘干再用。

（12）仪器较长时间不使用，应定期通电、预热。

（13）仪器用完之后，须拔去电源，套上仪器罩。

（王含彦　陈建业）

Experiment 2 Determination of $CuSO_4$ Concentration —Spectrophotometry Technique

【Purposes】

1. To master the use of type 721A spectrophotometer.
2. To learn the Lambert-Beer law and its deduction and application.
3. To know the structure and working principle of type 721A spectrophotometer.

【Principles】

Light is a kind of electromagnetic wave in nature. Different kinds of light have different wavelengths. Light which can be seen with naked eyes is known as the visible light and its wavelength ranges from 400nm to 750nm. Light with the wavelength less than 400nm is called the ultraviolet (UV) light and that with the wavelength greater than 750nm is called the infrared light.

The same substance has different light absorption abilities at different wavelengths of light, while different substances have different light absorption abilities at the same wavelength of light. It is called the substance's selective light absorption. Hence the substance takes on its own unique color, which is due to its selective light absorption reflecting on the person's visual sense. The color of the solution is associated with its concentration. The greater the concentration is, the deeper the color is, which means the substance absorbs more light. The correlation between the solution concentration and absorbance can be determined by the Lambert-Beer law. If a particular incident light is selected, the absorbance can be described by the following formula:

$$A=\varepsilon Cl$$

where A represents the absorbance; ε represents the molar absorptivity; C represents the concentration; l represents the thickness of solution. The formula shows that the absorbance of the solution is proportional to its concentration and thickness when a beam of monochromatic light passes through a kind of uniform and transparent solution. This is just the theoretical basis of spectrophotometry for the substance's quantitative analysis.

【Apparatus and Reagents】

1. Apparatus

(1) Lens paper and filter paper.
(2) Type 721A spectrophotometer and cuvette (1 cm thickness).
(3) Test tube and test tube rack.
(4) Measuring pipet.

2. Reagents

(1) Distilled water.
(2) Standard sample s (5% $CuSO_4$ solution): Dissolve 50g $CuSO_4$ in 1,000 mL distilled water and store it at room temperature.
(3) Unknown sample u: x% $CuSO_4$ solution of unknown concentration.

【Procedures】

1. Standard curve method

1) Making the standard curve.
(1) Add reagents into 6 test tubes respectively as the following (Table 2-1).

Table 2-1 The standard curve making of $CuSO_4$ solution

Reagents	Tubes					
	1	2	3	4	5	6
5% $CuSO_4$/mL	0.0	1.0	2.0	3.0	4.0	5.0
dH_2O/mL	6.0	5.0	4.0	3.0	2.0	1.0
Concentration/%						
Absorbance						

(2) Calculate the concentration of each tube and fill it into the table.

(3) Mix up the solution of each tube and measure the absorbance of each tube at wavelength of 650nm on a 721A spectrophotometer using tube 1 as the blank control. Repeat twice and fill the average value into Table 2-1.

(4) Make the standard curve with the concentration as the x axis and the absorbance as the y axis.

2) Sample assay: Measure the absorbance of unknown samples at 650nm. Repeat twice and take the average value to find out the concentration from the standard curve.

2. Standard control method

1) Absorbance assay: Measure the absorbance A_s of the standard solution and the absorbance A_u of the unknown sample solutions respectively at 650nm.

2) Calculation: According to the Lambert-Beer law, the standard solution $A_s=\varepsilon C_s L$ and the sample solution $A_u=\varepsilon C_u L$, so, $C_u=(A_u/A_s) \times C_s$.

【Question】

Compare the result of the standard curve method with that of the standard control method. Analyze the factors leading to errors. Propose the methods to reduce the errors.

Introduction of Spectrophotometry

Ⅰ. Principles

When a parallel beam of monochromatic light passes through a substance's solution, the light intensity of the transmitted light might become weak because part of the light has been absorbed by the solution. If the intensity of the incident light is defined as I_0, the absorbed light as I_a, the transmitted light as I_t, then the following formula can be gotten.

$$I_0=I_a+I_t$$

The light absorption is associated with both the concentration and the thickness of the solution. The scientists, J. H. Lambert and A. Beer, studied the relationship between the absorbance and the concentration or the thickness respectively.

1. Lambert law J. H. Lambert studied the quantitative relationship between the absorption intensity of the monochromatic light and the thickness of the solution layer in 1976. The transmitted light intensity can be expressed by the following formula:

$$I = I_0 e^{-k_1 l} \quad (2\text{-}1)$$

where I represents the transmitted light intensity; I_0 represents the incident light intensity; l represents the thickness of the solution; e represents the natural logarithm; k_1 represents the extinction coefficient.

Equation (2-1) shows that the intensity of light, as the monochromatic light passes through a solution, will exponentially decrease with the increasing thickness of the solution.

2. Beer law

A. Beer investigated the quantitative relationship between the absorbance of the monochromatic light and the concentration of the solution in 1852:

$$I = I_0 e^{-k_2 C} \tag{2-2}$$

where k_2 represents the extinction coefficient; C represents the concentration of the solution.

Equation (2-2) reveals the fact that the light intensity will decrease exponentially with the increase of the concentration of the solution as the monochromatic light passes through a solution.

Equations (2-1) and (2-2) together can get the Lambert-Beer law as follows.

$$\frac{I}{I_0} = e^{-\varepsilon Cl} \tag{2-3}$$

In this equation ε is the molar absorptivity, standing for the characteristic of the light absorbing substance in specific wavelength and specific solvent. ε changes when the wavelength or the solvent changes. I/I_0 is the transmittance T, which is generally expressed in percentage. So

$$T = \frac{I}{I_0} = e^{-\varepsilon Cl}$$

Take the logarithm,

$$-\lg T = -\lg\frac{I}{I_0} = \varepsilon Cl$$

$-\lg T$ is the absorbance, so

$$A = \varepsilon Cl \tag{2-4}$$

The Lambert-Beer law states that the amount of the light absorbance is proportional to the concentration and the thickness of the solution. So the concentration of the solution can be determined by the standard curve method or the standard control method.

Ⅱ. The basic structure of spectrophotometers

There are various spectrophotometers for the measurement of different spectra. All the spectrophotometers consist of five components. They are the light source, the monochromator, the cuvette, the detection system and the digital display or meter (Fig. 2-1).

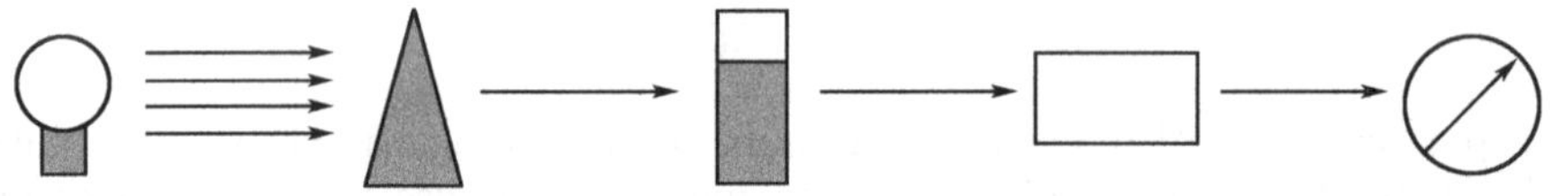

Fig. 2-1 The basic structure of spectrophotometers

1. The light source The light source must be the one that can supply the light with stable, enough luminous energy within the range of the wavelength suitable for the sample analysis. Both the tungsten lamp and the deuterium lamp are widely used as light sources. The former is suitable for 400–900nm spectral analysis, while the latter is suitable for 200–400nm spectral analysis. In general, the tungsten lamp is suitable for the spectral analysis of visible spectrum, near-ultraviolet light region and near-infrared light region, and the deuterium lamp is commonly used in the UV region.

Usually, the spectral analysis of the colorless substance uses the UV light source, which is called ultraviolet spectrophotometry. The spectral analysis of the colored substance uses the visible light source, which is called the visible spectrophotometry.

2. The monochromator This system consists of an array of the prism or the reflection grating, the slit, the focus lens, collimator, etc. Its function is to select the right wavelength of light, and guide the light into the sample pool and the detector. The prism is usually made of glass, quartz, etc. The glass prism can be used in the 350–2,000nm wavelength range and quartz lenses' available wavelength is in the range of the 185–4,000nm. The ultraviolet-visible spectrophotometer usually uses the quartz prism. This kind of prism has some disadvantages. For example, the dispersion of light changes with the wavelength. The arrangement of the spectrum is non-uniform and the transmission efficiency of light is lower. The grating is an alternative element and its distinguishability is uniform in the whole spectral range, which is more convenient to use (Fig. 2-2). Therefore, the grating monochromator is widely used in modern ultraviolet-visible spectrophotometers.

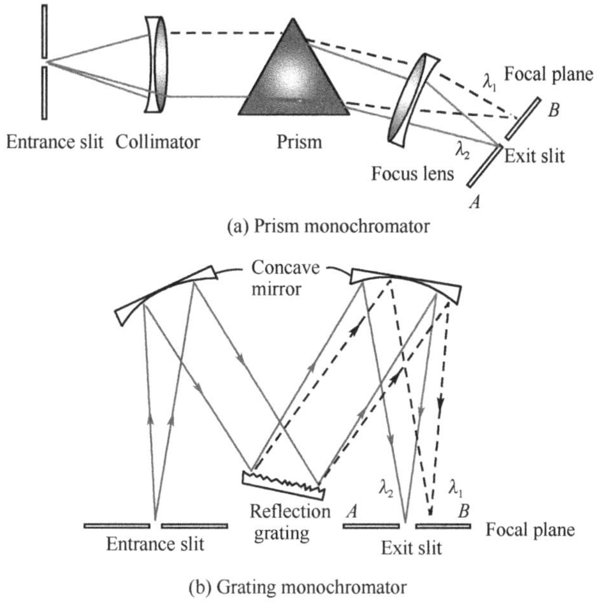

Fig. 2-2 The basic structure of the monochromator

3. The cuvette The cuvette that is made of glass or quartz is used for holding samples. The quartz cuvette is suitable for the visible and ultraviolet light region, and the glass one is only used in the visible light region. In order to reduce the light loss of reflection, the optical surface of the cuvette must be completely perpendicular to the direction of the light beam.

In the high-precision measurement, the selection of the cuvette should match particularly the ultraviolet region. Both the absorption characteristics and the optical path length of the cuvette influence the measurement results. Therefore, the optical surface of the cuvette must be protected from damage. Do not wipe its optical surface with your fingers or rough things, and wash it thoroughly with distilled water after assay.

4. The detection system This system detects the changes of the light intensity after the monochromatic light passes through the sample solution, then converts the light energy into the electrical energy, finally measures the results using an ammeter and shows the results on the displayer.

5. The digital display or meter The data from a detector are displayed by a readout device, such as a digital display or meter.

III. Operation of the spectrophotometer

The operation procedures of type 721A spectrophotometer are as follows.

(1) Place the instrument on a stable workbench, and keep the room dry and with no strong light.

(2) Be sure that the pointer of the electric meter is placed on the dial "0" position before connecting to power, otherwise turn the calibration screws to correct it.

(3) Turn on the power switch first, and then open the dark case cover of the cuvette to preheat it for more than 15min. Select the proper wavelength by rotating the knob, and adjust the

potentiometer to make the pointer at the "0" position. Fill a cuvette with distilled water, place it at the correct position of the dark box, and close the case cover to adjust the pointer at the "100%" position.

(4) Repeat the above steps for 3 times before the detection.

(5) Pull the rod gently to make the sample solution at the light path. Then read the absorbance which the pointer reaches.

(6) After the measurement, turn off the switch and unplug the power plug, take out and clean the cuvette with distilled water, put it back and close the dark case cover. Finally, cover the instrument well.

Ⅳ. Notes

(1) The instrument should be placed on a stable workbench. Keep the instrument from vibration, moist and strong light.

(2) It is better to fill about the two-thirds volume of the cuvette with the solution. If the solution spills outside, the surface of the cuvette and the machine must be wiped dry with lens paper to avoid the apparatus corrosion by the solution.

(3) Do not touch the optical surface of the cuvette with fingers or rough things.

(4) After finishing the measurement, the cuvette must be rinsed with distilled water immediately. If it does not work, soak the cuvette with the 5% neutral soap solution, detergent solution or fresh potassium dichromate lotion, then clean it with distilled water and place it upside down to dry in the air.

(5) Only the compatible cuvette should be used.

(6) Do not place the test tubes and reagents on the surface of the machine to avoid the apparatus corrosion.

(7) It is better to keep the optical density (OD) value in 0.1–1.0. If the OD value is not in 0.1–1.0, adjust the sample solution concentration by diluting or concentrating.

(8) Working time should not be too long to avoid the phototube fatigue. After determining a group of samples, open the dark case immediately.

(9) The instrument should not be used more than 2h continuously, if necessary turn off the instrument for half an hour.

(10) When determining an unknown solution, it is necessary to make the absorption spectrum curve first, and then choose the wavelength of maximum absorption peak as the measuring wavelength.

(11) The 721A spectrophotometer has two silica gel cartridges in the amplifier dark box and monochromator box, and a silica gel bag in the testing room, which should be checked frequently. If the silica gel is discolored, it should be replaced with new silica gel or dried and used again.

(12) If the instrument is not used for a long period of time, it should be periodically powered up and preheated.

(13) After the measurement, turn off the power and cover the instrument well.

(Wang Hanyan, Chen Jianye)

实验 3　血清蛋白乙酸纤维素膜电泳定量分析

【实验目的】

1. 掌握血清蛋白乙酸纤维素膜电泳与比色定量分析的基本原理、操作程序、技术要领和主要影响因素及其排除方法。

2. 熟悉血清蛋白乙酸纤维素膜电泳图谱的含义及临床意义。

3. 了解血清蛋白乙酸纤维素膜电泳图谱透明方法和定量分析。

【实验原理】

蛋白质是两性电解质，在 pH 小于等电点的溶液中带正电，在 pH 大于等电点的溶液中带负电。血清中所有蛋白质的等电点均低于 pH8.6，在大于或等于 pH8.6 的溶液中都带负电荷。因此，将血清蛋白放在 pH8.6 的缓冲液中进行乙酸纤维素膜电泳，它们将因为带负电荷而向正极泳动。不同血清蛋白的等电点不同、电荷量不等、分子形状各异以及分子质量不等，致使血清蛋白在电泳过程中的移动速度不同而彼此分离。电泳膜经染色、漂洗后，就会呈现出五条不连续的蛋白质区带图谱，从正极到负极依次为白蛋白（Alb）、α_1 球蛋白、α_2 球蛋白、β 球蛋白和 γ 球蛋白。

由于蛋白质含量与吸附的染料量在一定范围内呈正比，剪下各条蛋白质谱带，用碱性溶液洗下蛋白质吸附的染料，在 650nm 处比色读取光密度，就可计算出血清样品中各区带蛋白质的百分含量。此外，也可先对乙酸纤维素膜电泳图谱进行透明处理，然后对电泳图谱进行扫描分析，依据扫描曲线中各蛋白质区带的面积与总面积之比，计算出各区带蛋白质的百分含量。

【器材与试剂】

1. 器材

（1）低电压电泳仪与乙酸纤维素膜电泳槽。

（2）721A 型分光光度计。

（3）光密度扫描分析仪。

（4）乙酸纤维素膜（8.0cm×2.0cm）。

（5）点样器、镊子、2B 铅笔、粗滤纸、染色皿、脱色皿、载玻片等。

（6）试管（10mL）及试管架。

2. 试剂

（1）电极缓冲液（pH=8.6，离子强度 I=0.06）：称取巴比妥钠 12.76g，巴比妥 1.66g，溶解在 800mL 的蒸馏水中，再加蒸馏水定容至 1000mL，调节 pH 至 8.6。

（2）氨基黑 10B 染色液：取 0.5g 氨基黑 10B 溶于 50mL 甲醇中，加乙酸 10mL，再加蒸馏水定容至 100mL。

（3）脱色液：在 45mL 95%乙醇中加乙酸 5mL 和蒸馏水 50mL 混匀，室温储存。

（4）洗脱液：0.4mol/L NaOH 溶液。称取 40g NaOH，溶解于 800mL 蒸馏水中，定容

至 1000mL。

（5）透明液：A 液为 15mL 乙酸+85mL 95%乙醇；B 液为 25 mL 乙酸+75mL 95%乙醇。

【实验操作】

1. 电泳步骤

（1）乙酸纤维素膜准备：①用镊子取乙酸纤维素膜 1 张，用 2B 铅笔在光滑面一角编号，并在粗糙面距一端 1.5cm 处画一垂直细线作为点样线（图 3-1）；②将乙酸纤维素膜浸入巴比妥缓冲液中让其充分浸透；③用镊子从缓冲液中取出乙酸纤维素膜，轻轻夹于滤纸中吸去多余的液体。

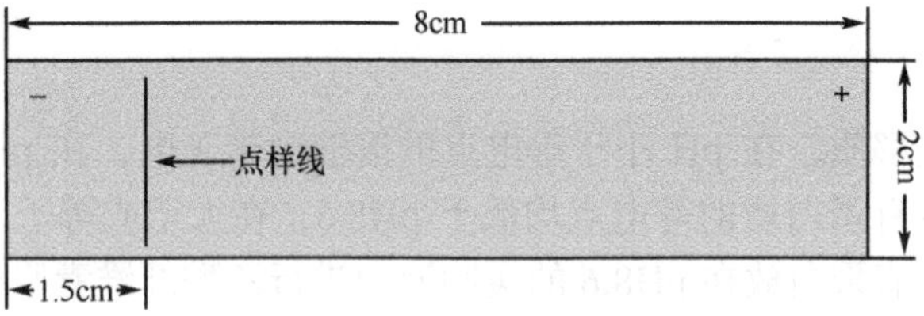

图 3-1　乙酸纤维素膜准备示意图

（2）盐桥制作：首先裁剪一些尺寸合适的滤纸，取双层滤纸先在电极缓冲溶液中浸湿，再将湿润的滤纸一端附着在电泳槽的支架上，另一端浸入缓冲溶液中，用玻棒驱除气泡，作为乙酸纤维素膜附着的“盐桥”。

（3）点样：将乙酸纤维素膜平铺于玻璃板上（粗糙面朝上），用加样器蘸取少许血清，垂直均匀地印于膜粗糙面的点样线上，上样量控制在 3μL 左右，让血清样品渗入膜中。

（4）上槽：将乙酸纤维素膜放置于电泳槽上应注意下列要点：①膜长边与电力线平行；②毛面朝下；③点样端置于负极，点样线与负极盐桥间保持约 0.5cm 间距；④膜面绷平，两端紧贴盐桥。

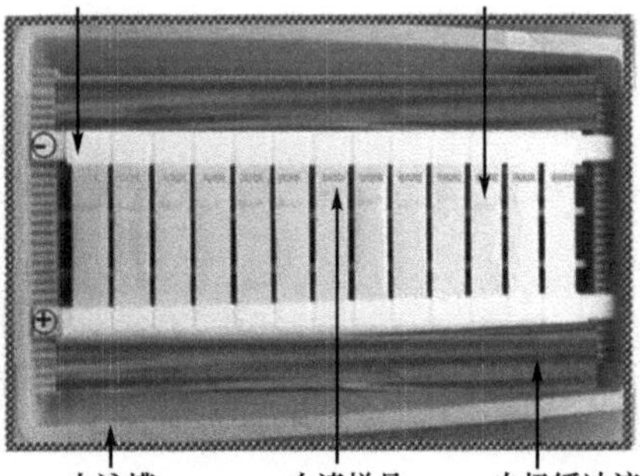

图 3-2　乙酸纤维素膜电泳上槽示意图

（5）平衡：关闭盖子，平衡 3～5min（图 3-2）。

（6）电泳：电极缓冲液 I=0.06，电压=110～130V，电流=0.4～0.6mA/cm，电泳时间=45～60min。

（7）染色：电泳结束后关闭电源，取出膜放入氨基黑 10B 染色液中染色 3～5min。

（8）脱色：从染色皿中取出已着色的电泳膜放入脱色皿内，用脱色液反复漂洗数次，直至背景底色透明、血清蛋白条带清晰为止，然后用水洗去脱色液，晾干备用（图 3-3）。

2. 定量分析

1）比色分析

（1）洗脱：①取 6 支试管依次编号为 0（空白）、Alb、α_1、α_2、β 和 γ，将电泳图谱按照 Alb、α_1、α_2、β 和 γ 蛋白区带剪开；②分别将各蛋白条带装入相应编号的试管中；③剪一条与 α_1 带宽大致相等的空白带放入空白管中；④各管分别加入 0.4mol/L NaOH 5mL，反复摇动几次，使染色带谱充分洗脱。

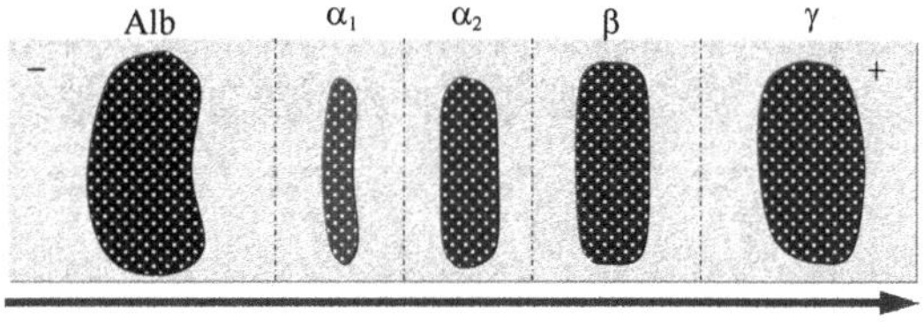

图 3-3　正常人血清蛋白乙酸纤维素膜电泳图谱

（2）比色测定：以空白液校正吸光度为零，分别读取 Alb、α_1 球蛋白、α_2 球蛋白、β 球蛋白及 γ 球蛋白各管在 650nm 波长下的吸光度。

（3）计算：

光密度总和（T）的计算：$T = T_{Alb}+T_{\alpha_1}+T_{\alpha_2}+T_{\beta}+T_{\gamma}$

各组分蛋白质百分数的计算：

白蛋白（%）=（T_{Alb}/T）×100%

α_1 球蛋白（%）=（T_{α_1}/T）×100%

α_2 球蛋白（%）=（T_{α_2}/T）×100%

β 球蛋白（%）=（T_{β}/T）×100%

γ 球蛋白（%）=（T_{γ}/T）×100%

2）扫描分析

（1）透明：从漂洗液中取出膜放入透明液 A 中 2min→转入透明液 B 中 1min→将膜平贴于玻璃板上 3～5min→待膜完全透明→扫描定量或晾干保存。

（2）扫描：将透明的乙酸纤维素膜在光密度扫描分析仪上进行扫描，得出电泳扫描曲线：距离-光密度曲线（图 3-4）。

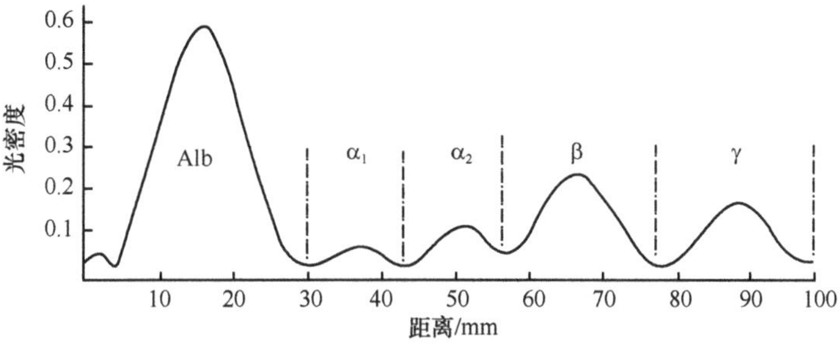

图 3-4　正常人血清蛋白乙酸纤维素膜电泳扫描曲线示意图

（3）定量：算出曲线每个峰的面积与总面积的百分比，得到各区带蛋白质占血清总蛋白的百分比。

【临床意义】

正常人血清蛋白乙酸纤维素膜电泳的百分含量如下：

白蛋白 57%～72%　　α_1 球蛋白 2%～5%　　α_2 球蛋白 4%～9%

β 球蛋白 6.5%～12%　　γ 球蛋白 12%～20%

血清蛋白乙酸纤维素膜电泳在临床上常用于分析血、尿等样品中的蛋白质，供临床上诊断肝、肾疾病等参考。例如肾病综合征患者，由于小分子量的血清白蛋白漏出并随尿液排出体外，导致乙酸纤维素膜电泳图谱中白蛋白区带明显变小变浅。又如，慢性肝炎和肝硬化患者，由于肝细胞受损，肝脏合成血清蛋白质的能力大大降低，使血清白蛋白显著降低，γ-球蛋白相对增加。另外，多发性骨髓瘤患者血清蛋白乙酸纤维素膜电泳图谱中可见异常球蛋白条带。

【思考题】

1. 为什么电泳时采用 pH8.6 的缓冲液？

2. 与正常的血清蛋白乙酸纤维素膜电泳图谱相比，肝、肾病患者的血清蛋白乙酸纤维素膜电泳图谱可能会发生什么变化？

3. 乙酸纤维素膜电泳应掌握哪些要点？

电泳技术概述

电泳指带电颗粒在电场力作用下向所带电荷相反电极的泳动。许多重要的生物分子如氨基酸、多肽、蛋白质、核苷酸和核酸等都含有可解离基团，在 pH 不等于其 pI 的条件下均带有电荷。在电场力作用下，它们会向着与其所带电荷相反的电极移动。电泳技术就是利用样品中各种分子因带电性质、分子因大小以及形状等有差异，在电场中的迁移速率不同，从而对样品分子进行分离、鉴定、纯化和制备的一种综合技术。

一、电 泳 原 理

设一带电粒子在电场中所受的力为 F，F 的大小取决于粒子所带电荷 Q 和电场强度 X，即

$$F=QX$$

按斯托克斯定律，一球形粒子运动时所受到的阻力 F' 与粒子运动的速率 V、粒子的半径 r、介质的黏度 η 的关系为

$$F'=6\pi r\eta V$$

当 $F=F'$ 时，达到动态平衡，即

$$QX=6\pi r\eta V$$

移项得：

$$V/X=Q/6\pi r\eta \quad (3\text{-}1)$$

V/X 表示单位电场强度时粒子运动的速率，称为迁移率（mobility），也称为电泳速率，以 μ 表示，即

$$\mu=V/X=Q/6\pi r\eta \quad (3\text{-}2)$$

由式（3-2）可见，粒子的迁移率在一定条件下取决于粒子本身的性质，即其所带电荷多少及粒子大小与形状，也就是取决于粒子的电荷密度。不同粒子一般具有不同的迁移率。在具体实验中，移动速率 V 为单位时间 t（以 s 计）内移动的距离 d（以 cm 计），即

$$V=d/t$$

电场强度 X 为单位距离（L，以 cm 计）内的电势差（E，以 V 计）。当距离为 1cm 时，电势差为 E，则

$$X=E/L$$

以 $V=d/t$、$X=E/L$ 代入式（3-2）即得

$$\mu=V/X=(d/t)/(E/L)=dL/Et$$

所以迁移率的单位为 $cm^2/(s\cdot V)$。

某物质（A）在电场中移动的距离为

$$d_A = Et \times \mu_A / L$$

另一物质（B）的移动距离为

$$d_B = Et \times \mu_B / L$$

两物质移动距离的差为

$$\Delta d = d_A - d_B = \frac{(\mu_A - \mu_B) \times Et}{L} \tag{3-3}$$

式（3-3）指出，物质 A、B 能否分离取决于两者的迁移率。如两者的迁移率相同，则不能分离，有差别则能分离。实验所选的条件如电压和电泳时间与两物质的分离距离呈正比，电场的长度（如滤纸长度）与分离距离成反比。

二、带电粒子在电场中的迁移泳动受多种因素的影响

影响带电粒子在电场中迁移的因素既包括带电粒子本身的性质，也包括缓冲液的性质、外加电场的性质以及支持介质的性质。下面简单讨论影响电泳的主要因素。

1. 生物大分子的性质　待分离生物大分子所带电荷的多少、分子大小和理化性质都会对电泳产生明显影响。一般而言，分子所带电荷越多、直径越小和形状越接近球形，其电泳迁移速率越快。

2. 缓冲液的性质　缓冲液 pH 直接影响生物大分子的解离程度和带电性质。缓冲液 pH 偏离生物大分子的等电点越远，生物大分子所带净电荷就越多，电泳时速率就越快。当缓冲液 pH 大于等电点时，生物大分子带负电荷，电泳时向正极移动；当缓冲液 pH 小于等电点时，生物大分子带正电荷，电泳时向负极移动。电泳还要求缓冲液的离子强度维持在一定范围内（0.02～0.2），离子强度过低则缓冲能力差，而离子强度过高则会形成较强的离子扩散层（即离子氛），使电泳速率降低。此外，缓冲液的黏度也会对电泳速率产生影响，总的趋势是缓冲液黏度越大，电泳时受到的阻力越大，电泳分离速率越慢。

3. 电场强度　电场强度指每厘米的电势差。一般而言，电场强度越大，电泳速率越快。但随着电场强度的增大，电流强度也增大，从而造成电泳过程产生的热量增多，最终导致介质温度升高，诱发一系列的不利影响：①样品和缓冲离子扩散速率增加，引起样品分离带变宽；②产生对流，引起待分离物的混合；③热敏感样品（如蛋白质）变性；④引起介质黏度、电阻降低等。降低电流强度可以减小产热，但会延长电泳时间，从而导致生物大分子扩散增加，同样影响分离效果。所以电泳实验中要选择适当的电场强度，同时可以通过冷却系统降低温度以获得较好的分离效果。

4. 电渗　液体在电场中相对于固体支持介质的移动称为电渗现象。支持介质表面存在一些带电基团，如滤纸表面含有羧基，琼脂糖凝胶表面有硫酸基，而玻璃表面常有 SiOH 基团等。这些基团电离后使支持介质表面带电，吸附一些带相反电荷的离子在电场作用下向电极方向移动，形成介质表面溶液的流动，这种现象就是电渗。当电渗方向与电泳方向相同时则加快电泳速率；当电渗方向与电泳方向相反时，则降低电泳速率。

5. 支持介质的筛孔　支持介质的筛孔大小对生物大分子的电泳迁移率有明显影响。生物大分子在筛孔大的介质中泳动速率快，反之，则泳动速率慢。

三、电泳技术的分类

电泳技术分类目前尚无统一标准，一般从实际和实用出发进行分类。

（1）根据工作目的和分离样品的数量多少分为分析电泳和制备电泳两大类。

（2）根据电泳时电压的高低分为高压电泳和常压电泳。高压电泳使用的电压在 500～1000V，电势梯度可高达 50～200V/cm。这类电泳分离速率快，但热效应较大，必须具备冷却装置。高压电泳主要适用于小分子化合物的快速分离。常压电泳使用的电压在 500V 以下，电势梯度为 2～10V/cm。这类电泳的分离速率较慢，但对电泳设备要求简单。临床检验上使用的电泳分析大都属于常压电泳。

（3）根据电泳中是否使用支持介质分为自由电泳和区带电泳。自由电泳不使用支持介质，电泳在溶液中进行。这类电泳又分为非自由界面电泳和自由界面电泳两类。非自由界面电泳指悬浮在溶液中的带电粒子（如各种细胞）通电后全部移动，不出现界面，如显微电泳等。自由界面电泳中被分离物质集中在某一层，形成各自的界面而进行定性或定量分析。自由界面电泳需要昂贵精密的电泳仪器，仅在少数特殊电泳如等电聚焦和等速电泳中使用。区带电泳都使用支持介质，根据支持介质不同分为纸电泳、乙酸纤维素膜电泳、薄层电泳和凝胶电泳等。此外，根据支持介质的装置形式不同又可分为水平板式电泳、垂直板式电泳、垂直盘状电泳、毛细管电泳、桥形电泳和连续流动电泳等。

（4）根据电泳系统 pH 是否连续分为连续 pH 电泳和不连续 pH 电泳。连续 pH 电泳是指电泳全过程中 pH 保持不变，如纸电泳和乙酸纤维素膜电泳等。不连续 pH 电泳是指电极缓冲液和电泳支持介质中的 pH 不同，甚至电泳支持介质不同区段的 pH 也不相同，如聚丙烯酰胺凝胶电泳、等电聚焦和等速电泳等。

（5）根据配套技术种类不同，分为免疫电泳、层析电泳、等电聚焦电泳、转移电泳、双向电泳和脉冲电场凝胶电泳等。

（6）根据电泳物质类别不同，分为细胞电泳、核酸电泳和蛋白质电泳等。

四、几种经典或新型的电泳技术介绍

1. 纸电泳和乙酸纤维素膜电泳

1）纸电泳：纸电泳是用滤纸作支持介质的一种早期电泳技术。尽管其分辨率比凝胶介质差，但由于操作简单，所以仍有很多应用，特别是在血清样品的临床检测和病毒分析等方面有重要用途。

纸电泳使用水平电泳槽。分离氨基酸和核苷酸时常用酸性缓冲液，分离蛋白质时常用碱性缓冲液。选用的滤纸必须厚度均匀，常用国产新华滤纸或进口 Whatman 1 号滤纸。点样位置在距滤纸一端 1～2cm 处。样品可点成圆形或长条形，而以长条形的分离效果较好。点样量为 5～100μg 或 5～10μL。点样方法有干点法和湿点法。湿点法是在点样前将滤纸用缓冲液浸湿，该法对样品浓度要求较高，不宜多次点样。干点法是在点样后再用缓冲液将滤纸喷湿，点样时可吹干后多次点样，因而可以用较稀的样品。电泳时要选择好正、负极，电压通常使用 2～10V/cm 的低压电泳，电泳时间较长。对于氨基酸和肽类等小分子物质，可使用 50～200V/cm 的高压电泳，电泳时间大大缩短，但必须解决电泳时的冷却问题，并要注意安全。

电泳完毕应立即测量滤纸的有效使用长度，然后烘干，用显色剂显色。定量测定的方法有洗脱法和光密度法。洗脱法是将样品条带剪下，用洗脱剂洗脱后进行比色测定。光密度法是将染色后的干滤纸用光密度计直接测定各样品条带的含量。

2）乙酸纤维素膜电泳：乙酸纤维素膜电泳与纸电泳相似，以乙酸纤维素膜作为支持介质。将纤维素的羟基乙酰化为乙酸甲酯，溶于丙酮后涂布成0.1～0.15mm厚度并具有均一细密微孔的薄膜。乙酸纤维素膜电泳与纸电泳相比具有以下优点：①乙酸纤维素膜对蛋白质样品吸附极少，无“拖尾”现象，染色后蛋白质条带清晰。②快速省时。乙酸纤维素膜亲水性比滤纸小，吸水少，电渗作用小，电泳时大部分电流通过样品传导，所以分离速度快，电泳时间短，完成全部电泳操作只需90min左右。③灵敏度高，样品用量少。血清蛋白电泳仅需2μL血清，蛋白质上样量少至0.1μg也可以得到清晰的电泳条带。临床医学常用于检测微量异常蛋白质的改变。④应用面广。可用于那些纸电泳不易分离的样品，如甲胎蛋白、溶菌酶、胰岛素及组蛋白等。⑤乙酸纤维素膜电泳染色后，用乙酸、乙醇混合液浸泡后可制成透明的薄膜，有利于光密度计和分光光度计扫描定量及长期保存。

由于乙酸纤维素膜电泳操作简单、快速与价廉，目前已广泛用于分析检测血浆蛋白、脂蛋白、糖蛋白、甲胎蛋白、体液蛋白、脑脊液蛋白、脱氢酶、多肽、核酸及其他生物大分子，为心血管疾病、肝硬化及某些癌症的鉴别诊断提供了可靠的依据，因而已成为医学和临床检验中的常规技术。

2. 琼脂糖凝胶电泳 琼脂糖凝胶可作为蛋白质和核酸的电泳支持介质，尤其适合于核酸的纯化和分析。例如，浓度为1%的琼脂糖凝胶的孔径对于蛋白质来说较大，阻碍作用较小，这时蛋白质分子大小对电泳迁移率的影响相对较小，所以适用于一些忽略蛋白质大小而只根据蛋白质天然电荷来进行分离的电泳技术，如免疫电泳和等电聚焦电泳等。琼脂糖凝胶也适合于DNA和RNA分子的分离与分析，由于DNA和RNA分子通常较大，所以在分离过程中会存在一定的摩擦阻碍作用，这时分子的大小会对电泳迁移率产生明显影响。例如，对于双链DNA，电泳迁移率的大小主要与DNA分子大小有关，而与碱基排列及组成无关。另外，一些低熔点琼脂糖凝胶可以在65℃时熔化，因此其中的样品如DNA可以重新溶解到溶液中而进行回收。

由于琼脂糖凝胶的弹性较差，难以从小管中取出，所以一般琼脂糖凝胶不适合于管状电泳。琼脂糖凝胶通常采用水平式板状凝胶用于等电聚焦和免疫电泳等蛋白质电泳以及DNA、RNA的分析。

3. 聚丙烯酰胺凝胶电泳 聚丙烯酰胺凝胶电泳（polyacrylamide gel electrophoresis，PAGE）是以聚丙烯酰胺凝胶作为支持介质的一种常用电泳技术。聚丙烯酰胺凝胶由单体丙烯酰胺和*N,N'*-亚甲基双丙烯酰胺聚合而成，聚合过程由自由基催化完成。催化聚合的常用方法有化学聚合法和光聚合法。化学聚合以过硫酸铵（AP）为催化剂，以四甲基乙二胺（TEMED）为加速剂。在聚合过程中，四甲基乙二胺催化过硫酸铵产生自由基，自由基引发丙烯酰胺单体聚合，同时*N,N'*-亚甲基双丙烯酰胺与丙烯酰胺链间产生交联，从而形成三维网状结构。

聚丙烯酰胺凝胶的孔径可调，常通过改变丙烯酰胺和*N,N'*-亚甲基双丙烯酰胺的浓度来进行控制。低浓度凝胶具有较大的孔径，如3%的聚丙烯酰胺凝胶对蛋白质没有明显的阻碍作用，可用于等电聚焦或DNA分离；高浓度凝胶的孔径较小，有分子筛的作用，一般用于不同分子量蛋白质的电泳分离。聚丙烯酰胺凝胶具有较强的机械韧性，凝胶的强度、弹性、透明度、黏度和孔径大小取决于丙烯酰胺和*N,N'*-亚甲基双丙烯酰胺的浓度以及丙

烯酰胺和 N,N'-亚甲基双丙烯酰胺之间的交联度。

非变性聚丙烯酰胺凝胶电泳可以使生物大分子在电泳过程中保持天然构象、电荷分布和生物活性，对生物大分子的鉴定具有十分重要的意义。此外，聚丙烯酰胺凝胶还具有以下突出优点：①可以任意控制胶浓度和交联度，用于分离不同分子量的生物大分子；②能把分子筛作用和电荷效应有机结合在一起，提高分离的灵敏度；③聚丙烯酰胺凝胶不含带电基团，化学惰性好，电泳时不会产生电渗作用；④透明度好，便于灰度检测和拍照；⑤机械强度好，有弹性，不易碎，便于操作和保存；⑥无紫外吸收，可用紫外分析仪对凝胶进行定量分析；⑦可作为固定化酶的惰性载体。

聚丙烯酰胺凝胶电泳分离蛋白质最初是在直径约 7mm、长约 10cm 的玻璃管中进行的，产生的条带像圆盘，故称为圆盘电泳。但由于玻璃管间的差异、灌胶时的差异导致各玻璃管间分离条件不一致，所以对各管样品进行比较时会出现较大误差。为了克服这种差异性，后来发明了垂直平板电泳。垂直平板电泳一次可以容纳 20 余个样品，电泳过程中样品所处的条件相对一致，样品间便于比较，重复性好。因而，垂直平板电泳很快得到广泛应用，常用于蛋白质和核酸的分离、鉴定及序列分析。

近年来发展很快的水平平板电泳与垂直平板电泳相比有很多相似之处，但也有其独特的优点，主要表现在：①凝胶可以直接平铺在冷却板上，这样容易使凝胶冷却；②可以加高电压以提高分辨率；③电泳速度快，通常只需 1h 左右，而圆盘电泳和垂直平板电泳一般需要 3～4h；④可以使用薄胶，加样少，染色快，灵敏度高，易保存，只要用甘油浸泡，干燥后即可长期保存不会龟裂；⑤适用各种电泳方式，用途广泛。

4. 十二烷基磺酸钠-聚丙烯酰胺凝胶电泳 十二烷基磺酸钠-聚丙烯酰胺凝胶电泳（SDS-PAGE）是最常用的定性分析蛋白质的电泳方法，特别适合用于蛋白质纯度检测和分子量测定。SDS-PAGE 是在要进行电泳分析的样品中加入含阴离子表面活性剂 SDS 和 β-巯基乙醇的样品处理液：SDS 可以断开分子内和分子间的氢键，破坏蛋白质的二、三级结构；β-巯基乙醇可以断开半胱氨酸残基间的二硫键，破坏蛋白质的四级结构。蛋白样品加入上样缓冲液后，置沸水浴中煮沸 3～5min，使 SDS 与蛋白质充分结合，使蛋白质变性、解聚、带上大量同种负电荷及形成棒状结构。样品处理液中通常加入溴酚蓝指示剂，用于控制电泳过程。此外，上样缓冲液中还可加入适量蔗糖或甘油以增大溶液密度，便于上样时样品溶液沉入样品凹槽底部。

制备凝胶时首先要根据待分离样品的分子量大小选择适当的分离胶浓度，一般分离大分子量蛋白质需要使用低浓度分离胶，分离小分子量蛋白质需要使用高浓度分离胶。当分离胶聚合以后，通常要在凝胶上面加上一层约 1cm 厚的浓缩胶，并在浓缩胶上插入样品梳，形成上样凹槽。浓缩胶的 pH 较低（通常为 6.8），浓度也较低（通常为 3%～5%），形成的孔径大，各种蛋白质都可以自由通过，常用于样品进入分离胶前将样品浓缩成很窄的条带。浓缩胶聚合后取出样品梳，上样后通电即可电泳。

聚丙烯酰胺凝胶电泳有两种系统，即连续系统与不连续系统，不连续系统中存在三种不连续性，即 pH 不连续、凝胶不连续、溶液离子组成不连续。样品在电泳过程中首先通过浓缩胶，在进入分离胶前由于等速电泳现象而被浓缩。进入分离胶后，由于聚丙烯酰胺的分子筛作用，小分子的蛋白质容易通过凝胶孔径，阻力小，迁移速率快，大分子蛋白质则受到较大的阻力而被滞后，这样蛋白质在电泳过程中就会根据各自分子量的大小而被分离。溴酚蓝指示剂为一种小分子物质，可以自由通过凝胶孔径，用它指示电泳的前沿位置。

有关聚丙烯酰胺凝胶电泳技术的具体操作，后有实验20详细介绍。

5. 等电聚焦 等电聚焦电泳是根据两性物质等电点不同而进行分离的一种电泳技术，具有极高的分辨率，可以分辨出等电点相差0.01的蛋白质，是分离蛋白质等两性物质的一种理想方法。等电聚焦的分离原理是通过在凝胶中加入两性电解质而形成不连续pH梯度，被分离样品在电泳过程中会自动聚集在与其等电点相对应的pH区域内，从而得以分离。

两性电解质是人工合成的一种复杂的多氨基-多羧基化合物，不同两性电解质具有不同的pH梯度范围。因此，要根据待分离样品的具体情况选择适当的两性电解质，使待分离样品中各个组分都介于两性电解质的pH范围之内。

等电聚焦具有极高的灵敏度和分辨率（最低检出量达10^{-10}g），可将人血清分出40～50条清晰的条带，特别适合于研究蛋白质微观不均一性。例如，一种蛋白质在SDS-PAGE中表现为一条带，而在等电聚焦中可被分为三条带。这可能是由于蛋白质存在单磷酸化、双磷酸化和三磷酸化形式。几个磷酸基团不会对蛋白质的分子大小产生明显影响，因此蛋白质在SDS-PAGE中表现为一条带，但它们所带的电荷有差异，所以在等电聚焦中可以检测到三条带。

等电聚焦还可以用于测定未知蛋白质的等电点，将一系列已知等电点的标准蛋白及待测蛋白同时进行等电聚焦。测定各个标准蛋白电泳条带到凝胶某一侧的距离对各自的等电点作图，即得到标准曲线。而后测定待测蛋白的距离，通过标准曲线即可求出其等电点。等电聚焦主要用于蛋白质的分离和纯化，虽然成本较高，但操作简单、纯化效率极高。

6. 双向电泳 双向电泳技术结合了等电聚焦技术和SDS-PAGE技术的双重优点，是分析蛋白质最有效的一种电泳手段。通常第一向电泳是等电聚焦，在细管中进行，蛋白质根据其等电点不同进行分离。而后将凝胶从管中取出，用SDS-PAGE进行第二向电泳。在第二向电泳过程中，蛋白质依据其分子量大小进行分离。这样各个蛋白质根据等电点和分子量不同而被分离、分布在双向图谱上。应用双向电泳，在细胞提取液的电泳图谱上可以分辨出1000～2000个蛋白点，有报道称最高可以分辨出5000～10 000个蛋白点，这与细胞中可能存在的蛋白质数量接近。双向电泳由于具有很高的分辨率，它可以直接从细胞提取液中检测某个蛋白。例如，将某个蛋白质的cDNA转入青蛙的卵母细胞中，通过对转入和未转入细胞的提取液进行双向电泳比较，转入cDNA的细胞提取液的双向电泳图谱中应存在一个特殊的蛋白质斑点，这样就可以直接检测cDNA的翻译结果。双向电泳是一项技术性很强的电泳技术，目前已有一些计算机控制系统可以直接记录并比较复杂的双向电泳图谱。

五、蛋白质的检测、鉴定及回收

1. 扫描与测定吸光度 通过扫描光密度仪对染色的凝胶扫描可以进行定量分析，确定样品中不同蛋白质的相对含量。扫描仪检测凝胶上不同迁移距离蛋白质条带的吸光度，得到距离-光密度曲线，曲线图上的峰对应各个染色蛋白质条带，峰面积的大小即代表蛋白质含量的多少。另一种简单方法是将染色蛋白质条带剪切下来，在50%吡啶溶液中摇晃过夜溶解染料，而后通过分光光度计测定吸光度，来估算蛋白质的含量。但应注意，只有在一定的浓度范围内蛋白质含量才与吸光度呈线性关系，不同蛋白质即使在含量相同的情况下染色程度也可能有所不同，所以分光光度法对蛋白质含量的测定只是一种半定量的方法。

2. 考马斯亮蓝染色法　检测蛋白质最常用的染色剂是考马斯亮蓝 R250，通常用体积比为 45∶45∶10 的甲醇∶水∶冰醋酸配制成 0.1%～0.25%（*W/V*）的考马斯亮蓝溶液作为染色液。这种酸-甲醇溶液使蛋白质变性，固定在凝胶中，防止蛋白质在染色过程中在凝胶内扩散，一般染色需 2h。脱色液同样是酸-甲醇混合物，但不含染色剂，脱色通常需在摇床上摇动过夜，其间更换脱色液 3～4 次。考马斯亮蓝染色灵敏度高，在聚丙烯酰胺凝胶中可以检测到 0.1μg 蛋白质形成的染色带。

3. 银染法　银染法比考马斯亮蓝染色的灵敏度高出 100 余倍，可以检测低于 1ng 的蛋白质，它通过银离子（Ag^+）在蛋白质上被还原成金属银形成黑色来指示蛋白质条带。银染可以直接进行也可以在考马斯亮蓝染色后进行，这样凝胶主要的蛋白点可以通过考马斯亮蓝染色分辨，而考马斯亮蓝染色检测不到的微小蛋白点再进行银染检测。

（宋永砚　陈建业）

Experiment 3 Quantitative Analysis of Serum Proteins Using Cellulose Acetate Membrane Electrophoresis

【Purposes】

1. To master the basic principles, operational procedures, technical points, main influence factors and elimination skills of serum protein quantitative analysis using cellulose acetate membrane electrophoresis and colorimetric quantitative analysis.

2. To learn the meaning of the serum protein cellulose acetate membrane electrophoresis map and its clinical significance.

3. To understand the transparent processing and quantitative analysis of the serum protein by cellulose acetate membrane profile.

【Principles】

Proteins are amphoteric electrolytes. In the solution with a pH lower than their isoelectric points (pIs) , protein molecules are positively charged. In the solution with a pH higher than their pIs, protein molecules are negatively charged. The pIs of all serum proteins are lower than the pH of 8.6. Hence, all serum proteins will be negatively charged when they are placed in the buffer with a pH greater than or equal to 8.6. In this case, the buffer with a pH of 8.6 is used to carry out cellulose acetate membrane electrophoresis for serum proteins which will migrate to the anode because they are negatively charged in this buffer. Different serum proteins have different pIs, electric quantities, molecular shapes and molecular weights. Therefore, they can be separated by electrophoresis due to different migration rates. After being dyed and rinsed, five discontinuous protein zones can be seen on the electrophoresis membrane. From the anode to the cathode, these zones include albumin (Alb) , α_1 globulin, α_2 globulin, β globulin and γ globulin respectively.

In a certain range, the protein content is proportional to the amount of the combined dye. Therefore, the percentage content of proteins in each zone of the serum can be calculated by cutting out protein zones, washing the dye with alkaline solution and reading the optical density (OD) at the wavelength of 650nm point on a spectrophotometer. In addition, the electrophoresis cellulose acetate membrane map can be scanned with an optical density scanner after the background of the membrane is cleared. Finally, the percentage content of each protein zone can be calculated based on the ratio of the area under each protein zone scanning curve relative to the total area.

【Apparatus and Reagents】

1. Apparatus

(1) Low-voltage electrophoresis apparatus and cellulose acetate membrane electrophoresis tank.

(2) Type 721A spectrophotometer.

(3) Optical density scanning analyzer.

(4) Cellulose acetate membrane (8.0cm×2.0cm).

(5) Sample applicator, tweezers, 2B pencil, coarse filter paper, staining dish, decolorizing dish and slide.

(6) Test tube (10 mL) and test tube rack.

2. Reagents

(1) Electrode buffer (pH=8.6, ionic strength I=0.06): 12.76g barbitone sodium and 1.66g barbital are dissolved in 800mL distilled water, add additional distilled water to 1,000mL, and adjust the pH to 8.6.

(2) Amino black 10B staining solution: Weigh 0.5g amino black 10B, dissolve it in 50mL methanol, add 10mL acetic acid and then add distilled water to 100mL.

(3) Decolorizing solution: Add 5mL acetic acid and 50mL distilled water into 45mL 95% ethanol, mix uniformly and store the solution at the room temperature.

(4) Elution solution: 0.4mol/L NaOH solution. Weigh 40g NaOH, dissolve it in 800mL distilled water, and add more distilled water to 1,000mL.

(5) Transparent solution: Solution A contains 15mL acetic acid + 85mL 95% ethanol; solution B contains 25mL acetic acid + 75mL 95% ethanol.

【Procedures】

1. Electrophoresis procedures

(1) Preparation of the cellulose acetate membrane: ①pick up the cellulose acetate membrane with tweezers, mark a number at the corner of the smooth face and draw a vertical thin line on the rough face 1.5 cm away from the edge as the sample line using a 2B pencil (Fig. 3-1); ②immerse the cellulose acetate membrane in the barbiturate buffer and make it fully soaked; ③take out the cellulose acetate membrane from the buffer with tweezers, and place it between two layers of filter paper to gently absorb the extra liquid.

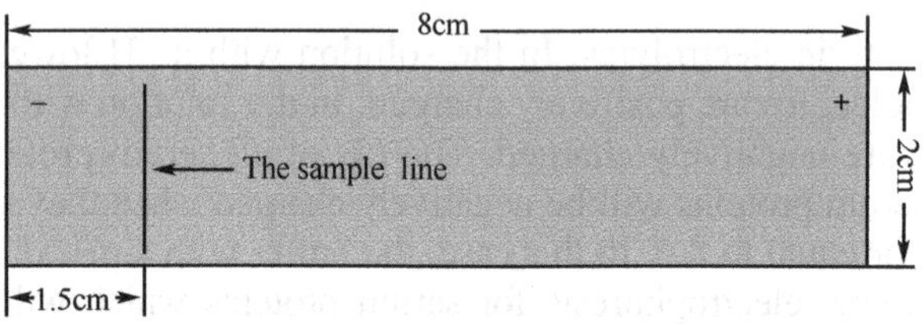

Fig. 3-1　The schematic diagram of the preparation of the cellulose acetate membrane

(2) Making a salt bridge: First, cut some filter paper of suitable size, take a double layer of filter paper and wet it in the electrode buffer. Next, attach one end of the double-layer wet paper to the rack of the electrophoresis tank and immerse the other end into the buffer. Finally, remove air bubbles from the paper strips using a glass rod. This successfully makes a "salt bridge".

(3) Sample application: Place the cellulose acetate membrane on a glass plate with the rough surface upward. Dip a small amount of the serum sample using a sample applicator and print the serum sample vertically and evenly on the sample line of the cellulose acetate membrane. The volume of the sample should be about 3μL and the serum sample should be allowed to infiltrate completely into the membrane.

(4) Tank placement: The following points should be stressed for this step: ①The long side of the membrane should be parallel to the power lines. ②The rough surface should be placed downward. ③Serum samples should be placed at the cathode side of the tank and the sample line should be about 0.5cm away from the cathode salt bridge. ④The cellulose acetate membrane should be stretched flat. Meanwhile, both ends of the membrane should be attached to the salt bridge.

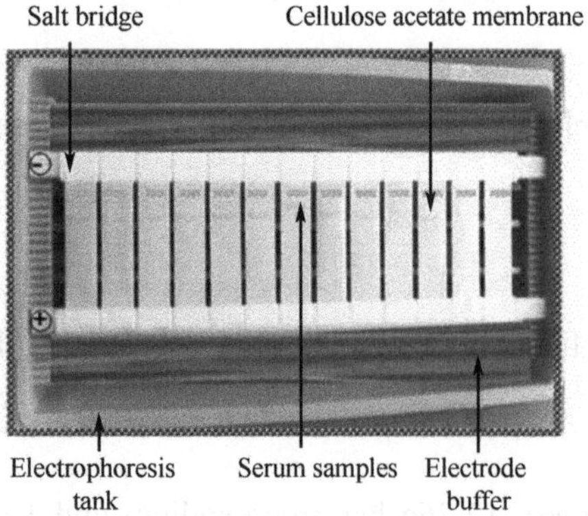

Fig. 3-2　The schematic diagram of the membrane placement on the tank

(5) Balancing: The cover should be closed and balanced for 3–5 min (Fig. 3-2).

(6) Electrophoresis: Electrode buffer I=0.06, Voltage=110–130V, Electric current=0.4–0.6mA/cm, Electrophoresis time=45–60 min.

(7) Staining: After electrophoresis, turn the power off, place the cellulose acetate membrane into the amino black 10B solution and stain it for

3–5min.

(8) Decolorization: Transfer the membrane from the staining dish to a decolorizing dish and rinse the membrane using the decolorizing solution for several times until the background becomes transparent and the serum protein bands are notable. Then, wash the decolorizing solution thoroughly with water and air dry the membrane for the next step (Fig. 3-3) .

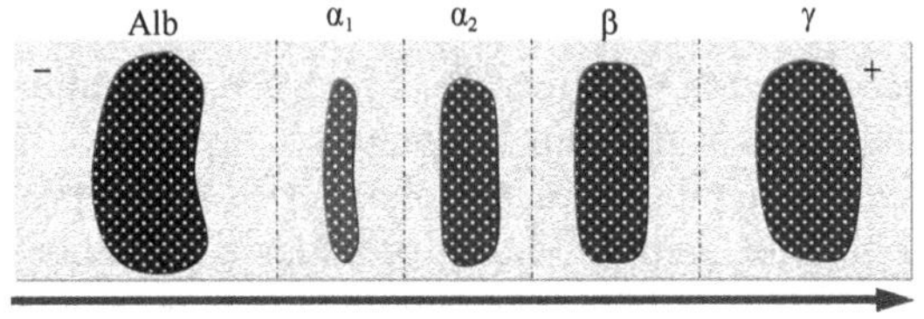

Fig. 3-3 The electrophoretic profile of serum proteins of normal humans separated using cellulose acetate membrane electrophoresis

2. Quantification analysis

1) Colorimetric analysis

(1) Elution: ①Label six tubes as 0 (blank) , Alb, α_1, α_2, β and γ, and then cut the Alb, α_1, α_2, β and γ protein zones from the electrophoretic profile. ②Place the protein band strips into their corresponding test tubes. ③Cut a blank strip with a size equal to the α_1 protein zone and place it in the blank tube. ④Add 5mL 0.4 mol/L NaOH into each tube, shake several times and completely elute off dyes from the membrane strips.

(2) Colorimetric assay: Correct for zero absorbance using the blank solution, read the absorbance of the Alb, α_1-globulin, α_2-globulin, β-globulin and γ-globulin at a wavelength of 650nm.

(3) Calculations

①Calculate the total optical density (T): $T = T_{Alb} + T_{\alpha_1} + T_{\alpha_2} + T_\beta + T_\gamma$.

②Calculate the percentage content for each protein component:

Albumin (%)=(T_{Alb}/T) ×100%

α_1 globulin (%)=(T_{α_1}/T) ×100%

α_2 globulin (%)=(T_{α_2}/T) ×100%

β globulin (%)=(T_β/T) ×100%

γ globulin (%)=(T_γ/T) ×100%

2) Scanning analysis

(1) Transparency: Transfer the membrane from the decolorizing solution to the transparent solution A for 2min → transfer the membrane to the transparent solution B for 1min → place the membrane strips on a glass plate for 3–5min→ let the membrane become completely transparent→ analyze them by scanning, or air dry and store.

(2) Scanning: Scan the transparent cellulose acetate membrane using an optical density scanning analyzer and obtain the electrophoresis scanning curve: the distance-optical density curve (Fig. 3-4) .

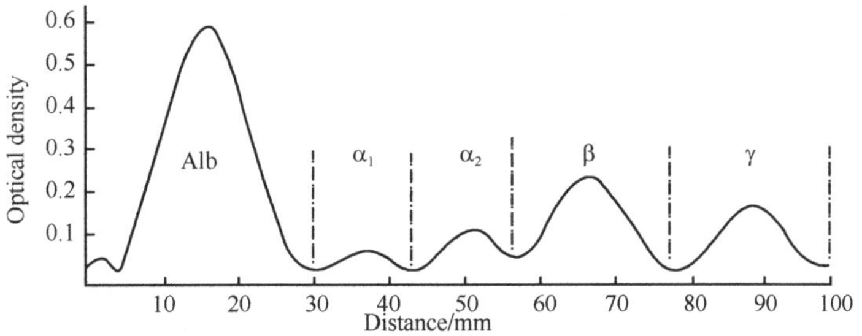

Fig. 3-4 The scanning curve of serum proteins of normal humans using the cellulose acetate membrane electrophoresis

(3) Quantification: Calculate the area of each peak of the curve as a percentage of the total area to obtain the percentage of total serum proteins in each zone.

【Clinical Significance】

The percentage contents of serum proteins of normal humans using cellulose acetate membrane electrophoresis are as follows:

Albumin(A) 57%–72% α_1 globulin 2%–5% α_2 globulin 4%–9%

β globulin 6.5%–12% γ globulin 12%–20%

In clinic, cellulose acetate membrane electrophoresis of serum proteins is usually applied to analyze proteins in blood or urine samples and it provides a reference for the clinical diagnosis of liver or kidney diseases. For example, the albumin zone in the cellulose acetate membrane electrophoresis is significantly smaller and weaker in patients with nephrotic syndrome because albumin, which has a small molecular weight, leaks out from serum into urine. In another example, serum albumin may be significantly reduced and γ globulin may be significantly increased in patients with chronic hepatitis and liver cirrhosis because of liver cell damage and the reduction of serum protein synthesis. In addition, abnormal globulin bands in serum protein cellulose acetate membrane electrophoresis are often seen in patients with multiple myeloma.

【Questions】

1. Why is a buffer with a pH of 8.6 used in serum protein cellulose acetate membrane electrophoresis?

2. What patterns will be observed in cellulose acetate membrane electrophoresis if serum proteins from patients with liver or kidney diseases are analyzed?

3. What key points should be mastered in cellulose acetate membrane electrophoresis?

Introduction to Electrophoresis

Electrophoresis refers to the process where charged particles move toward the opposite electrode under an electric field force. Many important biological molecules, such as amino acid, peptides, proteins, nucleotides and nucleic acid, contain ionizable groups that make these molecules carry charges at pHs other than their pIs. Charged molecules will move toward the opposite electrode under an electric field force. Electrophoresis is a comprehensive technique that separates, identifies, purifies and prepares charged molecules based on differences in the charge, the size or the shape, which cause the different mobility in the electric field.

Ⅰ. Principles

If the force of a charged particle in the electric field is set as F, the value of F is determined by the charge (Q) of the particle and the intensity of the electric field (X). That is:

$$F=QX$$

According to the Stokes' law, for a moving spherical particle, the relationship among factors including the resistance force (F'), the movement velocity (V), the radius of the particle (r) and the viscosity of the medium (η) is:

$$F'=6\pi r\eta V$$

When $F=F'$, dynamic balance is reached:

$$QX=6\pi r\eta V$$

Transposition of terms:

$$V/X=Q/6\pi r\eta \tag{3-1}$$

V/X indicates the moving rate of the particle in the electric field with one unit of intensity. V/X is designated as the mobility or the electrophoresis rate and is expressed as μ:

$$\mu=V/X=Q/6\pi r\eta \tag{3-2}$$

As shown in Equation (3-2) , the mobility ratio of a particle is dependent on its own characteristics, such as its charges, particle size and shape. In other words, the mobility ratio of a particle relies on its charge density. In general, different particles have different mobility. In a specific experiment, the moving rate (V) equals the distance (d, measured with cm) divided by time (t, measured with second):

$$V=d/t$$

The electric field intensity X equals the electric potential difference (E, measured with volt) divided by the unit of distance (L, measured with cm). When the distance is 1cm, the electric potential difference equals E.

$$X=E/L$$

The equations $V=d/t$ and $X=E/L$ are added to Equation (3-2) to obtain:

$$\mu=V/X=(d/t)/(E/L)=dL/Et$$

where the unit of the mobility is $cm^2/(s\cdot V)$.

The moving distance of particle A in the electric field is

$$d_A=Et\times\mu_A/L$$

The moving distance of particle B in the electric field is

$$d_B=Et\times\mu_B/L$$

The difference of the moving distances between particles A and B is

$$\Delta\,\Delta d = d_A - d_B = \frac{(\mu_A - \mu_B)\times Et}{L} \tag{3-3}$$

Equation (3-3) points out that the separation of two particles is dependent on their mobility. If these particles have different mobility, they can be separated; if they do not have different mobility, they are not able to be separated. Experimental conditions such as the voltage and the electrophoresis time are directly proportional to the isolating distance of the two particles. However, the length of the electric field (e. g. the length of filter paper) is inversely proportional to the isolating distance.

Ⅱ. The migration of charged particles in the electric field is influenced by multiple factors

Factors influencing the migration of charged particles in the electric field include the properties of the charged particle, the buffer, the electric field and the support medium. The effects of these factors on electrophoresis are as follows.

1. The properties of biomacromolecule

The number of charges, the molecular size and the physical and chemical properties of biomacromolecule to be separated have significant effects on electrophoresis. In general, the more the charge is, the smaller the diameter is and the closer the shape of the molecule to a sphere is, the faster the electrophoretic migration rate is.

2. The properties of the buffer

The degree of ionization and the charges of biomacromolecule are directly affected by the pH of the buffer. The larger the difference of the pH of the buffer from the pIs of the biomacromolecule is, the more net charges that are carried by biomacromolecule are, and the faster the moving rate is. In the buffer with a pH higher than the pI of the biomacromolecule, a negative charge will allow it to move to the cathode in the electric field. In the buffer with a pH lower than the pI of the biomacromolecule, a positive charge will allow it to move to the anode in the electric field. The ionic strength of the buffer should be maintained in a certain range (0.02–0.2). If the ionic strength is low, the pH buffer capacity of the buffer is weak. If the ionic strength is high, the strong ion-diffusion layer (namely the ion atmosphere) may be formed and the electrophoresis rate will slow down. In addition, the viscosity of the buffer will also affect the electrophoretic velocity. Generally, the greater the buffer viscosity is, the higher the electrophoresis resistance is and the slower the speed of electrophoresis is.

3. The electric field intensity The electric field intensity refers to the electric potential difference per centimeter. Generally speaking, the higher the electric field intensity is, the quicker the electrophoresis is. However, as the electric field strength increases, the electric current intensity also increases, which causes the electrophoresis process to generate more heat and ultimately leads to an increase in the temperature of the medium, inducing a series of adverse effects: ①the increase of the diffusion rate of samples and buffer ions, causing widened sample bands; ②the production of convection, causing the mixing of the samples which should be separated; ③denaturation of heat sensitive samples (e.g. proteins); ④the reduction of the medium viscosity and the electrical resistance. Heat can be reduced by lowering the current intensity but this will elongate the electrophoresis time and increase the diffusion of biomacromolecule, which will also affect separation efficiency. Thus, the proper electric field strength should be determined in a given electrophoresis experiment. To obtain excellent separation of samples, a cooling system can be used to lower the temperature.

4. The electroosmosis In the electric field, the relative movement of the solution to the fixed support medium is termed as the electroosmosis. The surface of the support medium contains charged groups. For example, there are carboxyl groups on the surface of the filter paper, sulfate groups on the surface of the agarose gel and SiOH groups on the surface of the glass. The ionization of these groups causes the surface of the supporting medium to become charged, adsorbing some of the oppositely charged ions to move in the direction of the electrode under the action of the electric field, and forming a flow of solution on the surface of the medium. This phenomenon is termed as the electroosmosis. When electroosmosis and electrophoresis are in the same direction, the electrophoretic velocity is accelerated. When electroosmosis and electrophoresis are in opposite directions, the electrophoretic velocity is reduced.

5. The sieve pore of the support medium The sieve pore size of the support medium has a significant influence on the mobility of electrophoresis. Biomacromolecules move faster in the support medium with bigger sieve pores. Otherwise, they move more slowly.

Ⅲ. Classification of electrophoresis

Presently, there is no standard classification for electrophoresis. Generally, it is classified by practical use.

(1) According to the experimental purpose and sample quantities, electrophoresis can be categorized as analytical electrophoresis and preparative electrophoresis.

(2) Based on the voltage used in electrophoresis, electrophoresis can be categorized as high voltage electrophoresis and ordinary voltage electrophoresis. Voltage settings used in high voltage electrophoresis are in 500–1,000V. The electric potential gradient can be up to 50–200V/cm. This type of electrophoresis quickly separates samples, but has great thermal effects and needs a cooling device. High voltage electrophoresis is mainly used in the separation of small molecules. The voltage used in ordinary voltage electrophoresis is lower than 500V. The electric potential gradient is 2–10V/cm. The separation rate of this electrophoresis is low, but equipment demands are simple. Ordinary voltage electrophoresis is usually used in clinical examinations.

(3) Based on the support medium used in electrophoresis, electrophoresis can be categorized as free electrophoresis and zone electrophoresis. Free electrophoresis does not use the support medium and samples that are separated move forward freely in the solution. This type of electrophoresis can also be categorized as non-free boundary electrophoresis and free boundary electrophoresis. Non-free boundary electrophoresis refers to that all the charged particles (such as cells) that are suspended in the solution move forward by current action. No zones are formed, such as micro-electrophoresis. Free boundary electrophoresis refers to that the specific sample to be separated gathers in one layer. Samples with different properties form their own zones and can be used for qualitative or quantitative analyses. Free boundary electrophoresis requires expensive instruments that are only used in special electrophoresis such

as isoelectric focusing or isotachophoresis. All zone electrophoresis uses the support medium. Based on the support medium used, zone electrophoresis can be categorized into paper electrophoresis, cellulose acetate membrane electrophoresis, thin layer electrophoresis or gel electrophoresis. In addition, zone electrophoresis can be categorized into horizontal electrophoresis, vertical electrophoresis, vertical disc electrophoresis, capillary electrophoresis, bridge-shaped electrophoresis or continuous flow electrophoresis.

(4) Based on the pH used in the electrophoresis system, electrophoresis can be categorized as continuous pH electrophoresis or non-continuous pH electrophoresis. Continuous pH electrophoresis refers to electrophoresis where the pH remains constant during the whole process, such as paper electrophoresis or cellulose acetate membrane electrophoresis. Non-continuous pH electrophoresis refers to electrophoresis where the electrode buffer and the support medium have different pHs and the different sections of the support medium have different pHs, such as polyacrylamide gel electrophoresis, isoelectric focusing and isotachophoresis.

(5) Based on the techniques used, electrophoresis can be categorized as immunity electrophoresis, chromatography electrophoresis, isoelectric-focusing electrophoresis, transferring electrophoresis, two-dimentional electrophoresis and pulsed-field gel electrophoresis.

(6) According to the sample types analyzed, electrophoresis can be categorized as cell electrophoresis, nucleic acid electrophoresis and protein electrophoresis.

Ⅳ. Brief introduction of several classic or novel electrophoresis techniques

1. Paper electrophoresis and acetate cellulose membrane electrophoresis

1) Paper electrophoresis. Paper electrophoresis is a kind of traditional electrophoresis that uses filter paper as a support medium. Although the resolution of paper electrophoresis is not as good as gel electrophoresis, its operation is very simple and it is still widely used especially in clinical serum sample examinations and virus analyses.

Paper electrophoresis needs a horizontal electrophoresis tank. The separation of amino acid and nucleotides usually uses the acidic buffer and the separation of proteins usually occurs in the alkaline buffer. The filter paper must have a uniform thickness. Chinese Xinhua filter paper and imported Whatman 1 filter paper are commonly used. The sample is added at a line that is 1–2cm away from the end of the paper. The sample can be added as a dot or a solid line, but a linear style has better separation efficiency than that of a dotted style has. The amount loaded is in 5–100μg or 5–10μL. Methods for adding samples include dry or wet methods. The wet method refers to the wet treatment of the filter paper before adding samples. The method requires a high sample concentration and is not suitable for multiple sample counts. The dry method refers to wetting the filter paper by spraying the buffer solution after adding the sample. The spot samples can be blown dry and spotted multiple times, thus allowing a thinner sample to be used. The anode and cathode need to be checked before electrophoresis and the voltage is usually 2–10V/cm with a long time. Electrophoresis for small molecules such as amino acid and peptides can use high voltages of 50–200V/cm. The electrophoresis time is reduced greatly but overheating in electrophoresis must be considered and safety issues must be avoided.

Measurement of the valid length of the filter paper, drying and colorizing with chromogenic reagent should be done immediately after electrophoresis. Quantitative methods include the elution and the optical density methods. The elution method includes cutting down the sample zone, eluting the samples from the paper and determining concentration by colorimetric assay. The optical density method refers to the direct measurement of the sample contents in each zone with a densitometer after staining.

2) Acetate cellulose membrane electrophoresis. Acetate cellulose membrane electrophoresis is similar to paper electrophoresis. It uses the acetate cellulose membrane as a support medium. The hydroxyl groups of cellulose are acetylated to form methyl acetate. Methyl acetate

is dissolved into acetone and then used to make the 0.1–0.15mm membrane with uniform and tiny pores. Compared with paper electrophoresis, acetate cellulose membrane electrophoresis has the following advantages: ①The cellulose acetate membrane hardly absorbs protein samples, no "tail" is produced and the stained protein band is clear. ②Acetate cellulose membrane electrophoresis is quick and saves time. The hydrophilicity of cellulose acetate membrane is smaller than that of filter paper so there is less water absorption and electroosmosis. Most of the current is transmitted by samples in electrophoresis so there is high separation efficiency and short electrophoresis time. The entire electrophoresis process takes only about 90min. ③Acetate cellulose membrane electrophoresis has high sensitivity and uses less samples. Serum protein electrophoresis only needs 2μL of serum. A clear electrophoresis map can be obtained with as little as 0.1μg of the serum sample. In the clinic, acetate cellulose membrane electrophoresis is usually used to detect changes in trace serum proteins. ④Acetate cellulose membrane electrophoresis has many applications in the medical field. It can be used to analyze samples not suitable for paper electrophoresis, such as α-fetoproteins, lysozymes, insulin or histones. ⑤The acetate cellulose membrane can be treated with acetic acid and ethanol to make it transparent after staining and can be used to measure the sample amount using a densitometer and spectrophotometer or be placed for long-term storage.

The cellulose acetate membrane electrophoresis has advantages such as its simple operation, less expensive and time-saving. It has been used to detect and analyze plasma proteins, lipoproteins, glycoproteins, α-fetoproteins, body fluids, cerebrospinal fluid, dehydrogenases, polypeptides, nucleic acid and other biomolecules. It provides a reliable basis for the diagnosis of cardiovascular diseases, liver cirrhosis and cancer. Therefore it has become a routine technique in medical and clinical examinations.

2. Agarose gel electrophoresis Agarose gel can be used as a support medium for protein or nucleic acid electrophoresis and is especially suitable for the purification and analysis of nucleic acid. 1% agarose gel has relatively large pores for protein particles, resulting in a small resistance effect. In immune electrophoresis and isoelectric focusing electrophoresis the mobility of proteins is mainly determined by the charges of proteins rather than the size. Agarose gel is also suitable to separate and analyze both DNA and RNA molecules. DNA and RNA are typically larger molecules that tend to encounter a resistant force from the gel. The size of DNA or RNA molecules has a great impact on the mobility. For example, the migration rate of double stranded DNA is mainly associated with the size of DNA molecules and not with nucleotide sequence and composition. In addition, some low melting point agarose gel melts at 65°C so samples such as DNA can be redissolved into the solution and collected.

Due to poor elasticity, it is difficult to remove the agarose gel from tubules making the gel not suitable for tubular electrophoresis. Agarose gel usually adopts a horizontal plate form and is used for protein electrophoresis including isoelectric focusing or immune electrophoresis, as well as the analysis of DNA and RNA molecules.

3. Polyacrylamide gel electrophoresis Polyacrylamide gel electrophoresis (PAGE) is a popular electrophoresis technique that uses polyacrylamide gel as a support medium. A polyacrylamide gel is formed by the polymerization of acrylamide monomer and bisacrylamide, and the polymerization process is catalyzed by free radicals. There are two commonly used methods to catalyze polymerization including chemical polymerization and photopolymerization. Chemical polymerization uses ammonium persulfate (AP) as a catalyst and *N*, *N*, *N'*, *N'*-tetramethy-lethylenediamine (TEMED) as accelerators. During polymerization, free radicals are produced from ammonium persulfate during the catalysis of TEMED. Free radicals trigger the polymerization of acrylamide monomers. At the same time, cross-linking between the methylene bisacrylamide and acrylamide chains is formed with methylene bonds, making the gel have a three dimensional net structure.

The pore size of the polyacrylamide gel can be adjusted by modulating the ratio of acrylamide to bisacrylamide. A low concentration gel has a larger pore size. For example, the pore size of 3% polyacrylamide gel is large, it almost has no resistance against the movement of protein molecules and it can be used for isoelectric focusing or separation of DNA. Gels with a high concentration have a smaller pore size and molecular sieve effect, which is generally used for the separation of proteins with different molecular weights. The mechanical toughness of a polyacrylamide gel is strong. Properties including gel strength, elasticity, transparency, viscosity and pore size are dependent on the concentration of acrylamide and bisacrylamide as well as the cross-linking degree between acrylamide and bisacrylamide.

Non-denaturing PAGE can maintain the native conformation, the charge distribution and the biological activity of large biomolecules and is important for the identification of biomacromolecule. In addition, a polyacrylamide gel also has the following advantages: ①The gel concentration and the cross-linking degree can be controlled to separate biomacromolecule with different molecular weights. ②The molecular sieve effects and charge effects can be effectively integrated into the same method to improve the sensitivity of separation. ③A polyacrylamide gel does not contain ionizable groups so no electroosmosis effects are presented in PAGE. ④A polyacrylamide gel has high transparency and it is easy to take images. ⑤A polyacrylamide gel has high mechanical strength and elasticity, it is not fragile, and it is easy to operate and store. ⑥A polyacrylamide gel does not absorb ultraviolet (UV) rays and can be used for quantitative analysis using a UV analyzer. ⑦A polyacrylamide gel can be used as an inert carrier for immobilized enzymes.

Initially, the separation of proteins by PAGE was performed in a glass tube with a diameter of about 7mm and a length of about 10cm. This is termed disc electrophoresis because protein zones have the appearance of discs. However, there has been error in the tubes due to inconsistency in separation conditions, which is produced from differences in glass tubes and in generating the gel. Vertical plate electrophoresis was later invented to replace disc electrophoresis. Vertical plate electrophoresis can accommodate more than 20 samples at one time. Conditions of samples during electrophoresis are relatively consistent, contributing to good repeatability and consistency. Therefore, vertical plate electrophoresis was widely applied for the isolation, identification and sequence analysis of proteins and nucleic acid.

Developed in recent years, horizontal plate electrophoresis has many similarities as vertical plate electrophoresis but it also has its own unique advantages including: ①The gel can be laid flat directly on the cooling plate, making it easy to cool the gel. ②The voltage can be elevated to improve the resolution. ③Horizontal plate electrophoresis is very fast and only needs about 1h for completion, while disc electrophoresis and vertical plate electrophoresis usually need 3–4h. ④A thin gel can be used and it has a series of advantages such as less samples being used, fast staining, high sensitivity and easy to save. The gel can be preserved for a long time and will not crack as long as it is soaked in glycerol and then naturally dries. ⑤Horizontal plate electrophoresis is suitable for various electrophoresis methods with wide applications.

4. SDS-PAGE Sodium dodecyl sulphate (SDS)-PAGE is the most commonly used electrophoresis method for qualitative analysis of proteins, especially for the detection of protein purity and molecular weight. In SDS-PAGE, SDS, an anion surfactant, and β-mercapto-ethanol are added to samples. SDS disconnects intramolecular and intermolecular hydrogen bonds and destroys secondary and tertiary structures of proteins. β-mercapto-ethanol can disconnect disulfide bonds between cysteine residues and destroy quaternary structures of proteins. Mixed with SDS and β-mercapto-ethanol, samples are boiled in a water bath for 3–5min, causing the denaturation and depolymerization of proteins, and covering a lot of negative charges on protein surfaces. Then, the rodlike structure of protein molecules is formed. Bromophenol blue is usually added to the sample to control the electrophoresis process. In addition, the proper amount of the sucrose or glycerol solution is added to the sample to increase the density of the solution, and then the sample is easy to sink into the bottom of the well during loading.

The concentration of separation gel is determined based on the molecular size of the sample. In general, a separation gel with a low concentration is selected for the separation of high molecular weight proteins whereas a separation gel with a high concentration is used to separate low molecular weight proteins. After polymerization of separation gel, a layer of stacking gel (about 1cm) is added to the separation gel with a comb inserted at the top to create sample wells. The pH (usually 6.8) and concentration (3%–5%) of stacking gel are lower than that of separation gel, so the pore size is relatively large and all protein molecules can pass through freely. The stacking gel is commonly used to concentrate the sample into a narrow zone before entering separation gel. After stacking gel is polymerized, the comb is removed and the gel is ready for electrophoresis.

PAGE has two types of systems, including a continuous system and a discontinuous system. A discontinuous system includes pH discontinuity, gel discontinuity and discontinuity of solution ionic composition. In the process of electrophoresis, samples are first moved through stacking gel and they are concentrated due to isotachophoresis. After entering separation gel, due to the molecular sieve action of polyacrylamide, small molecules of protein can easily pass through the pore size of the gel with little resistance and fast migration rate, while large molecules of protein are subjected to greater resistance and retarded. Hence, molecules can be separated based on their molecular size. Bromophenol blue can freely pass through the gel and it is used to indicate the leading line during electrophoresis. Operation of PAGE will be discussed in more detail in Exp.20.

5. Isoelectric focusing Isoelectric focusing separates substances based on the pIs of molecules. This technique has very high resolution and it can distinguish samples with pI differences as small as 0.01. Isoelectric focusing is an ideal method for separating proteins and other amphoteric substances. In isoelectric focusing, a discontinuous pH gradient is formed by adding ampholyte into the gel. In the electrophoresis process, the samples that will be separated can automatically move to corresponding pH regions, resulting in separation.

An amphoteric electrolyte is a complex, artificial compound with multi-amino and multi-carboxyl groups. Different amphoteric electrolytes have different pH gradient ranges. Therefore, the proper amphoteric electrolyte compound should be chosen before the experiment according to the properties of the samples that are to be separated. The pIs of the components should fall into the pH range of the amphoteric electrolyte compound.

Isoelectric focusing has very high sensitivity and resolution (minimum detection level of 10^{-10}g). Using this technique, human serum proteins can be divided into 40–50 clear bands. Isoelectric focusing is especially suitable to study protein heterogeneity in trace amounts. For example, proteins expressed in a single band in the SDS-PAGE can be divided into three bands using isoelectric focusing. This may be due to the presence of monophosphorylated, biphosphorylated and triphosphorylated forms of the protein. Phosphate groups have no clear influence on the molecular weights of proteins but they can change the protein charge significantly. So it shows a single band in SDS-PAGE but three bands in isoelectric focusing.

Isoelectric focusing can also be used to determine the pIs of unknown proteins. A series of standard proteins with known pIs and proteins with unknown pIs are added onto one gel where isoelectric focusing is performed. The standard curve is determined by the distance of each standard protein to one side and the corresponding pI. Then, the pI of the protein to be tested can be obtained from the standard curve by measuring the distance. Isoelectric focusing is mainly used for the separation and purification of proteins with the advantage of simple operation and high purification efficiency, although it has the disadvantage of a high cost.

6. Two-dimensional electrophoresis Two-dimensional electrophoresis (2-DE) has the advantages of both isoelectric focusing and SDS-PAGE and it is the most effective means to protein analysis. The first phase of 2-DE is isoelectric focusing carried out in a tubule where proteins are separated based on their pIs. Then, the gel is removed from the tubule and SDS-PAGE is used to separate during the second phase. In the second phase, proteins are separated based on their molecular sizes. Each protein can be separated and distributed in the bidirectional map. In the electrophoresis map of cell extracts, 1,000–2,000 protein spots can be detected using 2-DE. It has been reported that this technique can distinguish as many as 5,000–10,000 protein spots, which is probably close to the amount of proteins existing in cells.

A specific protein can be detected directly from cell extracts due to the high resolution of 2-DE. For example, after cDNA of a specific protein is transferred to frog oocytes, there should be a corresponding protein spot on the 2-DE map by comparing transferred and untransferred frog oocytes. This is a comprehensive technique and there have been some computer systems that directly record and compare the results of 2-DE.

V. Detection, identification and recovery of proteins

1. Scanning and measuring absorbance The quantitative analysis of different protein samples can be determined by scanning the stained gel with a densitometer. The absorbance of protein bands at different migration distances on the gel is measured by the scanner, and the distance-optical density curve is obtained. The peaks on the curve graph correspond to each stained protein band, and the size of the peak area represents the amount of protein content. Another simple method is to cut down stained protein bands, and shake it overnight in a 50% pyridine solution to dissolve the dye. Then, the absorbance of the solution are determined using a spectrophotometer and protein content can be estimated using absorbance. It should be noted that the protein concentration has a linear relationship with the absorbance in a certain concentration range only. Under the same degree of staining, the staining color of different proteins may differ. Hence, the sepectrophotometry is just a semi-quantitative method.

2. Staining by Coomassie brilliant blue The most commonly used protein staining reagent is Coomassie brilliant blue R250, which is composed of water, methanol and acetic acid in a volume ratio of 45 : 45 : 10. The final concentration of Coomassie brilliant blue R250 is 0.1%–0.25% (*W*/*V*). This acid-methanol solution can denature proteins and fix them in a gel to prevent their diffusion. Usually, the staining process requires 2h to be completed. Decolorizing solution also contains a mixture of acid and methanol but without the staining reagent. Decolorization usually requires overnight shaking on a shaker, with 3–4 changes of decolorizing solution in between. Staining with Coomassie brilliant blue has high sensitivity, which can detect protein bands with only 0.1μg of protein.

3. Silver staining The sensitivity of silver staining is 100 times greater than that of Coomassie brilliant blue staining. Proteins less than 1ng can be detected using this method. In silver staining, the protein band is visualized through black metallic silver which is formed through the reduction of silver ions (Ag^+) by reductive groups of the protein molecules. Silver staining can be directly carried out or stained after Coomassie brilliant blue staining. Major protein spots are differentiated with Coomassie brilliant blue staining, and minor protein spots not detected by coomassie brilliant blue staining are then detected with silver staining.

(Song Yongyan, Chen Jianye)

实验 4　离子交换层析

【实验目的】

1. 掌握离子交换层析操作技术。
2. 熟悉离子交换层析的一般工作原理。
3. 了解离子交换层析技术的应用。

【实验原理】

离子交换层析是用离子交换剂（具有离子交换性能的物质）作固定相，利用它与流动相中的离子进行可逆的交换性质来分离离子型化合物的层析方法。离子交换层析可分为两种：阳离子交换层析和阴离子交换层析。阳离子交换层析的固定相带负电基团，可与带正电荷的离子结合；阴离子交换层析的固定相带正电基团，可与带负电荷的离子结合。下面以阴离子交换为例说明离子交换层析的基本过程。阴离子交换剂的电荷基团带正电，装柱平衡后，可与缓冲溶液中的带负电的平衡离子结合。待分离溶液中可能有正电基团、负电基团和中性基团。加样后，负电基团可以与平衡离子进行可逆的置换反应，而结合到离子交换剂上。而正电基团和中性基团则不能与离子交换剂结合，随流动相流出而被去除。通过选择合适的洗脱方式和洗脱液（如增加离子强度的梯度洗脱），随着洗脱液离子强度的增加，洗脱液中的离子可以逐步与结合在离子交换剂上的各种负电基团进行交换，而将各种负电基团置换出来，随洗脱液流出。与离子交换剂结合力小的负电基团先被置换出来，而与离子交换剂结合力强的需要较高的离子强度才能被置换出来，这样各种负电基团就会按其与离子交换剂结合力从小到大的顺序逐步被洗脱下来，从而达到分离目的。

本实验用磺酸阳离子分离酸性氨基酸（天冬氨酸）、中性氨基酸（组氨酸）和碱性氨基酸（赖氨酸）的混合液。在特定的 pH 条件下，它们解离的程度不同，通过改变洗脱液的 pH 或离子强度可将其分别洗脱分离。

【器材与试剂】

1. 器材

层析柱、试管和试管架、滴管、烧杯、收集瓶、721A 型分光光度计、低速离心机。

2. 试剂

（1）苯乙烯磺酸钠树脂（强酸 1×8，100～200 目）。

（2）2mol/L HCl：量取 16.7mL 浓盐酸（12mol/L）加入蒸馏水定容至 100mL。

（3）2mol/L NaOH 溶液：称取 8g NaOH 溶于 100mL 蒸馏水中。

（4）柠檬酸缓冲液（pH5.8）：取柠檬酸 14.25g、NaOH 9.39g 和浓盐酸 5.25mL 溶于少量水后，用蒸馏水定容至 500mL，4℃保存。

（5）2mg/mL 标准氨基酸溶液：用 0.1mol/L 盐酸溶液分别配制 2mg/mL 的天冬氨酸（pI 2.74）、赖氨酸（pI 9.74）和组氨酸（pI 7.59）溶液。

（6）混合氨基酸溶液：将上述天冬氨酸、赖氨酸和组氨酸按照体积比为 1∶1∶1 的比例混合而成。

（7）显色剂：称取 2g 水合茚三酮溶于 75mL 乙二醇单甲醚中，加水至 100mL。

【实验操作】

1. 树脂的处理　根据层析柱的体积和所选用的树脂，以及膨胀后柱床体积，计算所需干树脂的重量，称好倾入 40～45℃热水中浸泡数小时，后用 60%乙醇溶液去掉其有机杂质，抽干，再用清水充分溶胀备用。

2. 离子交换柱的安装　取大小合适的层析柱，底部垫玻璃棉或者海绵圆垫，自顶部注入处理好的树脂悬浮液，关闭层析柱的出口，待树脂沉降后，放出过量的溶液，再加入一些树脂，至树脂沉积至合适的高度即可。于柱子顶部继续加入缓冲液，保持液面高出树脂表面 1cm 左右。

3. 加样　打开柱子下端的放液开关，使柱内液面刚好降至树脂面。在加样前，树脂顶部放一圆形滤纸片，然后将样品溶液（0.5mL 的混合氨基酸溶液）小心地加到圆形滤纸片上，待样品液面刚好进入树脂层内便立即加入少许柠檬酸缓冲液，以清洗黏附在覆盖层中的样品，并随之进入树脂层。当柱内液位接近树脂表面时便立即添加洗涤液进行洗涤操作。

4. 洗涤、洗脱及收集　用滴管小心地滴加 0.5mL 柠檬酸缓冲液（切勿搅动床面）进行洗涤（反复 2 次），以除去不被离子交换树脂吸附的杂质。继续滴加柠檬酸缓冲液进行洗脱，并将柱与洗脱收集瓶相连。开始用试管收集洗脱液，每管 1mL，共收集 60 管。

5. 检测　向各管收集液中加 1mL 显色剂并混匀，在沸水浴中准确加热 15min 后冷却至室温，再加 1.5mL 的 50%乙醇溶液。放置 10min，以蒸馏水为空白对照，测定 570nm 波长的吸光度。

6. 洗脱曲线　以洗脱液各管的吸光度为纵坐标，以洗脱液管号为横坐标绘制洗脱曲线。将混合的氨基酸洗脱曲线与标准的氨基酸洗脱曲线相对照，确定 3 个峰的位置，以及各峰为何种氨基酸。

【思考题】

1. 举例说明离子交换树脂工作的原理。
2. 如何保存树脂？

层析技术简介

一、层析技术概述

层析技术是一种分离混合物的实验技术，它利用混合物中各组分物理或化学性质的差异（如吸附能力、溶解度、分子形状、分子大小以及分子极性等），使各组分以不同的浓度分布在固定相和流动相中。各组分在流动相和固定相相对运动时，反复多次分配，最后彼此分离开来。

二、层析技术的分类

生物化学分析中常用的层析技术包括凝胶过滤层析、离子交换层析、亲和层析和薄层层析等。

1. 凝胶过滤层析　凝胶过滤层析又叫分子筛层析、排阻层析。它是利用凝胶颗粒对分子量和形状不同的物质进行分离的层析技术。小分子能够进入凝胶的内部，经过的路径长，需要更长的时间才能被洗脱；较大的分子不会掉进孔中因而被快速洗脱出来。

以葡聚糖凝胶层析为例，葡聚糖凝胶是由葡聚糖和甘油基以醚桥形式相互交联形成的具有三维网状结构的一种水不溶性大分子。通过控制交联剂环氧氯丙烷和葡聚糖的配比来获得不同网眼的凝胶。网眼的大小决定了被分离物质能够自由出入凝胶内部的分子量范围。不同型号的交联葡聚糖用 G 值表示（如 G-25、G-100 等），G 后面的数字为凝胶的吸水量乘以 10 得到的数字，如 G-25 表示此型号凝胶吸水量是 2.5mL/g 干胶。在具体的实验中根据欲分离物质大小及目的来选择合适的葡聚糖凝胶。待分离的物质中，各组分之间的分子量不同，在凝胶中移动的速度不同。分子量大的完全被排阻，不能进入凝胶颗粒内部，阻滞作用最小，随着溶剂在凝胶颗粒之间流动，因此流程最短，移动速度最快而最先流出层析柱；分子量小于凝胶分离下限的物质可完全渗入凝胶颗粒，阻力作用最大，流程最长，移动速度最慢，从层析柱中流出最晚。

2. 离子交换层析　离子交换层析主要根据分子所带电荷来分离。在这类层析中，树脂被用来与阴离子或阳离子共价交联。流动相中带相反电荷的溶质离子以静电作用被吸引到树脂上。在离子交换层析中，带电物质经过带相反电荷的柱材料而分离。交换柱上的电离基团与凝胶基质共价结合，且受到存在于缓冲液中的低浓度反离子的抵消。样品加到柱子上后，可与结合弱的反离子进行初始交换。只有洗脱液的离子强度不断增加或 pH 改变，目标蛋白才会从树脂上洗脱出来。

离子交换层析分为两种类型：阳离子交换和阴离子交换。在阳离子交换层析中，上到树脂上的蛋白质的迁移速率与蛋白质所带负电荷呈正比。也就是说，带更多负电荷的蛋白质运动更快、更容易被洗脱出来。相反，在阴离子交换层析中，带更多正电荷的蛋白质的移动速度更快，更容易被洗脱出来。

3. 亲和层析　亲和层析利用共价连接有特异配体的层析介质来分离混合物中能特异结合配体的目的分子。蛋白质是按各种蛋白质与连接在柱中树脂上的特异配体的结合能力来分离的。从柱上洗脱出那些不能与配体结合的蛋白质后，目的蛋白可用浓度逐渐增加的自由配体洗脱下来。在此类层析中，蛋白质和配体相互作用的特异性相当高，单个步骤就可提供最大程度的纯化。其不足之处在于需要为每种纯化的分子都制作一个柱子。

4. 薄层层析　薄层层析是将吸附剂、载体或其他活性物质均匀涂铺在平板（如玻璃板、塑料片、金属片等）上，形成薄层（常用厚度为 0.25mm 左右）后，在此薄层上进行层析分离的分析方法。薄层层析适用于少量样品（可低至 0.01μg），在制作薄层板时把吸附层加厚加大，可用来精制样品，因此特别适用于挥发性较小或较高温度易发生变化而不能用气相色谱分析的物质。制作薄层层析时，将样品溶液用毛细管点在薄层板的一端，置密闭槽中，加入适宜溶剂为流动相。由于毛细管原理，溶剂被吸上，沿板移动，并带动样品中各组分向前移动。由于各组分性质不同，移动距离不同，得到互相分离的组分斑点。可用适当方法使各组分在板上显示其位置，如组分本身有颜色，即可直接观察，否则可喷显色试剂或在紫外灯下观察荧光等办法确定。

（汤建才　陈建业）

Experiment 4 Ion Exchange Chromatography

【Purposes】

1. To master operation techniques of ion exchange chromatography.
2. To understand the general principle of ion exchange chromatography.
3. To learn the application of ion exchange chromatography.

【Principles】

Ion exchange chromatography is a method that uses ion exchanger (a substance that has ion exchange properties) as the stationary phase that can separate ionic compounds by reversible ion exchange between the stationary and mobile phases. There are two types of ion exchange chromatography including cation exchange chromatography and anion exchange chromatography. In cation exchange chromatography, the stationary phase contains negative groups that can bind positive ions. In anion exchange chromatography, the stationary phase contains positive groups that can bind negative ions. Anion exchange will next be used as an example to explain the basic process of ion exchange chromatography. Anion exchange resin contains positive groups that combine with negative ions in the buffer solution after the balance of a packing column. Positive, negative and neutral groups exist in the separated solution. After adding samples, the negative groups are reversibly replaced with balanced ions and are combined with ion exchange resin. The positive and neutral groups cannot combine with ion exchange resin or be removed with mobile phase flowing. By choosing a suitable elution method and eluent (such as the gradient elution) , ions in the eluent can be gradually exchanged with negative groups in the ion exchange resin with an increase of ionic strength in the elution solution. All types of negative groups are replaced from the ion exchange resin and flow out with the eluent. Negative groups that have a small binding force with ion exchange resin are first replaced, while groups that have high binding force with ion exchange resin need higher ionic strength to be displaced. Thus, a variety of negative groups will be gradually washed off based on their binding forces.

This experiment uses sulfonic acid cation-exchange resin to separate a mixture of acidic (aspartic acid) amino acid, neutral (histidine) amino acid and alkaline(lysine) amino acid. Under a specific pH, the degree of dissociation differs for the three kinds of amino acid so they can be eluted and separated by changes in pH and ionic strength.

【Apparatus and Reagents】

1. Apparatus

chromatography column, test tube and test tube rack, dropper, beaker, collecting bottle, type 721A spectrophotometer and low-speed centrifuge.

2. Reagents

(1) Sodium p-styrene sulfonate resin (strong acid 1×8; 100–200 mesh).

(2) 2mol/L HCl solution: Measure 16.7mL concentrated HCl (12mol/L) and add the distilled water to 100mL.

(3) 2mol/L NaOH solution: Weigh 8g NaOH and dissolve it in 100mL distilled water.

(4) Citrate acid buffer (pH5.8): Take 14.25g citric acid, 9.39g NaOH and 5.25mL concentrated HCl, dissolve them in a small amount of water, dilute the solution to 500mL with distilled water, and store it at 4°C.

(5) 2mg/mL standard amino acid solution: Prepare 2mg/mL aspartic acid (pI 2.74) , lysine (pI 9.74) and histidine (pI 7.59) solution, with 0.1mol/L HCl solution, respectively.

(6) Mixed amino acid solution: Mix the above standard amino acid solutions in a volume ratio of 1∶1∶1 to obtain the mixture.

(7) Chromogenic reagent: Dissolve 2g ninhydrin hydrate in 75mL ethylene glycol monomethyl ether and add up to 100mL with distilled water.

【Procedures】

1. Resin treatment Weigh the required resin powder according to the chromatographic column volume, the resin type and the expanded bed volume. Pour the resin into 40–45℃ water and soak for several hours. Remove organic impurities with 60% ethanol, dry and then add distilled water.

2. Installation of ion exchange columns Take a chromatography column and put glass wool or a circular sponge cushion at the bottom of the column. Pour the pretreated resin from the top into the column. Close the stopcock of the chromatography column, let the resin settle, open the stopcock to release the excessive solution, and then add more resin to the desired volume. Finally, add the buffer solution to wash the resin and keep the level of the liquid surface about 1cm higher above the resin bed.

3. Sample loading Open the stopcock and let the buffer solution flow out until the liquid level in the column just drops to the surface of the resin bed. Place a piece of circular filter paper on the top of the resin column before sample loading and then carefully add the sample (0.5mL mixed amino acid solution) directly onto the filter paper. Add a small amount of citrate acid buffer solution to clean the remaining sample in the cover layer after samples enter the resin layer. Immediately add more wash buffer when the buffer level in the column is close to the resin surface.

4. Washing, elution and collection Carefully add 0.5mL of the citric acid buffer using a dropper without disturbing the bed surface to wash the column resin and remove impurities not absorbed by the ion exchange resin (wash twice). Add the citric acid buffer to elute. Collect eluents with 60 test tubes that have 1mL of eluents in each tube.

5. Identification Add 1mL of the chromogenic reagent to each tube and mix well. Heat tubes in a boiling water bath for 15min and then let them cool to the room temperature. Then add 1.5mL of the 50% ethanol solution respectively and let them stand for 10min. Read the absorbance at 570nm using distilled water as the blank control.

6. The elution curve Plot the elution curve with the absorbance of each eluent tube as the vertical coordinate and the eluent tube number as the horizontal coordinate. Compare the elution curve of mixed amino acid with the elution curve of standard amino acid to determine the positions of threes peaks of amino acid and for what amino acid.

【Questions】

1. Explain the principles of ion exchange chromatography by giving an example.
2. How does one preserve the resin?

Introduction of Chromatography

Ⅰ. The overview of the chromatography technique

Chromatography is a laboratory technique used for the separation of mixtures. The separation principle is based on the differential physical or chemical properties of each component (such as adsorption capacity, solubility, molecular shape, molecular size and molecular polarity) , so that the various constituents of the mixture are differentially partitioned between the mobile and stationary phases. As the components move within the mobile and stationary phases, they are repeatedly distributed many times and are finally separated from each other.

II. Types of chromatography

There are several types of chromatography used in biochemical analysis including gel filtration chromatography, ion exchange chromatography, affinity chromatography and thin-layer chromatography.

1. Gel filtration chromatography Gel filtration chromatography, also known as molecular sieve chromatography or exclusion chromatography, separates molecules according to their different molecular weights and shapes. Smaller molecules can enter the interior pores of gel particles, pass through a long pathway and take a longer time to be eluted. Larger molecules do not enter the interior pores and are eluted faster.

Here, we will present the example of polydextran gel filtration chromatography. Polydextran gel is composed of a three-dimensional network structure and water insoluble macromolecules that are formed by dextran and glycerin that are cross-linked by glycerin ether bonds. Different kinds of gel for the mesh can be obtained by controlling the ratio of the cross-linking agent epichlorohydrin and dextran. The mesh size determines the relative molecular weight range of the separated materials that can freely enter the interior of the gel particles. Different types of cross-linked dextrans are represented by "G" values (e.g. G-25, G-100) that equal 10 times the water absorption rate of the gel. For example, G-25 indicates that the absorption of this type of gel is 2.5mL/g dry gel. In specific experiments, the selection of an appropriate polydextran gel is based on the size of the separated material and the experimental purpose. Components with different molecular weights have different moving speeds in the gel. A component with a molecular weight larger than the permitted upper range of the gel separation will not enter the interior of the gel and it will have a short but fast flow path where it flows out of the column first. Materials with a molecular weight less than the permitted lower range of the gel separation can completely enter the interior of the gel and face the largest resistance with a long and slow flow path, flowing out of the column last.

2. Ion exchange chromatography Ion exchange chromatography separates molecules based on their electrical charges. In this type of chromatography, the resin is used for covalent cross-linking with anions or cations. Oppositely charged solute ions in the mobile phase are attracted to the resin by electrostatic action. During ion exchange chromatography, substances are separated when they pass through a column with an opposite charge. The ionic groups of the exchanger column are covalently bound to the gel matrix and they are offset by counter ions with low concentrations in the buffer. When a sample is added to the column, an exchange with weakly bound counter ions begins. The target protein will be eluted from the resin only when the ionic strength of the eluent steadily increases or the pH changes.

There are two types of exchange chromatography including cation exchange chromatography and anion exchange chromatography. In cation exchange chromatography, the migration rate of proteins loaded onto the resin is proportional to the degree of negative charges on the proteins. Thus, proteins with more negative charges will move faster and be eluted easily. In contrast, in anion exchange chromatography, proteins with more positive charges will move faster and be eluted more easily.

3. Affinity chromatography Affinity chromatography is a type of chromatography that separates target molecules in mixtures by chromatography media that covalently binds to a specific ligand. The protein separation process is based on the combination force of proteins and specific ligands. After proteins that do not bind to the ligand are washed through the column, the bound target protein is eluted from the column by a higher concentration of the free ligands. With this type of chromatography, the interactions between the proteins and ligands are so specific, they afford the greatest degree of purification in a single step. The drawback of this technique is that an individual column is needed for each molecule to be purified.

4. Thin-layer chromatography Thin-layer chromatography is an analytical method for separating adsorbents, carriers or other active substances on a plate (such as a glass plate, plastic sheet, metal sheet) after uniformly coating it to form a thin layer (the common thickness is about

0.25 mm). Thin-layer chromatography is suitable for small amounts of samples (down to 0.01μg) and can be used to refine samples by increasing the thickness of the adsorbent layer during the preparation of thin-layer plates. Therefore, it is especially suitable for substances that cannot be analyzed by gas chromatography because they are less volatile or change easily at higher temperatures. To make a thin layer chromatography, the sample solution is spotted with a capillary tube at one end of the thin layer plate, and placed in a closed tank, and a suitable solvent is added as the mobile phase. Due to the capillary principle, the solvent is sucked up, moves along the plate, and drives the components of the sample forward. Due to the different properties of the components, the moving distances are different, and the components are separated from each other in spots. Appropriate methods can be used to make the components on the plate to show their position, such as the components themselves have color, can be directly observed, or else can spray coloring reagents or fluorescence in the ultraviolet lamp to determine the way to observe.

(Tang Jiancai, Chen Jianye)

第二章　基础性实验

实验 5　蛋白质的盐析与透析

【实验目的】

1. 了解蛋白质盐析与透析的原理。
2. 熟悉分离纯化蛋白质的方法。
3. 熟悉普通离心机的操作使用方法。

【实验原理】

蛋白质是亲水胶体，它在水溶液中的溶解度是由蛋白质周围亲水基团与水形成水化膜的程度，以及蛋白质分子间的静电排斥作用大小决定的。向蛋白质溶液中加入某种中性盐类，如$(NH_4)_2SO_4$、Na_2SO_4、NaCl 或 $MgSO_4$ 等，蛋白质分子会发生电荷中和（失去电荷）而使得其溶解度降低。当盐类的浓度足够大时，蛋白质胶粒脱水而沉淀，称为盐析。各种蛋白质分子的颗粒大小、亲水程度不同，故盐析所需要的盐浓度也不一样。球蛋白在半饱和硫酸铵溶液中即可析出，清蛋白则需在饱和硫酸铵溶液中才能沉淀。盐析是蛋白质分离纯化过程中的常用方法。

蛋白质胶体颗粒的直径范围为 1～100nm，不能透过半透膜。由于小分子物质能够透过，而蛋白质颗粒不能透过，所以可使蛋白质和小分子物质分开。这种技术称为透析，可除去和蛋白质混合的中性盐及其他小分子物质，是常用来纯化蛋白质的方法。

【器材与试剂】

1. 器材

（1）离心机。
（2）离心管。
（3）刻度移液管。
（4）150mL 小烧杯。
（5）玻璃纸或透析袋。

2. 试剂

（1）动物血清或血浆。
（2）饱和硫酸铵溶液。
（3）硫酸铵粉末。
（4）20% NaOH 溶液。
（5）0.1% $CuSO_4$ 溶液。
（6）奈斯勒试剂。

【实验操作】

（1）于洁净离心管中加入血清或血浆 1mL、饱和硫酸铵溶液 1mL，充分混匀。放置5min后，离心（速率为4000r/min）5min，沉淀即为球蛋白。

（2）上清液移入另一离心管中，分次加入少量硫酸铵粉末，充分混匀，至有少量硫酸铵不再溶解为止。放置5min后，离心（速率为4000r/min）5min。吸出上清液，沉淀是清蛋白。

（3）取 120mm×120mm 玻璃纸一张，折叠成袋状，用作透析袋。检查是否漏水。

（4）将上面制备得到的清蛋白沉淀溶解在 3mL 去离子水中。装入透析袋，置于盛有50mL水的小烧杯中，使袋内、外的液面处于同一水平面上，透析 15min。

（5）检查：①取2支试管，一管加水10滴，另一管加袋外液10滴，两管各加奈斯勒试剂2滴，摇匀。有黄色或黄褐色沉淀生成，表示有铵盐存在。②取3支试管，1号管加饱和硫酸铵上清液10滴，2号管加袋外液10滴，3号管加袋内液10滴，各管加20% NaOH溶液10滴，混匀。再分别各加0.1% $CuSO_4$溶液3～5滴，混匀。有紫红色出现，表示有蛋白质存在。

【注意事项】

蛋白质溶液用透析法去盐时，正负离子透过半透膜的速度不同。以硫酸铵为例，NH_4^+的透出较快，在透析过程中膜内SO_4^{2-}剩余而生成H_2SO_4，而使膜内蛋白质溶液呈酸性，足以达到使蛋白质变性的酸度。因此在用盐析法纯化蛋白质做透析去盐时，开始应用0.1mol/L的NH_4OH替代去离子水透析。

【思考题】

1. 透析时应怎样操作才可尽量除去盐类，并防止蛋白质变性?
2. 为什么要保持袋内液、袋外液在同一平面?

（张蜀敏　宋永砚）

Chapter II Fundamental Experiments

Experiment 5 Salt Out and Dialysis of Proteins

【Purposes】

1. To master the principles of salting out and dialysis of proteins.
2. To learn the methods of separation and purification of proteins.
3. To learn how to use a centrifuge.

【Principles】

A protein is a hydrophilic colloid and its solubility depends on both the distribution of hydrophilic amino acid residues on its surface as well as the repulsive electrostatic forces between protein molecules. The solubility of protein molecules will decrease when neutral salts, e.g. $(NH_4)_2SO_4$, Na_2SO_4, NaCl, $MgSO_4$, are added to the protein solution. When the salt concentration is increased, some of the water molecules are attracted by salt ions, which decreases the number of water molecules available to interact with charged areas of the protein. As a result of the increased demand for solvent molecules, the protein-protein interactions are stronger than the solvent-solute interactions and the protein molecules coagulate by forming hydrophobic interactions with one another. The salt concentration needed for the protein to precipitate out of the solution differs based on the varied size and solubility of protein. Globulins can be salted out in the half saturated ammonium sulfate solution, while the albumin precipitates in the saturated ammonium sulfate solution. Salting out is a useful method for separation and purification of proteins.

The diameter of protein particles ranges in size 1–100nm which is disabled to pass through the semipermeable membrane. By contrast, small molecules can freely diffuse across the membrane, thereby separated from proteins. This procedure is termed as dialysis. Dialysis is a common method for protein purification by removal of unwanted small molecules from macromolecules such as proteins.

【Apparatus and Reagents】

1. Apparatus

(1) Centrifuge.
(2) Centrifugal tube.
(3) Measuring pipet.
(4) Beaker (150mL).
(5) Cellophane or dialysis bag.

2. Reagents

(1) Animal serum or plasma.
(2) Saturated ammonium sulfate solution.
(3) Ammonium sulfate powder.
(4) 20% NaOH solution.
(5) 0.1% $CuSO_4$ solution.
(6) Nessler's reagent.

【Procedures】

(1) Add 1mL of animal serum or plasma and 1mL of saturated ammonium sulfate solution to a clean centrifugal tube and mix completely. Set aside for 5min. Centrifugate at 4,000 r/min for 5min. The globulin is precipitated at the bottom of the centrifugal tube.

(2) Transfer the supernatant to a clean centrifugal tube. Slowly add ammonium sulfate powder to the supernatant, and mix it well until a small amount of insoluble ammonium sulfate is observed. Set it aside for 5min. Centrifugate at 4,000 r/min for 5min. Remove the supernatant. Albumin is precipitated at the bottom of the centrifugal tube.

(3) Obtain a piece of cellophane (120mm×120mm) and fold it into a small bag that will be used as the dialysis bag. Check carefully to see whether the bag leaks water.

(4) Collect the pellet and suspend in 3mL deionized water. Transfer the solution into a dialysis bag, and then place it into a beaker with 50mL water. Keep the liquid surface inside and outside of the bag at the same level. Perform dialysis for 15min.

(5) Detection. ①Take two test tubes, add 10 drops of distilled water into one tube and 10 drops of solution from outside of the dialysis bag into another tube. Add 2 drops of Nessler's reagent into each tube and mix thoroughly. Yellow or tan precipitation indicates the existence of ammonium salt. ②Take three test tubes, add 10 drops of the saturated ammonium sulfate supernatant into the first tube, 10 drops of the solution from outside of the dialysis bag into the second tube and 10 drops of the solution from inside of the dialysis bag into the third tube. Add 10 drops of 20% NaOH solution into each tube. Mix it well. Finally, add 3–5 drops of 0.1% $CuSO_4$ solution into each tube and mix thoroughly. A purple color change suggests the presence of proteins in the solution.

【Notes】

During dialysis, positive and negative ions will pass through the semipermeable membrane at different speeds. For example, NH_4^+ passes through more quickly than SO_4^{2-}. The solution inside the bag will appear to be acidic after a while, which may lead to protein denaturation. Therefore, at the beginning of dialysis, NH_4OH (0.1mol/L) should be used instead of deionized water.

【Questions】

1. How do you remove salty ions thoroughly and prevent protein denaturation during dialysis?

2. Why should the surface of the solution inside and outside of the dialysis bag be kept at the same level?

(Zhang Shumin, Song Yongyan)

实验 6　双缩脲法测定血清蛋白总量

【实验目的】

1. 掌握双缩脲法测定血清蛋白总量的原理和方法。
2. 熟悉双缩脲法测定蛋白质含量的剂量-反应曲线制作方法。

【实验原理】

两分子尿素加热缩合成双缩脲（$H_2N—OC—NH—CO—NH_2$），其分子内含有两个相邻的肽键—CO—NH—，在碱性溶液中肽键可与 Cu^{2+}发生双缩脲反应，生成紫色络合物。

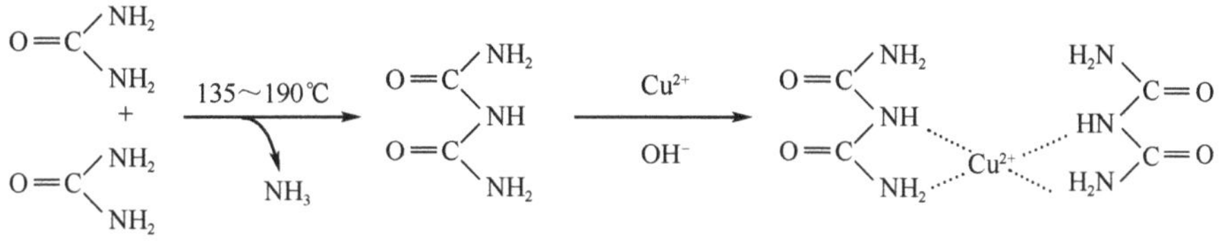

蛋白质分子内含有大量彼此相连的肽键（—CO—NH—），在碱性条件下同样能与 Cu^{2+}发生双缩脲反应，生成紫色络合物，其颜色深浅与蛋白质浓度呈正比，且在 540nm 处的吸光度与蛋白质含量在 10～120g/L 范围内有良好的线性关系。

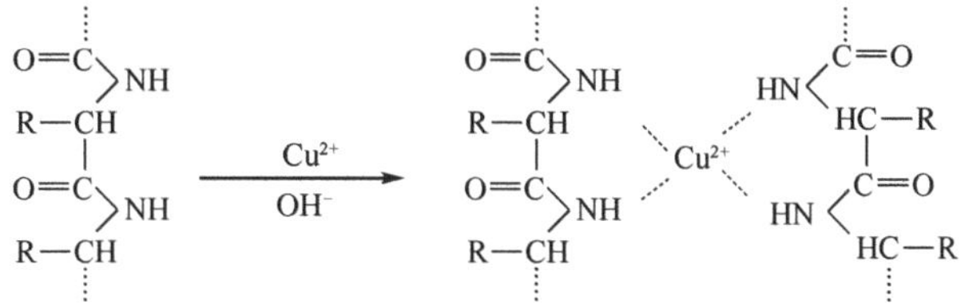

【器材与试剂】

1. 器材

（1）试管及试管架。

（2）刻度移液管。

（3）721A 型分光光度计。

2. 试剂

（1）0.9% NaCl 溶液：称取 0.9g NaCl，溶于 80mL 蒸馏水中，再加蒸馏水定容至 100mL。

（2）10% NaOH 溶液：称取 10g NaOH，溶于 80mL 蒸馏水中，再加蒸馏水定容至 100mL。

（3）双缩脲试剂：称取 1.5g 五水合硫酸铜（$CuSO_4 \cdot 5H_2O$）和 6g 酒石酸钾钠（$NaKC_4H_4O_6 \cdot 4H_2O$）溶于 500mL 蒸馏水中，在搅拌下加入 10% NaOH 溶液 300mL，再加蒸馏水稀释至 1000mL，混匀，置塑料瓶中保存。此试剂可长期保存备用。

（4）蛋白质标准液（10mg/mL）：称取 1g 牛血清白蛋白（BSA），溶于 100mL 蒸馏水中。置 4℃中保存备用。

（5）血清标本（1∶10）：准确吸取 0.2mL 血清，用 0.9% NaCl 溶液稀释至 2mL 备用。

【实验操作】

1. 加液　取 8 支干净试管，标明管号，按表 6-1 进行操作，每支试管重复操作 3 次。

表 6-1　双缩脲法测定血清蛋白总量　（单位：mL）

试剂	管号							
	B	S1	S2	S3	S4	S5	U1	U2
血清标本	—	—	—	—	—	—	0.5	0.5
蛋白质标准液	—	0.1	0.2	0.3	0.4	0.5	—	—
0.9% NaCl 溶液	0.5	0.4	0.3	0.2	0.1	—	—	—
双缩脲试剂	4.0	4.0	4.0	4.0	4.0	4.0	4.0	4.0

2. 比色　混匀各管，置 37℃水浴 20min，以 B 管（空白管）为对照管，于 540nm 处比色测定，记下各管吸光度，算出各平行管的平均吸光度。

3. 作图　以蛋白质浓度为横坐标，以平均吸光度为纵坐标，在坐标纸上绘出蛋白质双缩脲反应的剂量-反应曲线。

4. 求血清标本中的蛋白质浓度

（1）根据标准曲线计算：利用测定管的平均吸光度，在所绘的剂量-反应曲线上查出对应的蛋白质浓度，再乘以样品的稀释倍数。

（2）根据以下公式计算：

$$样品蛋白质总量（g/L）=\frac{A_U}{A_S}\times标准液的蛋白质浓度\times样品稀释倍数。$$

【思考题】

双缩脲法测定蛋白质含量的技术特点和临床意义是什么？

（张秀云　宋永砚）

Experiment 6 Determining the Total Protein in Serum Using the Biuret Method

【Purposes】

1. To master the principle and operation of the biuret method to determine the protein content.

2. To learn the method to generate a dose-response curve to determine the protein content using the biuret method.

【Principles】

When being treated at a high temperature, two urea molecules are condensed into a biuret (H_2N—OC—NH—CO—NH_2). There are two adjacent peptide bonds (—CO—NH—) in biuret molecules. In the alkaline solution, peptide bonds can react with Cu^{2+} to produce a purple complex.

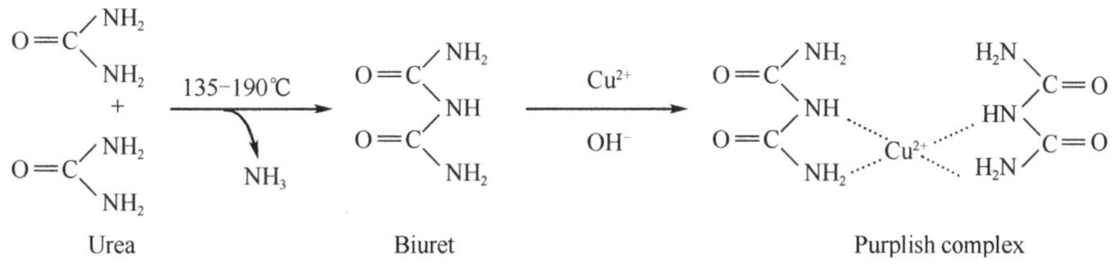

Protein molecules contain a large number of peptide bonds (—CO—NH—) and can react with Cu^{2+} to produce a purple complex under alkaline conditions. Color depth is proportional to the concentration of proteins and the absorbance at 540nm shows good linearity with the concentration of proteins in the 10-120g/L range.

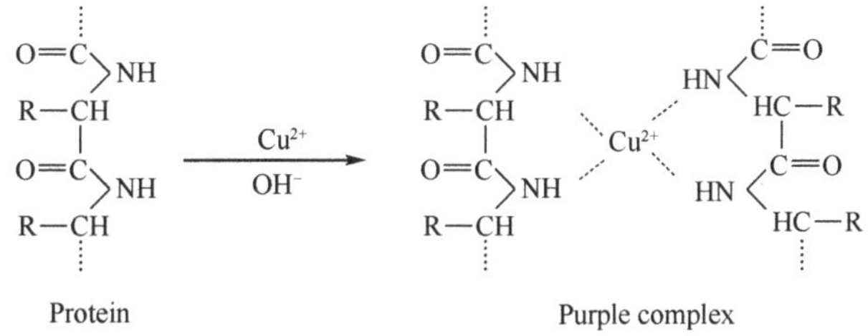

【Apparatus and Reagents】

1. Apparatus

(1) Test tubes and a test tube rack.

(2) Measuring pipet.

(3) Type 721A spectrophotometer.

2. Reagents

(1) 0.9% NaCl solution: Weigh 0.9g NaCl, dissolve it in 80mL distilled water and add distilled water up to 100 mL.

(2) 10% NaOH solution: Weigh 10g NaOH, dissolve it in 80mL distilled water and add distilled water up to 100 mL.

(3) Biuret reagent: Weigh 1.5g copper sulfate pentahydrate ($CuSO_4 \cdot 5H_2O$) and 6g

potassium sodium tartrate ($NaKC_4H_4O_6 \cdot 4H_2O$) , dissolve them in 500mL distilled water, add 300mL 10% NaOH with stirring, dilute the reagent to 1,000mL with distilled water and keep the reagent in a plastic bottle. The reagent can be stored for a long time at the room temperature.

(4) Standard protein solution (10mg/mL): Weigh 1g BSA, dissolve it in 100mL distilled water and store it at 4℃.

(5) Serum specimens (1∶10): Accurately take 0.2mL serum and dilute it to 2mL with 0.9% NaCl solution.

【Procedures】

1. Adding reagents Take 8 test tubes and add the reagents according to Table 6-1. Repeat the treatment three times for each tube.

Table 6-1 Determining total proteins in serum using the biuret method (Unit: mL)

Reagents	Tube numbers							
	B	S1	S2	S3	S4	S5	U1	U2
Serum specimens	—	—	—	—	—	—	0.5	0.5
Standard protein solution	—	0.1	0.2	0.3	0.4	0.5	—	—
0.9% NaCl solution	0.5	0.4	0.3	0.2	0.1	—	—	—
Biuret reagent	4.0	4.0	4.0	4.0	4.0	4.0	4.0	4.0

2. Colorimetricing assay Mix each tube well, and place the tubes in a 37℃ water bath for 20min. Adjust "0" using the B tube (blank tube) at a 540nm wavelength and measure the absorbance value of each tube. Calculate the average absorbance values of parallel tubes.

3. Making a standard curve Plot a dose-response curve for the protein biuret reaction on coordinate paper using the protein concentration as the abscissa (x), and the average absorbance as the ordinate (y) .

4. Calculating the protein concentration in serum specimens

(1) Calculating by the standard curve: Obtain the protein concentration of the serum sample corresponding to the absorbance by checking the standard curve, then multiplied by the diluted times.

(2) Calculate using the following equation:

$$\text{Protein content(g/L)} = \frac{A_U}{A_S} \times \text{Protein concentration of the standard protein solution} \times \text{Diluted times.}$$

【Question】

What are the technical features and clinical significance to determine protein content by using the biuret method?

(Zhang Xiuyun, Song Yongyan)

实验 7　酪蛋白等电点测定

【实验目的】

1. 掌握蛋白质的两性解离性质。
2. 熟悉测定蛋白质等电点的方法。
3. 了解蛋白质等电点的概念。

【实验原理】

蛋白质是两性电解质，其分子中含有的自由氨基及羧基均可电离。当溶液的 pH 小于蛋白质的等电点时，蛋白质带正电；当 pH 大于蛋白质的等电点时，蛋白质带负电；当 pH 等于蛋白质的等电点时，蛋白质所带电荷为 0，此时蛋白质的黏度和溶解度降低，可从溶液中沉淀析出。

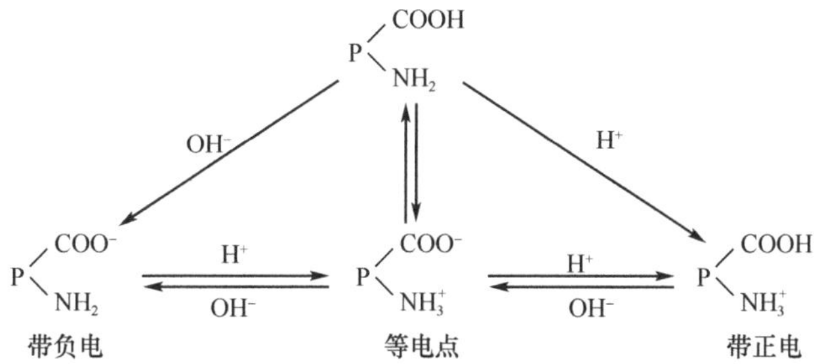

本实验借观察酪蛋白在不同 pH 的溶液中的溶解状态以测定其等电点。在乙酸缓冲液中，酪蛋白的溶解度最小时，该缓冲液的 pH 就是酪蛋白的等电点。

【器材与试剂】

1. 器材

（1）试管。

（2）试管架。

（3）刻度移液管（1.0mL、5.0mL 及 10mL）。

2. 试剂

（1）1mol/L 乙酸溶液：量取 6mol/L 乙酸溶液 10mL，加蒸馏水至 60mL，混匀即成。

（2）0.1mol/L 乙酸溶液：量取 1mol/L 乙酸溶液 10mL，加蒸馏水至 100mL，混匀即成。

（3）0.01mol/L 乙酸溶液：量取 0.1mol/L 乙酸溶液 10mL，加蒸馏水至 100mL，混匀即成。

（4）0.5%酪蛋白的乙酸钠（0.1mol/L）溶液：称取酪蛋白 0.25g，置于 50mL 容量瓶中，加水约 20mL 及 1mol/L NaOH 溶液 5mL，待酪蛋白完全溶解后，加入 1mol/L 乙酸溶液 5mL，用蒸馏水稀释至 50mL，混匀即成。

【实验操作】

（1）取 5 支试管，按表 7-1 分别加入各种试剂，充分混匀。

表 7-1　酪蛋白等电点测定

试剂	试管号				
	1	2	3	4	5
蒸馏水/mL	8.4	8.7	8	5	7.4
0.01mol/L 乙酸溶液/mL	0.6	—	—	—	—
0.1mol/L 乙酸溶液/mL	—	0.3	1.0	4	—
1mol/L 乙酸溶液/mL	—	—	—	—	1.6
0.5%酪蛋白的乙酸钠溶液/mL	1.0	1.0	1.0	1.0	1.0
各管 pH	5.9	5.3	4.7	4.1	3.5
静置 0min 时各管浊度					
静置 10min 时各管浊度					
静置 30min 时各管浊度					

沉淀量的多少可以分别用+、++、+++或者++++表示。含有最多沉淀的溶液 pH 便是酪蛋白的等电点（酪蛋白 pI 是 4.1～4.5）。

（2）记录每支试管在混匀后 0min、10min、30min 的沉淀量。找出沉淀最多而上清液最清亮的试管号及其 pH。该 pH 即是酪蛋白的等电点。

【思考题】

1. 是否所有蛋白质都可用此方法测定其等电点？
2. 你还知道其他测定蛋白质等电点的方法吗？

（张蜀敏　宋永砚）

Experiment 7　Determining the Isoelectric Point of Casein

【Purposes】

1. To master amphoteric electrolysis of a protein.
2. To learn methods to determine the isoelectric point of a protein.
3. To understand the concept of the isoelectric point of a protein.

【Principles】

Proteins are amphoteric electrolytes. The free amino groups and carboxyl groups in protein molecules can be ionized. Proteins are positively charged in a solution with a pH less than their isoelectric points, and proteins are negatively charged in solution with a pH higher than their isoelectric points. When the pH of the solution is equal to the isoelectric point of a protein, the net charge is zero. At this point, the proteins have minimum viscosity and solubility and are precipitated out of the solution.

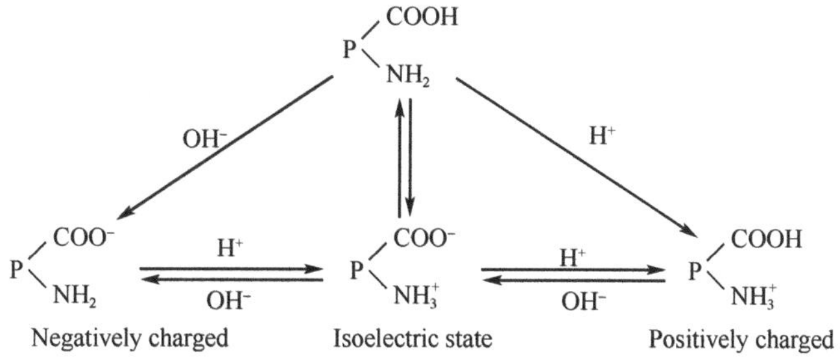

In this experiment, casein is used as an example to learn how to determine isoelectric points of proteins. The isoelectric point of casein is obtained by determining the pH where the protein exhibits minimum solubility.

【Apparatus and Reagents】

1. Apparatus

(1) Test tube.

(2) Test tube rack.

(3) Measuring pipet (1mL, 5mL and 10mL).

2. Reagents

(1) 1mol/L acetic acid solution: Measure 10mL acetic acid solution (6mol/L) , add distilled water to a final volume of 60mL and mix well.

(2) 0.1mol/L acetic acid solution: Measure 10mL acetic acid solution (1mol/L), add distilled water to a final volume of 100mL and mix well.

(3) 0.01mol/L acetic acid solution: Measure 10mL acetic acid solution (0.1mol/L) , add distilled water to a final volume of 100mL, and mix well.

(4) 0.5% casein solution in sodium acetate (0.1mol/L): Weigh 0.25g casein, place it in a 50mL volumetric flask and add 20mL distilled water and 5mL NaOH solution (1mol/L). After the casein is completely dissolved, add 5mL 1mol/L acetic acid solution, add distilled water to 50mL and mix well.

【Procedures】

(1) Take 5 test tubes and add reagents following Table 7-1, and mix them well.

Table 7-1 Determining the isoelectric point of casein

Reagents	Tube numbers				
	1	2	3	4	5
Distilled water/mL	8.4	8.7	8	5	7.4
0.01mol/L acetic acid solution/mL	0.6	—	—	—	—
0.1mol/L acetic acid solution/mL	—	0.3	1.0	4.0	—
1mol/L acetic acid solution/mL	—	—	—	—	1.6
0.5% casein solution in sodium acetate/mL	1.0	1.0	1.0	1.0	1.0
The pH of each tube	5.9	5.3	4.7	4.1	3.5
The turbidity of each tube after holding 0min					
The turbidity of each tube after holding 10min					
The turbidity of each tube after holding 30min					

The amount of precipitates can be indicated by +, ++, +++, or ++++. The pH of the tube that contains the maximum precipitate is the isoelectric point of casein (the pI of casein is 4.1–4.5).

(2) Record the amount of precipitates in each tube at 0min, 10 min and 30min respectively and mark the tube that has the maximum precipitate as well as the clearest and brightest supernatant. The pH of the solution in this tube is the pI of casein.

【Questions】

1. Can this method be used to determine the isoelectric points for all proteins?

2. Are there any other methods that can be used to determine the isoelectric point of a protein?

(Zhang Shumin, Song Yongyan)

实验 8　唾液淀粉酶专一性以及多种因素对酶活性的影响

【实验目的】

1. 掌握唾液淀粉酶的性质。
2. 了解酶活性的测定方法。

【实验原理】

酶具有高度专一性，一种酶只能催化一种或一类底物发生反应，如淀粉酶只能水解淀粉，不能水解蔗糖。当淀粉被淀粉酶彻底水解为还原性麦芽糖和葡萄糖时，能使班氏试剂的 Cu^{2+}还原成 Cu^{+}，生成砖红色的 Cu_2O 沉淀。淀粉酶的活性受温度、pH、激动剂、抑制剂、酶浓度以及作用时间等多种因素影响，因而水解淀粉生成一系列分子大小不同的糊精。这些不同程度的水解糊精可与碘反应生成紫色、棕色或红色络合物。通过上述特征性的反应，并以蔗糖等作对照，便可观察、验证淀粉酶是否具有专一性以及它的催化活性是否受到影响。

【器材与试剂】

1. 器材

（1）滴管、烧杯、试管（架）及试管夹。

（2）恒温水浴锅。

（3）脱脂棉、漏斗和纱布。

（4）白瓷反应板。

2. 试剂

（1）1%淀粉溶液：称取淀粉 1g，加少量蒸馏水调成糊状，加入煮沸的 0.3%NaCl 溶液至 100mL。

（2）1%蔗糖溶液：称取蔗糖 1g，加蒸馏水溶解至 100mL。

（3）班氏试剂：A 液：取柠檬酸钠 173g，无水碳酸钠 100g，加水 600mL，加热溶解，冷却后稀释至 850mL；B 液：取五水合硫酸铜（$CuSO_4 \cdot 5H_2O$）17.3g 溶于 100mL 预热的蒸馏水中，冷却后加水至 150mL。将 A 液缓慢倒入 B 液中混匀置试剂瓶备用。

（4）碘液：称取碘 4g、碘化钾 6g，溶于 1000mL 蒸馏水中，置棕色瓶内储存备用。

（5）各种 pH 缓冲液。①pH4.0 缓冲液：取 0.2mol/L Na_2HPO_4溶液 385.5mL，与 0.1mol/L 柠檬酸溶液 614.5mL 混匀。②pH6.8 缓冲液：取 0.2mol/L Na_2HPO_4溶液 772mL，与 0.1mol/L 柠檬酸溶液 228mL 混匀。③pH8.0 缓冲液：取 0.2mol/L Na_2HPO_4溶液 972mL，与 0.1mol/L 柠檬酸溶液 28mL 混匀。

（6）0.9% NaCl 溶液：称取 0.9g NaCl，溶于 80mL 蒸馏水，定容至 100mL。

（7）1% $CuSO_4$溶液：称取 1g $CuSO_4$，溶于 80mL 蒸馏水，定容至 100mL。

（8）1% Na_2SO_4溶液：称取 1g Na_2SO_4，溶于 80mL 蒸馏水，定容至 100mL。

【实验操作】

1. 唾液淀粉酶的收集与处理

1）制备唾液：实验者先将痰咳尽，用自来水漱口，以清除口腔内食物残渣，再在口腔内含蒸馏水约 15mL，并作咀嚼鼓漱运动，3min 后吐入垫有两层经润湿处理的脱脂纱布的漏斗内，过滤于小烧杯中备用。为与下面稀释唾液相区别，此称制备唾液。

2）煮沸唾液：取上述唾液约 2mL，盛入一中号试管中，置沸水浴煮沸 5min 备用。

3）稀释唾液：调整唾液淀粉酶活性，使之在 pH6.8、室温和既无激动剂又无抑制剂条件下作用 5min，水解淀粉至红色糊精为宜。具体做法是，取 12 凹白瓷反应板一块，按下列步骤操作。

（1）第 1 排每孔加 1 滴制备唾液，第二、第三和第四孔分别加生理盐水 1、2 和 3 滴，由稀到浓（第四→第三→第二顺序）小心混匀各孔，勿溅入相邻孔中。每混匀一孔便取其 1 滴放入同列的 2 排孔中，剩余稀释唾液应全部放回原孔。

（2）在盛有不同稀释度唾液的第 2 排各孔中，均加入 4 滴缓冲液（pH6.8）、2 滴 1% 的淀粉溶液和 2 滴蒸馏水，用（1）混匀法充分混匀，置 37℃下 5min。

（3）在第 2 排各孔中加碘液一滴，混匀，观察比较各孔颜色，以浅棕-红色对应的稀释倍数，用生理盐水稀释 3mL 制备唾液备用。

2. 唾液淀粉酶的专一性以及温度、pH、激动剂和抑制剂对唾液淀粉酶活性影响的观察

1）唾液淀粉酶的专一性观察

（1）取 3 支试管，按表 8-1 操作。

表 8-1　唾液淀粉酶专一性的实验观察　（单位：滴）

试剂	管号			试剂	管号		
	1	2	3		1	2	3
pH6.8 缓冲液	20	20	20	制备唾液	5	—	5
1%淀粉溶液	10	10	—	稀释唾液	—	5	—
1%蔗糖溶液	—	—	10				

（2）将上述各管混匀后，置 37℃水浴中保温 10min，然后每管加入班氏试剂 20 滴，再放入沸水浴中煮沸约 15min，观察各管颜色反应，并说明原因。

2）温度影响酶促反应的实验观察

（1）取 3 支试管，按表 8-2 操作。

表 8-2　温度影响酶促反应的实验观察　（单位：滴）

试剂	管号			试剂	管号		
	1	2	3		1	2	3
pH6.8 缓冲液	20	20	20	稀释唾液	5	5	5
1%淀粉溶液	10	10	10	保温 10min	37℃水浴	沸水浴	冰浴
预热 5min	37℃水浴	沸水浴	冰浴				

（2）将第一、第二管移入冰水浴中，待各管温度一致后速向各管加入碘液 1 滴，混匀后观察各管颜色的变化，并说明温度对酶促反应的影响。

3）pH 影响酶促反应的实验观察

（1）取 3 支试管，按表 8-3 操作。

表 8-3　pH 影响酶促反应的实验观察　（单位：滴）

试剂	管号 1	管号 2	管号 3	试剂	管号 1	管号 2	管号 3
pH4.0 缓冲液	20	—	—	1%淀粉溶液	10	10	10
pH6.8 缓冲液	—	20	—	稀释唾液	5	5	5
pH8.0 缓冲液	—	—	20				

（2）将上述各管混匀后，置 37℃水浴中保温 10min，然后每管加入碘液 1 滴，混匀后观察各管颜色的区别，并说明 pH 对酶促反应的影响。

4）激动剂和抑制剂影响酶活性的实验观察

（1）取 4 支试管，按表 8-4 操作。

表 8-4　激动剂和抑制剂影响酶活性的实验观察　（单位：滴）

试剂	管号			
	1	2	3	4
pH6.8 缓冲液	20	20	20	20
1%淀粉溶液	10	10	10	10
蒸馏水	10	—	—	—
0.9% NaCl 溶液	—	10	—	—
1% $CuSO_4$ 溶液	—	—	10	—
1% Na_2SO_4 溶液	—	—	—	10
稀释唾液	5	5	5	5

（2）将上述各管放入 37℃水浴中保温 10min，然后每管加入碘液 1 滴，混匀后观察各管颜色的区别，并说明激动剂和抑制剂对酶促反应的影响。

【思考题】

简述温度、pH、激动剂、抑制剂和酶浓度等因素对淀粉酶活性的影响。

（陈　竞　宋永砚）

Experiment 8 Specificity of Salivary Amylase and the Factors Affecting Enzyme Activities

【Purposes】

1. To master the properties of salivary amylase.
2. To learn the methods to determine enzyme activities.

【Principles】

Enzymes have high specificity and can only catalyze a specific or a class of substrates to react. For example, amylase can only catalyze hydrolysis of starch but not hydrolysis of sucrose. When starch is completely hydrolyzed, the produced maltose and glucose can make Cu^{2+} from Benedict's reagent to be Cu^{+} and generate brick red precipitates (Cu_2O). The activities of amylase can be affected by a number of factors such as temperatures, pHs, agonists, inhibitors,enzyme concentrations and duration of action. Therefore, dextrin with a series of different molecular sizes is produced in hydrolysis of starch. Dextrin can react with iodine and produce a purple, brown or red complex. Based on the characteristics of the reaction and using sucrose as a control, the specificity of amylase and whether its activities are affected can be observed and confirmed.

【Apparatus and Reagents】

1. Apparatus

(1) Dropper, beaker, test tube rack and a test tube holder.

(2) Thermostatic water bath cauldron.

(3) Absorbent cotton, funnel and gauze.

(4) White porcelain reaction disc.

2. Reagents

(1) 1% starch solution: Weigh 1g starch, add a small amount of water and mix. Add boiled 0.3% NaCl solution to 100 mL.

(2) 1% sucrose solution: Weigh 1g sucrose and add distilled water to 100mL.

(3) Benedict's reagents. Solution A: Weigh 173g sodium citrate and 100g sodium carbonate anhydrous, add 600mL distilled water, heat until it dissolves, cool down and dilute to 850mL. Solution B: Weigh 17.3g copper sulfate pentahydrate ($CuSO_4 \cdot 5H_2O$), dissolve it in 100mL preheated distilled water, and add water to 150mL after cooling. Slowly add solution A into solution B and store it in a reagent bottle for use.

(4) Iodine solution: Weigh 4g iodine and 6g potassium iodide, dissolve them in 1,000 mL distilled water and store the solution in a brown bottle for use.

(5) Buffers with different pHs.

①pH4.0 buffer: Take 385.5mL 0.2mol/L Na_2HPO_4 solution and 614.5mL 0.1mol/L citric acid solution, and mix well.

②pH6.8 buffer: Take 772 mL 0.2mol/L Na_2HPO_4 solution and 228mL 0.1mol/L citric acid solution and mix well.

③pH8.0 buffer: Take 972mL 0.2mol/L Na_2HPO_4 solution and 28mL 0.1mol/L citric acid solution and mix well.

(6) 0.9% NaCl solution: Weigh 0.9g NaCl, dissolve it in 80mL distilled water and add distilled water to 100mL.

(7) 1% $CuSO_4$ solution: Weigh 1g $CuSO_4$, dissolve it in 80mL distilled water and add distilled water to 100mL.

(8) 1%Na_2SO_4 solution: Weigh 1g Na_2SO_4, dissolve it in 80mL distilled water and add distilled water to 100mL.

【Procedures】

1. The collection and treatment of salivary amylase

1) Preparation of saliva

The subject should first clean his or her mouth with water. Then, the subject should drink about 15mL distilled water, rinse for 3min, spit it into the funnel with two layers of wet gauze and filter it into a small beaker for use. This is called prepared saliva to distinguish it from diluted saliva below.

2) Boiling saliva

Measure 2mL saliva, put it in a medium-sized tube and put the tube into a boiling water bath for 5min.

3) Diluting saliva

Adjust the activities of salivary amylase so that it can hydrolyze starch to red dextrin at the pH of 6.8 after reacting for 5 min, at the room temperature and without agonists or inhibitors. The adjusting method takes a piece of 12 concave white porcelain reaction disc and operates as follows.

(1) Add one drop of saliva to each hole of the first row, and add one, two and three drops of physiological saline to the second, third and fourth holes, respectively. Mix saliva in each hole from the diluted to the concentrated holes (the fourth to the third to the second holes) and be careful not to splash into the adjacent holes. After mixing, take one drop of saliva to the hole at the second row but in the same column and put the remaining diluted saliva back to the original hole.

(2) Add four drops of pH 6.8 buffer solution, two drops of 1% starch solution and two drops of distilled water in each hole at the second row, mix well and keep at 37°C for 5min.

(3) Add one drop of iodine solution to each hole at the second row, mix well and observe color depth of each hole. The diluted times of the hole with light brown to a red color will be used in later steps. 3mL diluted saliva according to diluted times needs to be prepared for later use.

2. Observation of specificity of salivary amylase and effects of temperatures, pHs, agonists and inhibitors on the activities of salivary amylase

1) The observation of specificity of salivary amylase

(1) Take 3 tubes, and operate according to Table 8-1.

Table 8-1 The observation of specificity of salivary amylase (Unit: drops)

Reagents	Tube numbers			Reagents	Tube numbers		
	1	2	3		1	2	3
pH 6.8 buffer	20	20	20	Prepared saliva	5	—	5
1% starch solution	10	10	—	Diluted saliva	—	5	—
1% sucrose solution	—	—	10				

(2) Mix each tube, keep them in a 37°C water bath for 10min, then add 20 drops of Benedict's reagent, place them back to a boiling water bath for 15min, and observe and explain the color change.

2) The observation of the effects of temperatures on the enzymatic reaction

(1) Take 3 tubes, and operate according to Table 8-2.

Table 8-2 The observation of the effects of temperatures on the enzymatic reaction (Unit: drops)

Reagents	Tube numbers		
	1	2	3
pH 6.8 buffer	20	20	20
1% starch solution	10	10	10
Preincubation for 5min	37°C water bath	Boiling water bath	Ice bath
Diluted saliva	5	5	5
Incubation for 10min	37°C water bath	Boiling water bath	Ice bath

(2) Transfer No. 1 and No. 2 test tubes into an iced water bath, add a drop of iodine solution to each tube immediately when the temperature of the tubes becomes the same, observe the color change and explain the influence of temperature on the enzymatic reaction.

3) The observation of the effects of pHs on enzymatic reaction

(1) Take 3 tubes, and operate according to Table 8-3.

Table 8-3　The observation of the effects of pH on the enzymatic reaction　(Unit: drops)

Reagents	Tube numbers			Reagents	Tube numbers		
	1	2	3		1	2	3
pH4.0 buffer	20	—	—	1% starch solution	10	10	10
pH6.8 buffer	—	20	—	Diluted saliva	5	5	5
pH8.0 buffer	—	—	20				

(2) After mixing up, keep the tubes in a 37°C water bath for 10min, then add a drop of iodine solution to each tube, mix well, observe the color change, and explain the influence of pHs on the enzymatic reaction.

4) The observation of the effects of agonists and inhibitors on the activities of amylase

(1) Take 4 tubes, and operate according to Table 8-4.

Table 8-4　The observation of the effects of agonists and inhibitors on the activities of amylase

(Unit: drops)

Reagents	Tube numbers			
	1	2	3	4
pH 6.8 buffer	20	20	20	20
1% starch solution	10	10	10	10
Distilled water	10	—	—	—
0.9% NaCl	—	10	—	—
1% $CuSO_4$ solution	—	—	10	—
1% Na_2SO_4 solution	—	—	—	10
Diluted saliva	5	5	5	5

(2) Place tubes in a 37°C water bath for 10min, then add a drop of iodine solution to each tube, mix well, observe the color change, and explain the influence of agonists and inhibitors on the enzymatic reaction.

【Question】

Describe the effects of temperatures, pHs, agonists, inhibitors and enzyme concentrations on the activities of amylase.

(Chen Jing, Song Yongyan)

实验 9　乳酸脱氢酶的递氢作用

【实验目的】

1. 掌握递氢体在生物氧化中的作用。
2. 熟悉酶溶液的制备方法。

【实验原理】

乳酸脱氢酶普遍存在于全身各组织细胞，尤以肌肉细胞为甚。在有辅酶Ⅰ存在时，乳酸脱氢酶可使乳酸脱氢转变成丙酮酸，其氢可经由辅酶Ⅰ、黄素酶传递给亚甲蓝，使之转变为甲烯白。由此产生的颜色变化即可证明乳酸脱氢酶的上述催化作用。

乳酸脱氢酶催化的是乳酸与丙酮酸之间的可逆反应，本实验采用 KCN（注意：剧毒）与丙酮酸反应生成丙酮酸氰醇而消耗反应体系中的丙酮酸，于是反应便不断朝着乳酸脱氢生成丙酮酸的方向进行。

【器材与试剂】

1. 器材

（1）实验家兔。

（2）手术剪、电炉、烧杯、乳钵、漏斗、纱布、活性炭、试管和刻度试管。

2. 试剂

（1）0.5% KCN：称取 0.5gKCN，加入 80mL 蒸馏水溶解，定容至 100mL。

（2）2%乳酸钠：称取 2g 乳酸钠，加入 80mL 蒸馏水溶解，定容至 100mL。

（3）0.04%亚甲蓝：称取 0.04g 亚甲蓝，溶解于 100mL 蒸馏水备用。

（4）0.9% NaCl：称取 0.9g NaCl，加入 80mL 蒸馏水溶解，定容至 100mL。

【实验操作】

1. 辅酶溶液的制备　先将盛有 6mL 水的试管置于沸水浴中，约 5min 后，取实验用兔一只，静脉注射空气致死，迅速剪下腿部肌肉 8～10g，去除筋膜，剪成碎块，立即投放于沸水浴中的热水试管里，煮沸 4～5min 以破坏肌肉中酶的活性，这一步应尽量迅速。之后，取出试管，将内容物倒入乳钵中，研成细浆，两层纱布过滤，收集滤液（内含备用的辅酶Ⅰ）。

2. 乳酸脱氢酶溶液的制备　再取兔腿部肌肉 8～10g，置于乳钵中，加沙少许，加 0.9%NaCl 8mL 一同研成匀浆，收集滤液（内含乳酸脱氢酶及黄素酶等）。滤液中加活性炭约 0.5mg，混匀，放置 15min，其间摇动数次，以吸去辅酶。最后，滤去活性炭，留取滤液备用。

3. 观察乳酸脱氢酶的递氢作用　取 4 支试管，标上号码，依次加入下列各溶液（表 9-1）。

表 9-1　乳酸脱氢酶的递氢作用

试剂	管号			
	1	2	3	4
乳酸脱氢酶/mL	0.5	0.5	0.5	—
辅酶 I /mL	—	0.5	0.5	0.5
0.5%KCN/mL	0.5	0.5	0.5	0.5
2%乳酸钠/mL	0.5	0.5	—	0.5
0.04%亚甲蓝/滴	2	2	2	2
蒸馏水/mL	0.5	—	0.5	0.5

将各管混匀，时时观察各管的颜色变化。

【注意事项】

KCN 是剧毒物质，吸入、口服或经皮吸收均可引起急性中毒。实验操作时，若不慎污染皮肤或眼睛，立即用大量清水冲洗 20 分钟以上，就医。

【思考题】

1. 为什么制备辅酶溶液时要加热而制备酶溶液时不加热？
2. KCN 在本实验中起什么作用？KCN 为什么有剧毒？
3. 你能写出本实验涉及的生物化学反应吗？

（陈　竞　宋永砚）

Experiment 9 The Hydrogen Transferring Effect of Lactate Dehydrogenase

【Purposes】

1. To comprehend the function of a hydrogen carrier in biological oxidation.
2. To learn how to prepare the enzyme solution.

【Principles】

Lactate dehydrogenase (LDH) is widely distributed throughout the body and is mainly found in muscle tissue. In the presence of coenzyme Ⅰ, LDH can catalyze the dehydrogenation of lactic acid to pyruvic acid. The hydrogen produced in this reaction contributes to the conversion of methylene blue to methylene white by the hydrogen transferring effect of coenzyme I and flavoenzyme.

LDH catalyzes the reversible reaction between lactic acid and pyruvic acid. In this experiment, pyruvic acid is removed by the condensation reaction with KCN(Note: highly toxic). Hence, the reaction continues where lactic acid is converted to pyruvic acid.

【Apparatus and Reagents】

1. Apparatus

(1) Experimental rabbit.

(2) Surgical scissors, electric stove, beaker, mortar, funnel, gauze, activated carbon, test tube and graduated test tube.

2. Reagents

(1) 0.5% KCN: Weigh 0.5g KCN, dissolve it in 80mL distilled water and add distilled water to 100mL.

(2) 2% sodium lactate: Weigh 2g sodium lactate, dissolve it in 80mL distilled water and add distilled water to 100mL.

(3) 0.04% methylene blue: Weigh 0.04g methylene blue and dissolve it in 100mL distilled water.

(4) 0.9% NaCl: Weigh 0.9g NaCl, dissolve it in 80mL distilled water and add distilled water to 100mL.

【Procedures】

1. Preparation of the coenzyme solution First, place the test tube containing 6mL of water into a boiling water bath for about 5min. Next, euthanize an experimental rabbit by injecting air into its vein, quickly dissect 8-10g of leg muscle, remove the fascia, cut the muscle into pieces and immediately place the tissue into the test tube containing hot water. After boiling for 4-5min, the enzyme activity in muscle is destroyed. Remove the tube from the hot bath, pour the mixture into a mortar and grind it into a homogenate. Filter the homogenate with two layers of gauze and collect the filtrate (containing coenzyme I) .

2. Preparation of lactate dehydrogenase solution Place another 8–10g of rabbit leg muscle into a mortar, grind it into a homogenate with sand and 8mL 0.9% NaCl and collect the filtrate (containing lactate dehydrogenase and flavoenzyme). Add about 0.5mg of activated carbon to the filtrate, mix well and keep it at the room temperature for 15min while shaking several times to remove coenzyme. Finally, filter to remove activated carbon and keep the filtrate for use.

3. Observation of hydrogen transferring effect of LDH Number 4 tubes and add the following solutions according to Table 9-1.

Table 9-1 The hydrogen transferring effect of LDH

Reagents	Tube numbers			
	1	2	3	4
LDH/mL	0.5	0.5	0.5	—
Coenzyme Ⅰ/mL	—	0.5	0.5	0.5
0.5%KCN/mL	0.5	0.5	0.5	0.5
2% sodium lactate/mL	0.5	0.5	—	0.5
0.04% methylene blue/drops	2	2	2	2
Distilled water/mL	0.5	—	0.5	0.5

Mix well and observe the color change.

【Notes】

KCN is a highly toxic substance and can cause acute poisoning by inhalation, oral or percutaneous absorption. If you accidentally contaminate your skin or eyes during experimental operations, immediately flush with plenty of water for more than 20 minutes and seek medical attention.

【Questions】

1. Why does the preparation of coenzyme solutions require heating while the preparation of enzyme solutions does not?
2. What role does KCN play in this experiment? Why is KCN poisonous?
3. Write the biochemical reactions involved in this experiment.

(Chen Jing, Song Yongyan)

实验 10　血清胆固醇总量的测定（硫铁磷法）

【实验目的】

1. 掌握血清胆固醇总量的测定方法，包括脂溶性物质的定量提取、使用易燃有机溶剂的注意事项及胆固醇的显色。

2. 熟悉测定原理及影响因素。

3. 了解血清胆固醇总量的正常范围及临床意义。

【实验原理】

经无水乙醇处理后，脂蛋白中的载脂蛋白被变性沉淀，胆固醇及其酯释放至血清中。血清中的胆固醇及其酯与浓硫酸及 Fe^{3+}作用，生成紫红色化合物。紫红色化合物在 550nm 处有最大吸光度，吸光度与胆固醇及其酯的含量呈正比。将已知浓度的胆固醇标准溶液经同样处理后，根据浓度之比等于吸光度之比，即可求出血清胆固醇总量。

【器材与试剂】

1. 器材

（1）试管（架）：0.75cm×10cm，5cm×15cm。

（2）刻度移液管：5mL，0.1mL。

（3）721A 型分光光度计。

2. 试剂

（1）显色剂。①储存液：称取六水合三氯化铁（$FeCl_3 \cdot 6H_2O$）2.5g 溶于 81%浓磷酸中，并加浓磷酸至 100mL。置于棕色瓶内于室温下储存。②工作液：取原液 8mL，加浓硫酸至 100mL。可在室温保存 6～8 周。

（2）胆固醇标准液。①储存液：称取胆固醇 100mg 置于小烧杯中，加入 80mL 无水乙醇，稍加温使其溶解。待冷却后定量转移至 100mL 的容量瓶中，然后加无水乙醇至 100mL。混匀储存于棕色瓶中，4℃冰箱内保存（此液含胆固醇 1mg/mL）。②工作液：将储存液由冰箱取出，待其温度与室温相近后，取出 4mL 移至 100mL 的容量瓶中，加无水乙醇至 100mL，再加蒸馏水 2mL。混匀，贮于棕色瓶中（此液含胆固醇 0.0392mg/mL）。

（3）浓硫酸（分析纯）和无水乙醇（分析纯）。

【实验操作】

（1）准确吸取血清 0.1mL，放入小试管中。对准血清吹入 5.0mL 无水乙醇，使蛋白质分散成细小的沉淀颗粒，用力振摇 10s，放置 5min 再摇匀，过滤到刻度试管中至 2mL。

（2）取 3 支试管，按表 10-1 操作。

表 10-1　测定血清胆固醇浓度

试剂	管号		
	1（空白管）	2（标准管）	3（测定管）
抽提上清液/mL	—	—	2.0
胆固醇标准液/mL	—	2.0	—
无水乙醇/mL	2.0	—	—
显色剂/mL	2.0	2.0	2.0
吸光度	0	A_1	A_2

注：显色剂应沿管壁缓慢加入

（3）立即振摇 10～15s，室温静置 15min，然后在 550nm 波长处以空白管调节零点，测定各管吸光度。

（4）计算：血清胆固醇总量（mg/dL）$=\dfrac{\dfrac{A_2}{A_1}\times\dfrac{0.0392}{2}}{\dfrac{1}{2}\times\dfrac{0.1}{5+0.1}}=\dfrac{(A_2/A_1)\times 0.0392}{0.0196}\times 100$

【临床意义】

用本法测得的正常人空腹血清胆固醇总量为 151～233mg/dL。血清胆固醇含量常随生理或病理情况而改变。当患甲状腺功能减退、2 型糖尿病、动脉粥样硬化症时，血清胆固醇含量增高；相反，当患甲状腺功能亢进、恶性贫血、营养不良及肝脏疾病时，其含量降低。

【注意事项】

1. 胆固醇的显色反应会受水分和温度的影响。因此，所用的试管、刻度移液管及比色杯均需干燥。浓硫酸若放置过久，因吸水而使颜色反应减弱。如室内温度低于 15℃时，可先将上清液放在 37℃水浴中，然后显色。

2. 加入显色剂必须与乙醇分成两层，然后混合。显色剂每加一管立刻混匀，不可三管加完后再混合，混合的手法也要一致。

3. 有机溶剂不得溅落在实验台上或实验架上，避免腐蚀实验设备。

4. 使用时应断绝火源或远离火源。若不慎起火，应立即断绝火源，并用湿布盖住器皿口，以隔绝空气，严重时可用消防砂或其他防火设备。

【思考题】

1. 胆固醇的提取过程中应注意什么问题？

2. 实验过程中所用容器为何必须保持干燥？

（宋永砚　杨映雪）

Experiment 10 Determining Total Serum Cholesterol (By Sulphur-Iron-Phosphorus Reagent)

【Purposes】

1. To master methods used to determine the total serum cholesterol, including extracting fat soluble materials, precautions operating flammable organic solvents and the coloring reaction of cholesterol.

2. To learn measurement principles and influencing factors.

3. To understand the normal range of total serum cholesterol and understand its clinical significance.

【Principles】

When treated with anhydrous ethanol, apolipoproteins in lipoproteins are denatured and precipitated, cholesterol and cholesterol esters are released into serum. Cholesterol and cholesterol esters can react with concentrated sulfuric acid and Fe^{3+} to produce purple red compounds. The purple red compounds have the maximum light absorption at a 550nm wavelength, and the absorbance value is proportional to the content of cholesterol and its esters. A standard cholesterol solution with a known concentration is treated the same way. According to the equation where the ratio of concentrations equals the ratio of absorbance, total serum cholesterol can be calculated.

【Apparatus and Reagents】

1. Apparatus

(1) Test tube (rack): 0.75cm×10 cm, 5cm×15cm.

(2) Measuring pipet: 5mL, 0.1mL.

(3) Type 721A spectrophotometer.

2. Reagents

(1) Chromogenic agent. ①The stock solution: Weigh 2.5g of ferric trichloride hexahydrate ($FeCl_3 \cdot 6H_2O$) and dissolve it in 81% concentrated phosphoric acid and add concentrated phosphoric acid up to 100mL. Store it at the room temperature in a dark bottle. ②The working solution: Take 8mL of the stock solution, and slowly add concentrated sulfuric acid to make the final volume of 100mL. The working solution can be stored at the room temperature for 6–8 weeks.

(2) Standard cholesterol solution. ①The stock solution: Weigh 100mg of cholesterol and place it in a small beaker, add 80mL of anhydrous ethanol, and heat slightly to help dissolve. After cooling, transfer it to a 100mL volumetric flask and add anhydrous ethanol to 100mL. Mix well and store it in a dark bottle at 4°C (this solution contains 1mg/mL cholesterol). ②The working solution: Transfer 4mL of the stock solution to a 100mL volumetric flask when its temperature is close to the room temperature, add anhydrous ethanol to 100mL and add another 2mL of distilled water. Mix well and store it in a dark bottle (this solution contains 0.0392mg/mL cholesterol) .

(3) Concentrated sulfuric acid (analytical reagent, AR) and anhydrous ethanol (AR) .

【Procedures】

(1) Accurately add 0.1mL of serum to a small test tube. Add 5.0mL of anhydrous ethanol

into the test tube towards the serum to force serum proteins to disperse into tiny sediments. Shake the test tube vigorously for 10s. Let the tube sit in a test-tube rack for 5 min and shake it again. Filter the mixture into a test tube to 2mL.

(2) Take 3 test tubes and operate according to Table 10-1.

Table 10-1 Determining total serum cholesterol

Reagents	Tube numbers		
	1(Blank)	2(Standard)	3(Sample)
Extraction solution/mL	—	—	2.0
Standard cholesterol solution/mL	—	2.0	—
Anhydrous ethanol/mL	2.0	—	—
Chromogenic agent/mL	2.0	2.0	2.0
Absorbance value	0	A_1	A_2

Note: The chromogenic agent should be slowly added along the test tube wall.

(3) Shake the tubes for 10–15s. Place tubes at the room temperature for 15min. Adjust "0" with the blank tube at the 550nm wavelength and measure the absorbance values of the standard tube (A_1) and the sample tube (A_2) .

(4) Calculation: total serum cholesterol (mg/dL) $= \dfrac{\dfrac{A_2}{A_1} \times \dfrac{0.0392}{2}}{\dfrac{1}{2} \times \dfrac{0.1}{5+0.1}} = \dfrac{(A_2 / A_1) \times 0.0392}{0.0196} \times 100$

【Clinical significance】

The total fasting serum cholesterol measured by this method is 151–233 mg/dL in healthy individuals. The content of serum cholesterol changes based on physiological or pathological conditions. Increased serum cholesterol levels can be detected in patients with hypothyroidism, type 2 diabetes and atherosclerosis. In contrast, reduced serum cholesterol levels can be detected in patients with hyperthyroidism, pernicious anemia, malnutrition and liver disease.

【Notes】

1. The chromogenic reaction of cholesterol can be affected by moisture and temperature. Hence, all glassware, such as test tubes, measuring pipets and cuvettes, should be dried before use. The purple red compounds produced in the reaction may be reduced due to water absorption, if the concentrated sulfuric acid has been stored for a long period of time. If the room temperature is below 15°C, the supernatant should be warmed in a 37°C water bath before adding the chromogenic reagent.
2. Chromogenic agent and anhydrous ethanol must be kept at two layers before mixing. Mixing should be done immediately after the chromogenic agent is added to each tube. Avoid mixing them at the same time until the chromogenic agent has been added to all three tubes. The mixing operation also needs to be consistent.
3. The reagents used in this experiment may corrode the lab bench and the experimental shelf, so beware of splashing the reagents.
4. Stay far away from a fire source while using the organic solution. All reagents should be kept away from fire. If a fire happens accidentally, the fire source should be cut off immediately and a wet cloth can be used to cover the glassware mouth to cut air exposure. In severe cases, fire-extinguishing sand or other fire equipment should be used.

【Questions】

1. What problems should be focused on during cholesterol extraction?
2. Why should all containers or glassware be kept dry during this experiment?

(Song Yongyan, Yang Yingxue)

实验 11　血清谷丙转氨酶（GPT）活性测定

【实验目的】

1. 掌握血清谷丙转氨酶活性测定的基本原理。
2. 熟悉血清谷丙转氨酶活性测定的具体操作方法。
3. 了解血清谷丙转氨酶活性测定的临床意义。

【实验原理】

谷丙转氨酶（GPT），又称为丙氨酸转氨酶（ALT），能催化 L-丙氨酸与 α-酮戊二酸作用生成 L-谷氨酸和丙酮酸：

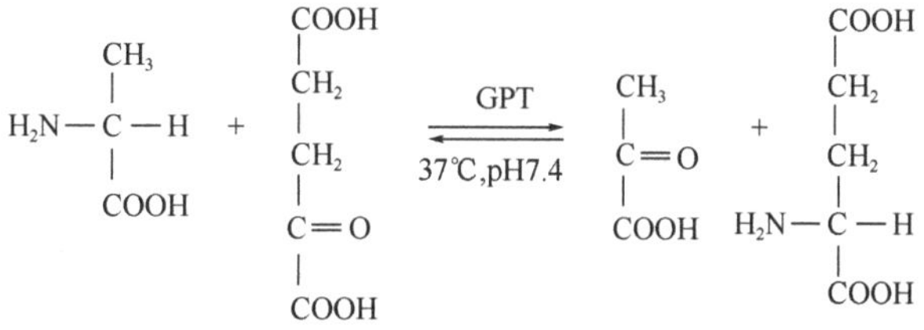

L-丙氨酸　　α-酮戊二酸　　丙酮酸　　L-谷氨酸

生成的丙酮酸可与 2, 4-二硝基苯肼作用生成丙酮酸-2, 4-二硝基苯腙，后者在碱性环境中呈红色，其颜色的深浅在一定范围内与丙酮酸的生成量及 GPT 活性的高低呈正比关系。因此可测定溶液的吸光度 A_{530}，并将其与同样处理的丙酮酸标准液相比较，进而计算出血清中 GPT 的活性。

【器材与试剂】

1. 器材

（1）试管。
（2）刻度移液管。
（3）恒温水浴。
（4）离心机。
（5）721A 型分光光度计。

2. 试剂

（1）0.1mol/L pH7.4 磷酸盐缓冲液：① 溶液 A（0.1mol/L Na_2HPO_4 溶液）：称取 Na_2HPO_4 14.22g 或 $Na_2HPO_4 \cdot 2H_2O$ 17.8g 溶解于 800mL 蒸馏水中，并稀释至 1000mL，4℃保存。②溶液 B（0.1mol/L KH_2PO_4 溶液）：称取 KH_2PO_4 13.61g 溶解于蒸馏水中，并稀释至 1000mL，4℃保存。取 420mL 溶液 A 和 80mL 溶液 B 混匀，即为 0.1mol/L pH7.4 的磷酸盐缓冲液。4℃保存。

（2）标准丙酮酸（含丙酮酸 2.0μmol/mL）：取标准丙酮酸钠 11mg，用 0.1mol/L pH7.4 的磷酸盐缓冲液溶解，定容至 50mL。此液须当日用当日配。

（3）GPT 底物液（含 α-酮戊二酸 2μmol/mL 及 L-丙氨酸 200μmol/mL）：取 α-酮戊二酸 29.2mg、L-丙氨酸 1.7g，用 0.1mol/L pH7.4 磷酸盐缓冲液溶至 100mL。4℃保存。

（4）2, 4-二硝基苯肼溶液：取 2, 4-二硝基苯肼（分析纯）19.8mg，用 1mol/L HCl 溶至 100mL，置棕色瓶中 4℃保存。

（5）0.4mol/L NaOH 溶液：称取 1.6g NaOH 溶于蒸馏水至 100mL。

（6）人/猪血清。

【实验操作】

（1）取干净试管 4 支，标明管号，按表 11-1 进行操作（样品管可做 2～3 支平行管）。

表 11-1　谷丙转氨酶活性测定　（单位：mL）

试剂	管号			
	1（空白管）	2（对照管）	3（标准管）	4（样品管）
血清标本	—	—	—	0.2
标准丙酮酸	—	—	0.2	—
磷酸盐缓冲液	0.2	—	—	—
GPT 底物液	0.5	0.5	0.5	0.5
	37℃水浴 30min			
2，4 二硝基苯肼	0.5	0.5	0.5	0.5
血清	—	0.2	—	—
	37℃水浴 20min			
0.4mol/L NaOH	5.0	5.0	5.0	5.0

（2）比色：混匀表 11-1 中的各管，置室温下 10min 后比色，以 1 号管调零，于 530nm 处比色测定，记下各管吸光度。

（3）血清标本中 GPT 活性按下式计算：以 1mL 血清在 37℃，与底物作用 30min 生成 1.0μmol 丙酮酸所需的 GPT 量为 1 个活性单位，则：

$$\text{GPT 活性单位/dL}=\frac{\bar{A}_4-\bar{A}_2}{A_3}\times 0.4\times\frac{100}{0.2}$$

【思考题】

血清中谷丙转氨酶的测定有何临床意义？

（张秀云　杨映雪）

Experiment 11 Determining Glutamic-Pyruvic Transaminase (GPT) Activity in Serum

【Purposes】

1. To master the principles of determing GPT activity.
2. To learn how to determine GPT activity.
3. To understand the clinical significance of GPT activity.

【Principles】

GPT, also known as alanine aminotransferase (ALT), can catalyze L-alanine (L-Ala) and α-ketoglutaric acid to form L-glutamic acid (Glu) and pyruvic acid:

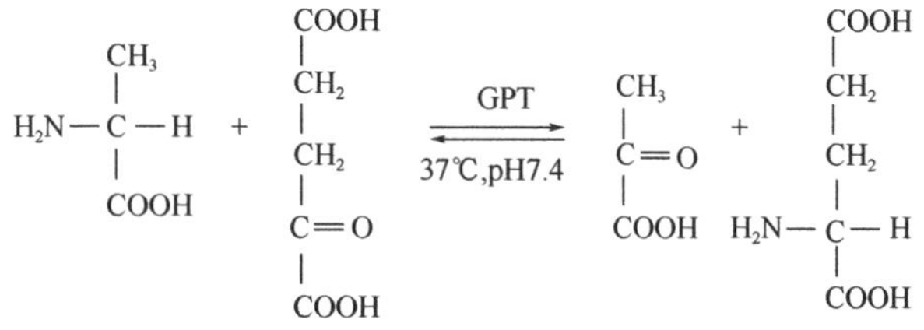

L-Ala α-ketoglutaric acid pyruvic acid L-Glu

Pyruvic acid can react with 2,4-dinitrate phenylhydrazine to form pyruvate-2, 4-dinitrate phenylhydrazone, which turns red under alkali conditions. The depth of the color is proportional to the quantity of pyruvic acid or GPT activity. Therefore, the activity of glutamic-pyruvic transaminase can be measured spectrophotometrically by comparing the absorbance at 530nm with a standard pyruvic acid solution equally treated.

【Apparatus and Reagents】

1. Apparatus

(1) Test tube.
(2) Measuring pipet.
(3) Thermostatic water bath.
(4) Centrifuge.
(5) Type 721A spectrophotometer.

2. Reagents

(1) 0.1mol/L pH7.4 phosphate buffer: ① Solution A (0.1mol/L Na_2HPO_4 solution): Dissolve 14.22g of Na_2HPO_4 or 17.8g of $Na_2HPO_4 \cdot 2H_2O$ in 800mL of distilled water, then dilute it to 1,000mL with distilled water and store it at 4°C. ②Solution B (0.1mol/L KH_2PO_4 solution): Dissolve 13.61g of KH_2PO_4 in distilled water, add it to 1,000mL, and store it at 4°C. Mix 420mL of solution A and 80mL of solution B to yield the 0.1mol/L pH7.4 phosphate buffer and store it at 4°C.

(2) Standard pyruvic acid solution (containing 2.0μmol/mL pyruvic acid): Dissolve 11.0mg of pure sodium pyruvate in 0.1mol/L pH7.4 phosphate buffer, add it to 50mL. It should be prepared the same day for use.

(3) GPT substrate solution (containing 2μmol/mL α-ketoglutaric acid and 200μmol/mL L-Ala): Dissolve 1.7g of L-Ala and 29.2mg of α-ketoglutaric acid into 0.1mol/L pH7.4 phosphate buffer, add it to 100mL and store it at 4°C.

(4) 2,4-dinitrate phenylhydrazine solution: Dissolve 19.8mg of 2,4-dinitrate phenylhydrazine (AR) in 1mol/L HCl, add it to 100mL and store it in a dark bottle at 4°C.

(5) 0.4mol/L NaOH solution: Dissolve 1.6g of NaOH in distilled water and add it to 100mL.

(6) Human/porcine serum.

【Procedures】

(1) Label 4 clean test tubes and add reagents based on Table 11-1 (each sample should have 2-3 replicates) .

Table 11-1 Determining GPT Activity (Unit: mL)

Reagents	Tube numbers			
	1 (Blank)	2 (Control)	3 (Standard)	4 (Sample)
Serum	—	—	—	0.2
Standard pyruvic acid solution	—	—	0.2	—
Phosphate buffer	0.2	—	—	—
GPT substrate solution	0.5	0.5	0.5	0.5
	Keep in a 37°C water bath for 30min			
2,4-dinitrate phenylhydrazine	0.5	0.5	0.5	0.5
Serum	—	0.2	—	—
	Keep in a 37°C water bath for 20min			
0.4mol/L NaOH	5.0	5.0	5.0	5.0

(2) Colorimetric assay: Mix and place all tubes treated in Table 11-1 at the room temperature for 10min. Determine the absorbance and keep a record of each tube at 530nm using tube 1 to adjust "0".

(3) Calculate the GPT activity in serum as follows. One-unit activity of GPT is defined as the amount of enzyme in 1.0mL serum that catalyzes the substrate to generate 1.0μmol pyruvic acid at 37°C for 30min. Then

$$\text{GPT activity unit/dL}=\frac{\bar{A}_4-\bar{A}_2}{A_3}\times 0.4\times\frac{100}{0.2}$$

【Question】

What is the clinical significance for determining GPT activity in serum?

(Zhang Xiuyun, Yang Yingxue)

实验 12　血清二氧化碳结合力的测定——Van Slyke 酸碱滴定法

【实验目的】

1. 掌握测定血清 CO_2 结合力的 Van Slyke 酸碱滴定法。
2. 熟悉血清 CO_2 结合力测定原理。
3. 了解血清 CO_2 结合力作为酸碱平衡指标的临床意义。

【实验原理】

取一定量血清与已知量标准稀盐酸作用，使其中 HCO_3^- 转化成 H_2CO_3，再充分振摇驱除 H_2CO_3 分解放出的 CO_2。之后用不含碳酸盐的 NaOH 滴定剩余的盐酸，并与同样处理的等量标准稀盐酸的滴定结果相比较，即可获得血清中 HCO_3^- 所耗的盐酸量，进而算出血清中的[HCO_3^-]。

【器材与试剂】

1. 器材

（1）锥形瓶。

（2）刻度移液管。

（3）滴定管。

2. 试剂

（1）不含 CO_2 的 0.9% NaCl 溶液：取 0.9g NaCl 溶于煮沸过的蒸馏水，稀释至 100mL。加塞保存，用前再煮沸冷却。

（2）0.03%苯酚红指示剂。

（3）0.01mol/L HCl 标准溶液。

（4）0.01mol/L NaOH 标准溶液（不含 CO_2）。

（5）液体石蜡。

【实验操作】

取锥形瓶 5 只，编号 0、A、B，0 号 1 只，A、B 号各 2 只。

（1）在 0 号瓶中加入不含 CO_2 的 0.9% NaCl 溶液 20mL、0.03%苯酚红 7 滴和液体石蜡 1 滴（液体石蜡覆盖液面以防止空气中的 CO_2 溶入）。然后用吸管插在液体石蜡层下加入血清 1.0mL。轻轻转动锥形瓶，使液体混匀，并以此瓶显示的颜色作为观察滴定终点的参考色。

（2）于 A 号瓶中加入血清 1.0mL、0.01mol/L HCl 标准溶液 5mL，用力振摇 1min 以上，之后加入 0.9% NaCl 溶液 10mL 和 0.03%苯酚红 7 滴，混匀，用 0.01mol/L NaOH 标准溶液滴定。在接近终点时用 0.9% NaCl 溶液补液至 21mL，继续滴定至终点颜色，保持至少 30s 不褪。记录所消耗的 NaOH 体积为 V_A。

（3）于 B 号瓶中加入 0.9% NaCl 溶液 1mL、0.01mol/L HCl 标准溶液 5mL，用力振摇，加 0.9% NaCl 溶液 10mL，0.03%苯酚红 7 滴，混匀，用 0.01mol/L NaOH 标准溶液滴定。在接近终点时，加 0.9% NaCl 溶液补液至 21mL，再滴定至终点颜色，保持至少 30s 不褪。记录所消耗的 NaOH 体积为 V_B。

（4）计算：血清[HCO_3^-]（mmol/L）=（V_B-V_A）×0.01×1000/1.0

【思考题】

1. Van Slyke 酸碱滴定法的实验原理是什么？如何提高该法测定的准确性？

2. 何谓血清 CO_2 结合力？有何重要的生理意义和临床意义？为什么代谢性酸中毒时 CO_2 结合力降低，而呼吸性酸中毒时 CO_2 结合力反而会升高？

（汤建才　杨映雪）

Experiment 12 Determining CO_2 Combining Power in Serum—Van Slyke Acid-Base Titration

【Purposes】

1. To master the Van Slyke acid-base titration method.
2. To learn the principles of this method.
3. To understand the clinical significance of taking CO_2 combining power of serum as an acid-base equilibrium index.

【Principles】

A certain quantity of serum reacts with standard diluted hydrochloric acid (HCl) , causing HCO_3^- to be transformed into H_2CO_3. Mix and stir to remove CO_2 formed from H_2CO_3 decomposition. Carbonate-free NaOH is used to titrate surplus hydrochloric acid and compare with similar processing to an equal amount of standard HCl. Based on the amount of HCl consumed by HCO_3^-, the concentration of HCO_3^- in the serum can be calculated.

【Apparatus and Reagents】

1. Apparatus

(1) Erlenmeyer flask.

(2) Measuring pipet.

(3) Buret.

2. Reagents

(1) CO_2-free 0.9% NaCl solution: dissolve 0.9g of NaCl in boiled distilled water, dilute it to 100mL and store it in a container with a cork. Boil again and cool down before use.

(2) 0.03% phenol red indicator.

(3) 0.01mol/L HCl standard solution.

(4) CO_2-free 0.01mol/L NaOH standard solution.

(5) Liquid paraffin.

【Procedures】

Take 5 erlenmeyer flasks, and label them as “0, A, B”. “A” and “B” should have 2 repeats.

(1) For flask “0”, add 20mL of CO_2-free 0.9% NaCl solution, 7 drops of 0.03% phenol red and one drop of liquid paraffin (the liquid paraffin covers the liquid surface to prevent CO_2 in the air from dissolving). Then, a pipet should be inserted into the liquid under the liquid paraffin layer to add 1.0mL of serum. Shake the conical flask gently to mix and use the color of the bottle as the end point reference in the titration.

(2) For flask “A”, add 1.0mL of serum and 5mL of 0.01mol/L standard HCl solution and shake vigorously for more than 1min. Add 10mL of 0.9% NaCl solution and 7 drops of 0.03% phenol red to the flask and mix well. Titrate with 0.01mol/L of standard NaOH solution. When near the end point, add 0.9% NaCl solution to the liquid and make the final volume to 21mL. Then, continue to titrate to the end point. Be sure that the color does not fade at least for 30s. Record the volume of NaOH consumed for titration as V_A.

(3) For flask “B”, add 1mL of 0.9% NaCl and 5mL of 0.01mol/L standard HCl solution, and shake vigorously. Add 10mL of 0.9% NaCl solution and 7 drops of 0.03% phenol red in the

flask, mix well, and then titrate with 0.01mol/L NaOH standard solution. When near the end point, add 0.9% NaCl solution in the liquid and make the volume to 21mL. Then, continue to titrate to the end point. Be sure that the color does not fade at least for 30s. Record the volume of NaOH consumed for titration as V_B.

(4) Calculation: Serum [HCO_3^-] (mmol/L)=(V_B-V_A) ×0.01×1,000/1.0

【Questions】

1. What is the principle of the Van Slyke acid-base titration? What can be done to enhance its accuracy?

2. What is CO_2 combining power? What is its important physiological and clinical significance? Why is the CO_2 combining power reduced in metabolic acidosis while the CO_2 combining power is elevated in respiratory acidosis?

(Tang Jiancai, Yang Yingxue)

实验 13　肝脏中酮体的生成和检测

【实验目的】

验证肝脏中酮体生成作用，掌握酮体测定方法。

【实验原理】

酮体包括乙酰乙酸、β-羟丁酸及丙酮。它是肝脏在空腹或碳水化合物摄入较少时利用脂肪酸产生的，此时细胞利用酮体代替葡萄糖作为能量。

本实验利用丁酸作为底物，与肝组织匀浆（含有酮体生成酶系）保温后即有酮体生成。酮体可与含硝普钠的显色剂反应产生紫红色化合物(Rothera 测试法)。而经同样处理的肌肉匀浆，则不产生酮体，因此不发生显色反应。

【器材与试剂】

1. 器材

（1）匀浆器。

（2）试管及试管架。

（3）水浴锅。

（4）白瓷反应板。

2. 试剂

（1）0.9% NaCl 溶液。

（2）洛克溶液：NaCl 0.9g、KCl 0.042g、$CaCl_2$ 0.024g、$NaHCO_3$ 0.02g、葡萄糖 0.1g，将以上药品混合溶于蒸馏水中，溶解后加蒸馏水至 100mL。

（3）0.5mol/L 丁酸溶液：45mL 正丁酸用 0.1mol/L NaOH 液中和至 pH=7.6，并用蒸馏水稀释至 1000mL。

（4）pH7.6 磷酸盐缓冲液。①溶液 A（1/15 mol/L 的 KH_2PO_4 溶液）：称取 KH_2PO_4 9.078g，用蒸馏水溶解定容至 1000mL。②溶液 B（1/15 mol/L 的 Na_2HPO_4 溶液）：称取 $Na_2HPO_4 \cdot 2H_2O$ 11.876g（或 $Na_2HPO_4 \cdot 12H_2O$ 23.894g）用蒸馏水溶解定容至 1000mL。将溶液 A 和 B 按 1.4∶8.6（V/V）比例混合即为 pH7.6 磷酸盐缓冲液。

（5）15%三氯乙酸溶液：称取 500g 三氯乙酸溶于 227mL 蒸馏水中，再与蒸馏水按 3∶20（V/V）比例稀释。

（6）显色粉：硝普钠 1g、无水碳酸钠 30g、硫酸铵 50g 混合后研碎。

【实验操作】

（1）样品的制备：将兔处死，迅速收集肝脏和肌肉组织，用 0.9% NaCl 溶液清洗。称取 5g 肌肉组织，剪碎，放入匀浆器中，加入 15mL 0.9% NaCl 溶液（按每克组织 3mL 加入），制备成肌匀浆。用同样的步骤制备肝匀浆。

（2）取试管 4 支，编号后按表 13-1 加入各种试剂。

表 13-1　酮体的生成　（单位：滴）

试剂	管号			
	1	2	3	4
洛克溶液	15	15	15	15
0.5mol/L 丁酸溶液	30	—	30	30
pH7.6 磷酸盐缓冲液	15	15	15	15
肝匀浆	20	20	—	—
肌匀浆	—	—	—	20
蒸馏水	—	30	20	—

（3）将上述 4 支试管摇匀后，放置于 37℃恒温水浴中保温 40～50min。

（4）取出各管，各加入 15%三氯乙酸 20 滴，摇匀混合，3000r/min 离心 5min。

（5）分别取出上述各管离心后上清液放于白瓷反应板上，每凹放入显色粉一小匙，观察所产生的颜色反应，并说明不同现象产生的原因。

【思考题】

1. 酮体仅供肝外某些组织氧化供能，为什么？
2. 有哪些其他的检测酮体存在和含量的方法？

（易　芳　杨映雪）

Experiment 13 Production and Detection of Ketone Bodies in the Liver

【Purpose】

To verify the ketogenesis effect in the liver and master the detection of ketone bodies.

【Principles】

Acetoacetic acid, β-hydroxybutyric acid and acetone are collectively termed as ketone bodies. These are produced by the liver from fatty acid during periods of low food intake (fasting) or carbohydrate restriction, where cells use ketone bodies as energy instead of glucose.

This experiment uses butyric acid as the substrate and ketone body can be achieved by keeping the liver tissue homogenate (containing ketogenic enzyme system) warm. Ketone bodies can react with sodium nitroprusside to produce a purple red compounds (Rothera's test), while butyric acid incubated with muscle homogenate cannot produce ketone bodies and shows no color change with the same processing procedure.

【Apparatus and Reagents】

1. Apparatus

(1) Homogenizer.

(2) Test tube and test tube rack.

(3) Water bath cauldron.

(4) White porcelain reaction plate.

2. Reagents

(1) 0.9% NaCl solution.

(2) Locke's solution: Take 0.9g of NaCl, 0.042g of KCl, 0.024g of $CaCl_2$, 0.02g of $NaHCO_3$ and 0.1g of glucose, mix and dissolve them in distilled water and dilute it to 100mL.

(3) 0.5mol/L butyric acid solution: Add 45mL of butyric acid to 0.1mol/L NaOH solution. Adjust the pH=7.6 using 0.1mol/L NaOH solution and dilute it with distilled water to 1,000mL.

(4) pH7.6 phosphate buffer: ①Solution A (1/15mol/L KH_2PO_4 solution): 9.078g of KH_2PO_4 is diluted with distilled water to 1,000mL. ② Solution B (1/15mol/L Na_2HPO_4 solution): 11.876g of $Na_2HPO_4 \cdot 2H_2O$ or 23.894g of $Na_2HPO_4 \cdot 12\ H_2O$ is diluted with distilled water to 1,000mL. Mix solution A and solution B as 1.4∶8.6 (*V/V*) to yield phosphate buffer with a pH7.6.

(5) 15% trichloroacetic acid solution: Dissolve 500g of trichloroacetic acid into 227mL of dH_2O, and then dilute it with dH_2O by 3∶20(*V/V*).

(6) Chromogenic powder: Combine 1g of sodium nitroprusside, 30g of Na_2CO_3 and 50g of ammonium sulfate, mix and grind them.

【Procedures】

(1) Preparation of liver homogenate and muscle homogenate: Euthanize a rabbit and quickly collect the liver tissue and muscle tissue. Wash with 0.9% NaCl solution. Weigh 5g of the muscle tissue, cut the tissue into small pieces, place them in a homogenizer, add 15mL of

0.9% NaCl solution (3mL for each gram of tissue) and grind it into smooth homogenate. Follow the same procedure to prepare liver tissue homogenate.

(2) Label 4 test tubes and add reagents based on Table 13-1.

Table 13-1 Ketogenesis detection (Unit: drops)

Reagents	Tube numbers			
	1	2	3	4
Locke's solution	15	15	15	15
0.5mol/L butyric acid solution	30	—	30	30
pH7.6 phosphate buffer	15	15	15	15
Liver tissue homogenate	20	20	—	—
Muscle tissue homogenate	—	—	—	20
Distilled water	—	30	20	—

(3) Mix the 4 tubes and place them into a 37°C water bath for 40–50min.

(4) Remove test tubes, add 20 drops of 15% trichloroacetic acid solution into each one. Mix and centrifugate them at 3,000r/min for 5min.

(5) After centrifugation, transfer the supernatant of each tube into the white porcelain reaction plate and add a small amount of color powder. Observe and record the color change. Explain reasons for the different results.

【Questions】

1. Ketone bodies are oxidized to generate energy only in some kinds of tissue out of liver. Why?

2. Is there any other method used to detect the presence and quantity of ketone bodies?

(Yi Fang, Yang Yingxue)

实验 14　PCR 扩增髓鞘碱性蛋白基因

【实验目的】

1. 掌握 PCR 的基本原理与实验技术方法。
2. 熟悉 PCR 技术的应用。

【实验原理】

聚合酶链式反应（PCR）是体外合成扩增 DNA 片段的一种方法。PCR 的原理很简单，包括三步反应的循环过程：①变性，把双链模板 DNA 加热至 95～100℃；②退火，引物与解链 DNA 结合（通常在 55℃进行）；③延伸，DNA 聚合酶催化新链 DNA 的合成（通常在 72℃进行）。一个典型的循环需要 3～5min，然后再重复 20～40 次。PCR 体系中的混合物包括缓冲液、核苷酸、引物、酶以及来源于特定标本的核酸。

PCR 技术具有灵敏、特异、快速以及操作简便等诸多优点，因此，它自 1985 年问世以来被迅速而广泛地用于分子生物学的各个领域。例如，PCR 技术可用于阐明基因结构和基因表达，鉴定疾病相关的基因或者病原体，遗传疾病的产前鉴定，以及在法医、农业、考古学领域中的 DNA 指纹鉴定。

【器材与试剂】

1. 器材

（1）PCR 仪。
（2）离心机。
（3）微量移液器。
（4）PCR 管。

2. 试剂

（1）10×扩增缓冲液。
（2）*Taq* DNA 聚合酶。
（3）2mmol/L dNTP 混合物，含 dATP、dCTP、dGTP、dTTP 各 2mmol/L。
（4）含有待扩增 DNA 模板的大肠杆菌菌液。
（5）正引物（2μmol/L），反引物（2μmol/L）。
（6）蒸馏水。

【实验操作】

1. 引物及模板　本实验待扩增片段为人髓鞘碱性蛋白基因 cDNA（序列号：NM_001025081.2）。髓鞘碱性蛋白在神经系统的髓鞘形成过程中发挥重要作用。

待扩增序列（共 591bp）：

```
ATGGCGTCAC AGAAGAGACC CTCCCAGAGG CACGGATCCA AGTACCTGGC CACAGCAAGT
ACCATGGACC ATGCCAGGCA TGGCTTCCTC CCAAGGCACA GAGACACGGG CATCCTTGAC
TCCATCGGGC GCTTCTTTGG CGGTGACAGG GGTGCGCCCA AGCGGGGCTC TGGCAAGGTA
```

```
CCCTGGCTAA AGCCGGGCCG GAGCCCTCTG CCCTCTCATG CCCGCAGCCA GCCTGGGCTG
TGCAACATGT ACAAGGACTC ACACCACCCG GCAAGAACTG CTCACTACGG CTCCCTGCCC
CAGAAGTCAC ACGGCCGGAC CCAAGATGAA AACCCCGTAG TCCACTTCTT CAAGAACATT
GTGACGCCTC GCACACCACC CCCGTCGCAG GGAAAGGGGA GAGGACTGTC CCTGAGCAGA
TTTAGCTGGG GGGCCGAAGG CCAGAGACCA GGATTTGGCT ACGGAGGCAG AGCGTCCGAC
TATAAATCGG CTCACAAGGG ATTCAAGGGA GTCGATGCCC AGGGCACGCT TTCCAAAATT
TTTAAGCTGG GAGGAAGAGA TAGTCGCTCT GGATCACCCA TGGCTAGACG C
```

PCR 引物序列：

正引物：5′TTCAAGCTTATGGCGTCACAGAAGAGAC3′

反引物：5′CCACGCGTCGACTGGCGTCTAGCCATGGGT3′

2. PCR 程序

（1）在冰浴中，按以下次序将各成分加入一无菌 PCR 管中：

10×扩增缓冲液	5μL
dNTP 混合物	4μL
正引物	2μL
反引物	2μL
Taq 聚合酶	1μL
DNA 模板（50ng/μL）	1μL

加蒸馏水至 50μL。

（2）将上述混合液置 PCR 仪中 95℃温育 5min，以使模板 DNA 完全变性。

（3）按以下方法进行 25～30 次循环的 PCR 扩增：

变性：94℃ 30s

退火：55℃ 30s

延伸：72℃ 1min

（4）最后在 72℃保温 5min。结束反应后，PCR 产物可直接电泳检测或-20℃长期保存。

【注意事项】

1. 所有试剂都应该没有核酸和核酸酶的污染。
2. 试剂和缓存液首先应该进行大体积配制，然后每次扩增反应时分装适量的体积。
3. PCR 加样应在冰上进行，并且要充分混匀。

【思考题】

PCR 扩增与细胞内 DNA 复制有何异同？

（郭冬梅　杨映雪）

Experiment 14 Amplification of the Myelin Basic Protein Gene Using PCR

【Purposes】

1. To learn the basic principles of PCR and to master the experimental technology of PCR.
2. To understand the practical applications of PCR.

【Principles】

The polymerase chain reaction (PCR) is a method for *in vitro* amplification of specific DNA fragments. The principle of PCR is simple, requiring a three-step cycling process: ①Denaturation: heat the double-stranded DNA to 95–100°C. ②Annealing: primers are attached to the dissociated DNA strands (usually at 55°C). ③Extension: DNA polymerase catalyzes the synthesis of new strands of DNA (usually at 72°C). A cycle typically takes 3–5min and is repeated 20–40 times. The PCR system contains a mixture of buffers, nucleotides, primers, enzymes and nucleic acid from a specimen.

Due to the sensitivity, specificity, rapidity and simplicity of the reaction, PCR has been used in a variety of applications in molecular biology since it was invented in 1985. For example, PCR has been used in characterizing the structure and expression of genes, identifying disease-causing genes and pathogens, prenatally diagnosing inherited diseases and DNA fingerprinting in forensics, agriculture and archaeology.

【Apparatus and Reagents】

1. Apparatus

(1) PCR thermocycler.
(2) Centrifuge.
(3) Micropipette.
(4) PCR tube.

2. Reagents

(1) 10× amplification buffer.
(2) *Taq* DNA polymerase.
(3) dNTP mixture (2mmol/L) containing dATP, dCTP, dGTP, dTTP (each 2mmol/L).
(4) *E. coli* liquid containing DNA template to be amplified.
(5) Forward primer (2μmol/L) and reverse primer (2μmol/L).
(6) Distilled water.

【Procedures】

1. Primers and templates The cDNA of the human myelin basic protein gene (Accession: NM_001025081.2) is used as the template in this PCR amplification. Myelin basic protein (MBP) is a protein believed to be important in the process of the myelination of nerves in the nervous system.

Target region for amplification (591bp):

```
ATGGCGTCAC AGAAGAGACC CTCCCAGAGG CACGGATCCA AGTACCTGGC CACAGCAAGT
ACCATGGACC ATGCCAGGCA TGGCTTCCTC CCAAGGCACA GAGACACGGG CATCCTTGAC
TCCATCGGGC GCTTCTTTGG CGGTGACAGG GGTGCGCCCA AGCGGGGCTC TGGCAAGGTA
CCCTGGCTAA AGCCGGGCCG GAGCCCTCTG CCCTCTCATG CCCGCAGCCA GCCTGGGCTG
```

```
TGCAACATGT ACAAGGACTC ACACCACCCG GCAAGAACTG CTCACTACGG CTCCCTGCCC
CAGAAGTCAC ACGGCCGGAC CCAAGATGAA AACCCCGTAG TCCACTTCTT CAAGAACATT
GTGACGCCTC GCACACCACC CCCGTCGCAG GGAAAGGGGA GAGGACTGTC CCTGAGCAGA
TTTAGCTGGG GGGCCGAAGG CCAGAGACCA GGATTTGGCT ACGGAGGCAG AGCGTCCGAC
TATAAATCGG CTCACAAGGG ATTCAAGGGA GTCGATGCCC AGGGCACGCT TTCCAAAATT
TTTAAGCTGG GAGGAAGAGA TAGTCGCTCT GGATCACCCA TGGCTAGACG C
```

Sequences of primers:
Forward primer: 5′TTCAAGCTTATGGCGTCACAGAAGAGAC3′
Reverse primer: 5′CCACGCGTCGACTGGCGTCTAGCCATGGGT3′

2. PCR procedure

(1) In a sterile 0.5mL PCR tube (The tubes should be kept on ice until the PCR is started) , mix the ingredients in the following order:

10× amplification buffer	5μL
dNTP mixture	4μL
Forward primer	2μL
Reverse primer	2μL
Taq DNA polymerase	1μL
DNA template (50ng/μL)	1μL

Add distilled water to the total volume of 50μL.

(2) Incubate the tubes in a thermocycler at 95℃ for 5min to completely denature the template.

(3) Perform 25–30 cycles of PCR amplification as follows:

Denaturation	94℃	30s
Annealing	55℃	30s
Extension	72℃	1min

(4) Finally incubate for an additional 5min at 72℃. PCR products can be analyzed by electrophoresis using an agarose gel electrophoresis or be stored at −20℃ for a long term.

【Notes】

1. All reagents should be free of nucleic acid and nuclease contamination.

2. Buffers and reagents should be prepared in large volumes and dispensed in appropriate amounts for each amplification reaction.

3. PCR sampling should be on ice and be mixed well.

【Question】

What are the differences and similarities between PCR amplification and DNA replication in cells?

(Guo Dongmei, Yang Yingxue)

实验 15　DNA 琼脂糖凝胶电泳

【实验目的】

掌握琼脂糖凝胶电泳检测 DNA 的方法。

【实验原理】

琼脂糖凝胶电泳是分离、纯化、鉴定 DNA 片段的典型方法，其特点为简便、快速。与蛋白质的电泳原理类似，DNA 分子在高于其等电点的 pH 溶液中带负电荷，在电场中向正极移动。除电荷效应外，DNA 在电场中的迁移速率还与凝胶浓度（表 15-1）以及 DNA 分子大小及构象有关。对于线形 DNA 分子，其电场中的迁移率与其分子量的对数值成反比。核酸染料 GoldView 分子可插入 DNA 的碱基之间，并在紫外灯下呈现荧光。核酸染料可以在凝胶凝固前加入，或者电泳结束后再对凝胶进行染色。通过这种方法，DNA 在凝胶中的位置可以在 254～365nm 的紫外灯下进行观察。DNA 样品在点样前须和上样缓冲液混合。上样缓冲液中包括密度较大的化合物如甘油、蔗糖或者聚蔗糖等，其作用是增加样品 DNA 的密度，使之更容易沉到点样孔底部。上样缓冲液中还包括指示剂如二甲苯蓝和溴酚蓝等，以反映样品的泳动情况。

表 15-1　分离的线性 DNA 片段长度变化范围与凝胶浓度的关系

琼脂糖凝胶浓度/%	分离的线性 DNA 片段大小/kb	琼脂糖凝胶浓度/%	分离的线性 DNA 片段大小/kb
0.3	60～5	1.2	6～0.4
0.6	20～1	1.5	4～0.2
0.7	10～0.8	2.0	3～0.1
0.9	7～0.5		

【器材与试剂】

1. 器材

（1）水平电泳槽。

（2）电泳仪。

（3）凝胶图像分析系统。

（4）微波炉。

（5）锥形瓶。

（6）制胶槽和梳子。

（7）微量移液器。

2. 试剂

（1）DNA 样品。

（2）DNA 分子量标准。

（3）5×三羟甲基氨基甲烷-硼酸-乙二胺四乙酸（TBE）缓冲液：54g 三羟甲基氨基甲

烷、27.5g 硼酸、4.6g 乙二胺四乙酸二钠溶于蒸馏水中，定容至 1L。电泳时稀释至 0.5×使用。

（4）6×上样缓冲液：溴酚蓝 25mg 及 3mL 甘油溶于 5mL 5×TBE 溶液中，以 5×TBE 溶液定容至 10mL。

（5）GoldView。

（6）琼脂糖。

【实验操作】

（1）称取 0.7g 琼脂糖于锥形瓶中，加入 100mL 0.5×TBE 溶液。在微波炉中加热溶化。

（2）待凝胶冷却至 50℃左右，加入 GoldView 1～2 滴，混匀。把凝胶倒入制胶槽中，并插入相应的梳子。

（3）室温下 30～45min 后凝胶完全凝结，小心拔出梳子，将凝胶安放在电泳槽内，胶孔端靠近负极；向电泳槽中倒入 0.5×TBE 电泳缓冲液，直到没过胶面。

（4）在 DNA 样品中加入 6×上样缓冲液，混匀后，用移液器将样品混合液缓慢加入被浸没的凝胶加样孔内。

（5）盖上电泳槽盖子，接通电源，红线连正极（红），黑线连负极（黑），100V 电压。根据指示剂泳动的位置判断是否终止电泳，一般前端染料到胶长的 2/3 处即可，需要 30～40min。

（6）电泳完毕，关上电源，戴上手套取出制胶槽和凝胶。

（7）在凝胶图像分析系统上观察凝胶，通过与 DNA 分子量标准比较后可以得知样品 DNA 的大小。

【思考题】

DNA 在电场中的迁移率取决于哪些因素？

（郭冬梅　易　芳）

Experiment 15 DNA Agarose Gel Electrophoresis

【Purpose】

To learn how to analyze DNA by agarose gel electrophoresis.

【Principles】

Due to its rapidity and simplicity, agarose gel electrophoresis is widely used to separate, purify and identify DNA fragments. Similar to protein electrophoresis, DNA is negatively charged at a high pH (>pI) and moves to the anode in an electric field. Besides the charging effect, the migration of DNA is also affected by the gel concentration (Table 15-1) , as well as the size and conformation of the DNA electrophoresis. Linear DNA moves at a rate that is inversely proportional to the logarithm of the molecular weight. Nucleic acid dyes GoldView can bind to DNA and fluoresce under UV light. GoldView may be added to the agarose solution before it solidifies or the DNA gel may be stained later after electrophoresis. In this way, the location of DNA within the gel can be visualized by illumination with a 254–365nm UV light. Loading buffer is mixed with the DNA sample before sampling. The loading buffer contains dense compounds, such as glycerol, sucrose, or ficoll, which raise the density of the sample so that the DNA sample may sink to the bottom of the well. The loading buffer also contains dyes such as xylene cyanol and bromophenol blue which are used to monitor the progress of electrophoresis.

Table 15-1 Relationship between the range of variation in length for separated linear DNA fragments and gel concentration

Concentration of agarose gel/%	Size of separated linear DNA fragments/kb	Concentration of agarose gel/%	Size of separated linear DNA fragments/kb
0.3	60-5	1.2	6-0.4
0.6	20-1	1.5	4-0.2
0.7	10-0.8	2.0	3-0.1
0.9	7-0.5		

【Apparatus and Reagents】

1. Apparatus

(1) Horizontal electrophoresis tank.
(2) Electrophoresis apparatus.
(3) Gel image analysis system.
(4) Microwave.
(5) Erlenmeyer flask.
(6) Gel tray and comb.
(7) Micropipette.

2. Reagents

(1) DNA sample.
(2) DNA Marker.
(3) 5×TBE buffer: Dissolve 54g of trihydroxymethyl aminomethane (Tris) base, 27.5g of boric acid and 4.6g of $EDTANa_2$ in distilled water and dilute it to 1,000mL. A working solution should be diluted to 0.5× prior to electrophoresis.
(4) 6×loading buffer: Dissolve 25mg of bromophenol blue and 3mL glycerol in 5mL

5×TBE buffer and dilute it to 10mL.

(5) GoldView.

(6) Agarose.

【Procedures】

(1) Weigh 0.7g of agarose and add 100mL 0.5×TBE buffer to a flask. Dissolve the agarose in a microwave.

(2) Cool the gel solution to 50°C and add 1–2 drops of GoldView. Pour the gel into a gel tray and insert the proper comb.

(3) Let the gel cool at the room temperature until it is completely solidified, which may takes 30–45min. Carefully remove the comb and place the gel in the gel tray with the wells closest to the cathode end. Fill the electrophoresis tank with 0.5× TBE buffer until the gel is immersed.

(4) Add 6×loading buffer to DNA samples, mix well and carefully load the sample mixture into the gel wells with the micropipette.

(5) Cover the electrophoresis tank. Connect the electrode wires to the power supply, ensuring that the positive electrode (red) and negative electrode (black) are correctly connected. Turn on the power supply to 100V. Keep the power on until the blue dye approaches 2/3 length of the gel, which may takes 30–40min.

(6) Turn off the power and carefully take out the tray and gel with gloves on.

(7) Observe the gel with a gel image analysis system. Determine the size of sample DNA by comparing to the DNA Marker.

【Question】

What factors affect the migration of DNA in an electric field?

(Guo Dongmei, Yi Fang)

第三章　综合性实验

实验 16　血清免疫球蛋白的分离、纯化和鉴定

【实验目的】

1. 掌握分离纯化蛋白质的基本原理和基本过程。
2. 熟悉盐析、离心、层析等生物化学基本技术在蛋白质分离纯化中的应用。

【实验原理】

血清蛋白按电泳法一般可分为清蛋白、α_1球蛋白、α_2球蛋白、β球蛋白和γ球蛋白五类，免疫球蛋白大多存在于γ球蛋白中。盐析可将不同的蛋白质进行粗分（盐析原理见实验 5），对于血清蛋白而言，50%饱和硫酸铵溶液中，球蛋白沉淀出来，清蛋白仍溶解在溶液中，通过离心可得到球蛋白沉淀。

通过盐析得到的蛋白质携带大量的硫酸铵，会妨碍蛋白质进一步纯化，必须去除。由于蛋白质与硫酸铵分子量相差悬殊，可用透析或凝胶过滤层析法将两者分开。本实验用葡聚糖凝胶 G-25（Sephadex G-25）脱去球蛋白中的盐分。此类凝胶颗粒具有多孔网状结构，当溶液通过凝胶柱时，溶液中分子直径大的蛋白质直接通过凝胶柱，而分子直径小的无机盐能进入凝胶颗粒的网孔之中。因此在洗脱过程中，小分子的盐会被阻滞而后洗脱出来，从而可达到去盐的目的。

纯化后的蛋白质中含有α球蛋白、β球蛋白和γ球蛋白，三种球蛋白的等电点不同。α球蛋白、β球蛋白的等电点小于 6.0，γ球蛋白的等电点为 7.2 左右，因此在 pH6.5 的缓冲溶液中，α、β 球蛋白带负电荷，而 γ 球蛋白正电荷，利用离子交换层析可将其分离。在 pH 为 6.5 时，二乙氨乙基（DEAE）-纤维素带正电荷：

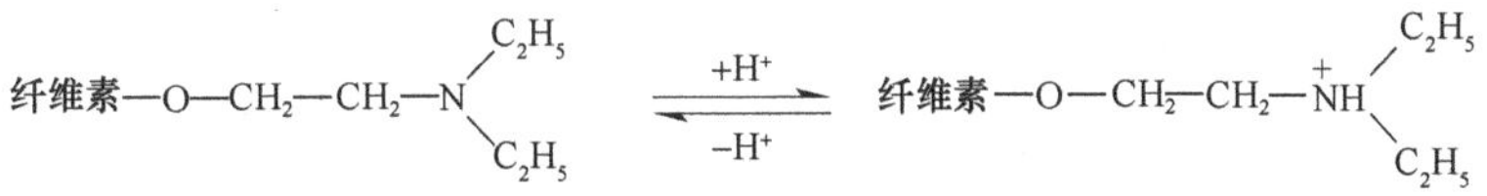

因此，DEAE-纤维素能吸附带负电荷的阴离子，故称为阴离子交换层析柱。当蛋白质溶液流经层析柱时，带负电荷的α球蛋白和β球蛋白被吸附结合；带正电荷的γ球蛋白则直接从层析柱随洗脱液流出，使γ球蛋白粗制品进一步被纯化。

要检验γ球蛋白是否纯净单一，可将纯化前后的γ球蛋白进行电泳鉴定。

【器材与试剂】

1. 器材

（1）葡聚糖凝胶 G-25 层析柱。
（2）DEAE-纤维素阴离子交换层析柱。
（3）离心机及离心管。

（4）试管。

（5）刻度移液管。

（6）洗耳球。

（7）白瓷反应板。

2. 试剂

（1）血清样品。

（2）0.9% NaCl 溶液。

（3）饱和$(NH_4)_2SO_4$溶液：称取固体$(NH_4)_2SO_4$（分析纯）850g 置于 1000mL 蒸馏水中，在 70～80℃水中搅拌溶解，室温中放置过夜，瓶底析出白色结晶，上清液即为饱和$(NH_4)_2SO_4$溶液。

（4）0.0175mol/L pH6.5 磷酸盐缓冲液（pH6.5 PBS）：①溶液 A：称取 $NaH_2PO_4 \cdot 2H_2O$ 2.730g 溶于蒸馏水，并定容至 1000mL。②溶液 B：称取 $Na_2HPO_4 \cdot 12H_2O$ 6.269g 溶于蒸馏水，并定容至 1000mL。

取溶液 A 77.5mL、溶液 B 22.5mL，混匀后即成 0.0175mol/L pH6.5 的磷酸盐缓冲液。

（5）葡聚糖凝胶 G-25：按每 100mL 凝胶床需干的 25g 葡聚糖凝胶 G-25，置于锥形瓶中，按每克干胶加入蒸馏水约 30mL，轻轻摇匀并于沸水浴中加热 1h，或于室温浸泡 24h，搅拌后稍静置，倾去上清细粒，用蒸馏水漂洗后继续用 0.0175mol/L 磷酸盐缓冲液（pH6.5）浸泡。

（6）奈斯勒试剂（参见实验 5）。

（7）双缩脲试剂（参见实验 6）。

【实验操作】

1. 分离球蛋白——盐析及离心　取血清 2mL 于试管中，加 0.9% NaCl 溶液 2mL，边搅拌混匀边缓慢滴加饱和$(NH_4)_2SO_4$溶液 4mL，混匀后于室温中放置 10min，3000r/min 离心 10min。样品分为两部分，球蛋白沉淀，而清蛋白保留在上清液中。小心倾去上清液，重复洗涤一次，于沉淀中加入 0.0175mol/L 磷酸盐缓冲液（pH6.5）1mL 使之溶解。此液即为粗提的球蛋白溶液。

2. 脱盐——交联葡聚糖凝胶柱层析

（1）装柱：洗净的层析柱保持垂直位置，关闭止水旋塞，将已处理的凝胶加入层析柱内，打开止水旋塞，凝胶随柱内溶液慢慢流下而均匀沉降到层析柱底部，最后使凝胶床达 20cm 高，床面上保持有洗脱液，关闭止水旋塞。装柱过程中，若凝胶沉积不均匀，或出现气泡，可再次打开止水旋塞，加入洗脱液，搅动柱床，使凝胶随缓冲液流下而重新沉积。

（2）上样与洗脱：打开止水旋塞，当柱上的缓冲液面刚好下降至凝胶床表面时关闭止水旋塞，用长滴管吸取球蛋白溶液，小心缓慢地加到凝胶床表面。打开止水旋塞，将流速控制在 0.5mL/min 以使样品进入凝胶床内。关闭止水旋塞，小心加入少量缓冲液，洗柱内壁。打开止水旋塞，待缓冲液进入凝胶床后再加少量缓冲液。如此重复三次，以洗净内壁上的样品溶液。然后可加入适量缓冲液开始洗脱。加样开始应立即用试管收集洗脱液，每管 1mL。

（3）NH_4^+与蛋白质的检查：按洗脱液的收集顺序每管取一滴，分别滴入白瓷反应板中，每孔加双缩脲试剂 2 滴，出现紫色表示有蛋白质析出，由此可估计蛋白质在各管中的分布及浓度；取另一白瓷反应板，每孔加奈斯勒试剂 1 滴，出现黄色代表含有 NH_4^+。

合并球蛋白含量高的各管，混匀。除留少量作电泳鉴定外，其余用 DEAE-纤维素阴离子交换柱进一步纯化。

3. 纯化——DEAE-纤维素阴离子交换层析　用 DEAE-纤维素装柱 8～10cm 高度，并用 PBS 缓冲液（pH6.5）平衡，然后将脱盐后的球蛋白溶液缓慢加于 DEAE-纤维素阴离子交换柱上，用同一缓冲液洗脱、分管收集。用双缩脲试剂检查蛋白质分布情况。收集所得即为纯化后的 γ 球蛋白（详细操作步骤参见实验 4）。

4. 浓缩　经 DEAE-纤维素阴离子交换柱纯化的 γ 球蛋白液往往浓度较低，不利于后续鉴定。将较浓的 γ 球蛋白溶液汇聚于一管，按每毫升加 0.2～0.25g 葡聚糖凝胶 G-25 干胶，摇动 2～3min，3000r/min 离心 5min。上清液即为浓缩的 γ 球蛋白溶液。

5. 鉴定——乙酸纤维素膜电泳　取乙酸纤维素膜 3 条，用点样器垂直点样。样品是血清、脱盐后的球蛋白、纯化的 γ 球蛋白液（详细过程参见实验 3）。比较电泳结果。

【思考题】

1. 本实验中，影响免疫球蛋白纯度的因素有哪些？如何加以控制？
2. 根据免疫球蛋白的性质和特点，还有其他什么方法可将其分离？

（王含彦　易　芳）

Chapter III Integrated Experiments

Experiment 16 Separation, Purification and Identification of Serum Immunoglobulin

【Purposes】

1. To master the basic principles and processes of protein separation and purification.

2. To understand the basic biochemical techniques involved in protein separation and purification, including salting-out, centrifugation and chromatography.

【Principles】

Serum proteins can be divided into five categories by electrophoresis: albumin, α_1 globulin, α_2 globulin, β globulin and γ globulin. Immunoglobulins mostly exist in γ globulin. Salting-out is a method that can be used to separate proteins from serum (for the principle of salting-out, please refer to Exp. 5). For serum proteins, globulin can be precipitated by 50% saturated ammonium sulfate solution, while albumin is still dissolved. Therefore, globulin precipitation can be separated from other proteins by centrifugation after salting-out.

Proteins obtained by salting-out carry a large amount of ammonium sulfate, which interferes with further protein purification and must be removed. Considering that the protein greatly differs from the ammonium sulfate in molecular weight, dialysis or gel filtration chromatography can be used for separation. In this experiment, dextran gel G-25 (Sephadex G-25) is used to remove salts from proteins. The dextran gel particle has a porous network structure. When the solution to be purified passes through the gel column, proteins with large molecular weights directly flow out of the column, while salts with small molecular weights enter into the gel. Therefore, during the process of elution, proteins will stream out first and salts will move more slowly streaming out later, which separates proteins from salts.

Purified proteins contain α globulin, β globulin and γ globulin with different isoelectric points (pIs). Both the pIs of α globulin and β globulin are less than 6.0, while the pI of γ globulin is about 7.2. In a buffer solution of pH6.5, α globulin and β globulin are negatively charged, and γ globulin are positively charged, which can be separated using ion exchange chromatography. At a pH of 6.5, diethylaminoethyl (DEAE) cellulose is positively charged:

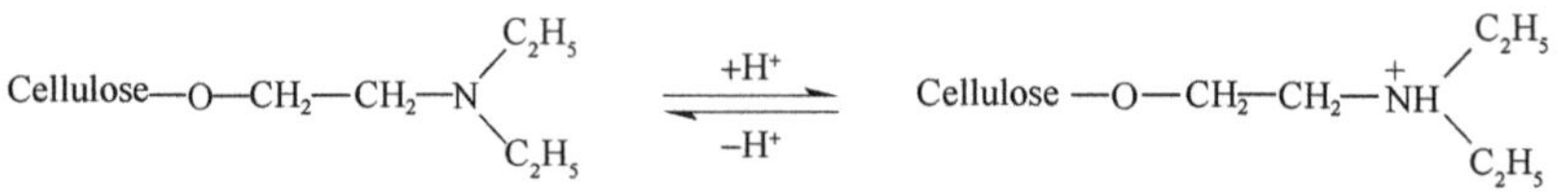

DEAE-cellulose, which can absorb anions, is termed as an anion exchange chromatography column. When a protein solution flows through the column, both α globulin and β globulin with negative charges are absorbed and γ globulin with positive charges directly flows out, following the eluent. In this way, γ globulin in crude products is further purified.

To test whether γ globulin products are pure, protein samples before and after purification can be observed using electrophoresis.

【Apparatus and Reagents】

1. Apparatus

(1) Dextran gel G-25 chromatography column.

(2) DEAE-cellulose anion exchange chromatography column.
(3) Centrifuge and centrifugal tube.
(4) Test tube.
(5) Measuring pipet.
(6) Ear wash bulb.
(7) White porcelain reaction plate.

2. Reagents

(1) Serum sample.
(2) 0.9% NaCl solution.
(3) Saturated $(NH_4)_2SO_4$ solution. Weigh 850g of solid $(NH_4)_2SO_4$ (AR), add it to 1,000mL distilled water, and stir and dissolve it at 70–80°C. Place at the room temperature overnight until white crystals form and the supernatant is saturated $(NH_4)_2SO_4$ solution.

(4) 0.0175mol/L pH6.5 phosphate buffer saline (pH6.5 PBS). ①Stock solution A: Dissolve 2.730g of $NaH_2PO_4 \cdot 2H_2O$ in distilled water, dilute it to 1,000mL. ②Stock solution B: Dissolve 6.269g of $Na_2HPO_4 \cdot 12H_2O$ in distilled water, dilute it to 1,000mL.

Mix 77.5mL of solution A and 22.5mL of solution B to yield 0.0175mol/L PBS (pH6.5).

(5) Dextran gel G-25. Take an appropriate amount of dry gel based on a ratio of 25g gel for every 100mL of gel bed volume and add 30mL distilled water for 1g gel. Gently mix and keep in a boiling water bath for 1h or soak it at the room temperature for 24h. Next, stir to remove bubbles, let the solution sit and then discard fine particles in the supernatant. Soak the rest gel with 0.0175mol/L PBS (pH6.5) after washing with distilled water.

(6) Nessler's reagent (Refer to Exp. 5).
(7) Biuret reagent (Refer to Exp. 6).

【Procedures】

1. Separating globulins—salting-out and centrifugation Pipette 2mL of serum into a test tube, add 2mL of 0.9% NaCl and mix well while slowly adding 4mL of saturated $(NH_4)_2SO_4$ dropwise. Keep it at the room temperature for 10min and centrifugate it at 3,000r/min for 10min. The sample in the tube is divided into two parts including globulin precipitates in the bottom and albumin in the supernatant. Carefully discard the supernatant, repeat washing, then add 1mL of PBS (pH 6.5) to dissolve precipitates and obtain crude extract from serum globulin.

2. Desalting—dextran gel column chromatography

(1) Column preparation: Fix a clean column on the burette stand perpendicularly, turn off the stop cock, add the treated gel into the column, turn on the stop cock, and gel particles uniformly and slowly move towards the bottom as they flow through the column. Do not turn off the stop cock until a 20cm height in the gel bed is reached. Make sure to keep some eluting solution on the gel surface. If the gel deposits are uneven or contain bubble during the process, turn on the cock, add the eluting solution and stir the gel column to make it deposited with the buffer flow.

(2) Sample loading and eluting: Turn on the cock and release the buffer. As soon as the liquid level reaches the surface of the gel bed, turn off the cock. Pipette the globulin solution obtained from salting-out with a rubber dropper and carefully release it onto the gel bed surface. Turn on the cock and adjust to a flow rate of 0.25mL/min to enable the sample to enter the gel bed. Turn off the cock and carefully add the buffer to wash the inner wall of the column. Turn on the cock, and after the buffer enters the gel bed, add extra buffer. Repeat three times to wash the sample on the inner wall. Begin eluting by adding an appropriate amount of buffer. At the same time, collect the eluent using test tubes (1mL for each tube).

(3) Detection of NH_4^+ and proteins: Place a drop of eluent to each well of a white porcelain reaction plate in the order of collecting tubes for the NH_4^+ test and 2 drops for the biuret test. If a purple color appears, there is presence of proteins and the distribution and

concentration of proteins in the collecting tubes can be estimated. Add one drop of Nessler's reagent to the well of another white porcelain reaction plate and the appearance of yellow precipitate indicates the presence of NH_4^+.

Collect and mix the solutions rich in globulin together. Purify the solution using a DEAE-cellulose anion exchange column except for a small portion that will be used in electrophoresis analysis.

3. Purification—DEAE-cellulose anion exchange chromatography Fill the column with DEAE-cellulose at a height of 8-10cm and balance with PBS (pH6.5). Pipette the globulin obtained from desalting with a dropper and release it gently into the DEAE-cellulose anion exchange column. Use PBS (pH6.5) to elute and collect the solution using test tubes. A biuret reagent should be used to detect the protein. The production is purified γ globulin (chromatography refer to Exp.4) .

4. Concentration Purified γ globulin solution using chromatography often has a low concentration that is not convenient for following identification. Collect all the solution in one tube and add Sephadex G-25 dry gel at a ratio of 0.2–0.25g gel per milliliter solution. Next, mix and centrifugate it at 3,000r/min for 5min. The supernatant is the concentrated γ globulin solution.

5. Identification—cellulose acetate membrane electrophoresis Use three pieces of cellulose acetate membrane and add a vertical sample line with a sample applicator. Samples are serum, globulin after desalting and γ globulin after purification (please refer to Exp. 3). Compare the results obtained from electrophoresis.

【Questions】

1. What are the factors affecting purity of immunoglobulins? How do you improve purity?
2. According to the nature and characteristics of immunoglobulins, what other options can be used to separate proteins?

(Wang Hanyan, Yi Fang)

实验 17　碱性磷酸酶的分离纯化及其 K_m 值测定

【实验目的】

1. 掌握碱性磷酸酶分离纯化及其 K_m 值测定的方法。
2. 了解碱性磷酸酶在临床疾病诊断方面的应用。

一、碱性磷酸酶的分离纯化

【实验原理】

酶提取、分离与纯化的方法和蛋白质相似。一般有中性盐盐析法（如硫酸铵盐析等）、电泳法（如聚丙烯酰胺凝胶电泳等）、层析法（如葡聚糖凝胶层析等）和有机溶剂法（如乙醇、丙酮、乙醚、正丁醇等）等。通常要用多种方法配合使用，才能得到纯净的酶。

本实验主要利用有机溶剂沉淀法从肝组织匀浆中提取碱性磷酸酶，因为不同蛋白质在不同浓度的有机溶剂中的溶解度不同，又称为“有机溶剂分段沉淀法”。常用的有机溶剂有乙醇和丙酮。本方法首先用低浓度乙酸钠溶液制备肝匀浆，用乙酸镁保护和稳定碱性磷酸酶的活性。其次，为了去除其他杂蛋白，加入正丁醇至 20%终浓度，让杂蛋白留在肝匀浆滤液中。碱性磷酸酶溶于 30%和 33%的乙酸溶液，离心去掉沉淀，碱性磷酸酶则留在上清液中。碱性磷酸酶不溶于 50%和 60%的乙酸溶液，离心去掉上清液，碱性磷酸酶则存在于沉淀中。反复用不同浓度的乙酸溶液使碱性磷酸酶溶解/沉淀，可去掉绝大部分杂蛋白，得到碱性磷酸酶的初级纯化产品。

应用有机溶剂提取分离碱性磷酸酶，最重要的就是要控制好适当的温度。高温易引起酶分子变性失活。用有机溶剂制备肝匀浆时会产生大量的热。因此，宜冰浴中制备匀浆，匀浆研磨过程宜慢，避免产生大量的热能使温度升高。

【器材与试剂】

1. 器材

（1）天平。

（2）手术剪。

（3）研钵、研磨杵、石英砂。

（4）刻度移液管、试管。

（5）离心机、离心管。

（6）制冰机或冰箱。

（7）玻璃棒、滤纸、漏斗。

2. 试剂

（1）0.5mol/L 乙酸镁溶液：称取乙酸镁 107.23g 溶于蒸馏水中，稀释至 1000mL。

（2）0.1mol/L 乙酸钠溶液：称取乙酸钠 8.2g 溶于蒸馏水中，稀释至 1000mL。

（3）0.01mol/L 乙酸镁-0.01mol/L 乙酸钠溶液：取 0.5mol/L 乙酸镁 20mL、0.1mol/L 乙

酸钠 100mL，混合后加蒸馏水稀释至 1000mL。

（4）正丁醇（分析纯试剂）。

（5）丙酮（分析纯试剂）。

（6）96%乙醇（分析纯试剂）。

（7）0.01mol/L pH8.8 三羟甲基氨基甲烷缓冲液：称取 12.1g 三羟甲基氨基甲烷，用少量蒸馏水溶解，然后稀释至 1000mL，得 0.1mol/L 三羟甲基氨基甲烷缓冲液。取 100mL 0.1mol/L 三羟甲基氨基甲烷缓冲液，加 790mL 蒸馏水，再加 100mL 0.1mol/L 乙酸钠混匀，用 1%乙酸调 pH 至 8.8，最后用蒸馏水稀释至 1000mL。

【实验操作】

（1）AKP 的分离纯化操作步骤如图 17-1 所示（以下操作均在 0～4℃进行）。

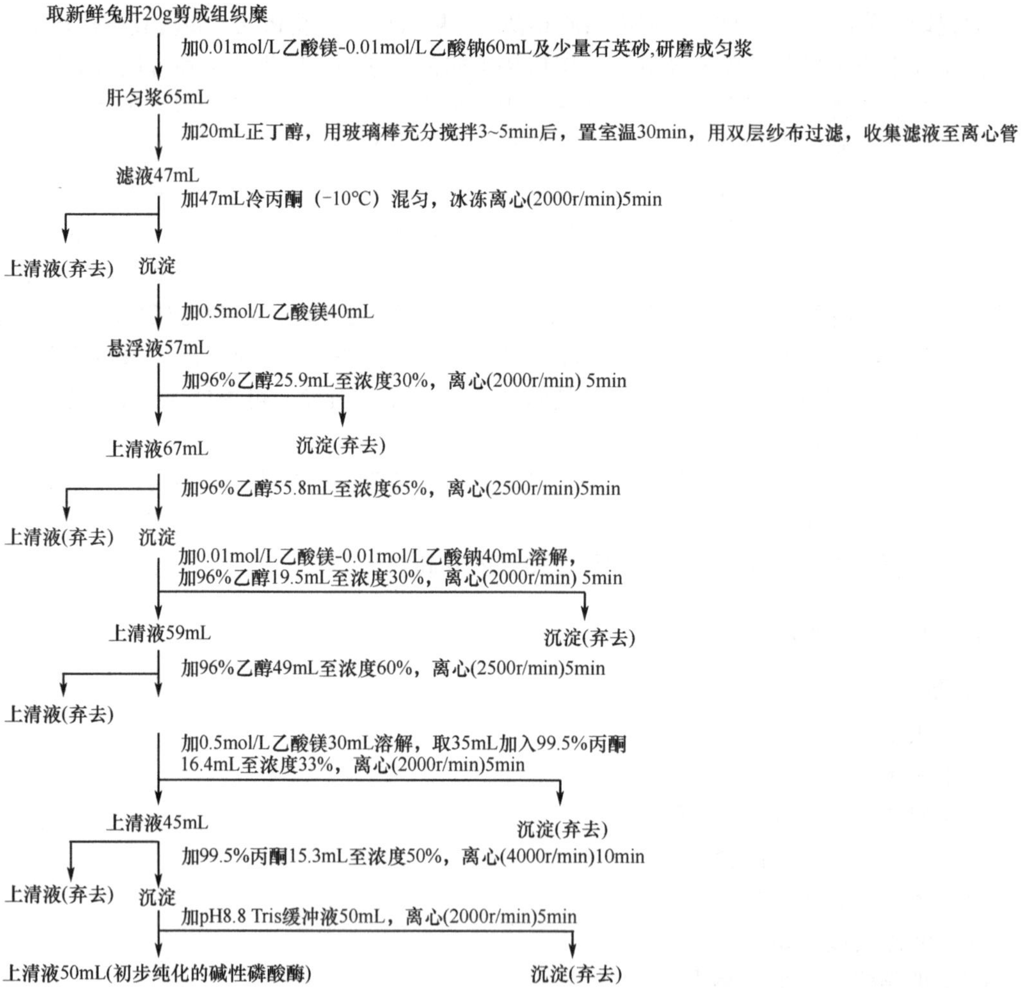

图 17-1　分离纯化碱性磷酸酶的操作流程

（2）将分离提取的碱性磷酸酶分装 2mL/瓶，冰冻干燥保存或液体保存也可，但均置于-60℃低温冰箱保存。测其 K_m 值时稀释 5～7 倍。

【注意事项】

（1）应加有机溶剂的体积计算公式为

$$X=V_0\times（C_s'-C_s''）/C_s-C_s'$$

式中，X 代表应加有机溶剂体积；V_0 代表溶液原始体积；C_s 代表有机溶剂的百分浓度；C_s' 代表有机溶剂在混合液中的终浓度；C_s'' 代表有机溶剂在混合液中的初始浓度。

（2）蛋白质在高浓度的有机溶剂中容易发生变性，所以分离和纯化蛋白质的过程宜在低温条件下进行。

二、碱性磷酸酶的 K_m 值测定

【实验原理】

K_m 值是酶促反应中一个重要的动力学参数。为了准确测定 K_m，可通过对米氏方程进行演变得到多种直线方程。其中 Lineweaver- Burk 作图法是最常用的（图 17-2），即以 $1/V$ 对 $1/[S]$ 作图，直线在横轴的截距为 $-1/K_m$，根据在横轴上的截距，可以计算出该酶的 K_m。

$$\frac{1}{V}=\frac{K_m+[S]}{V_{max}[S]}=\frac{K_m}{V_{max}}\frac{1}{[S]}+\frac{1}{V_{max}}$$

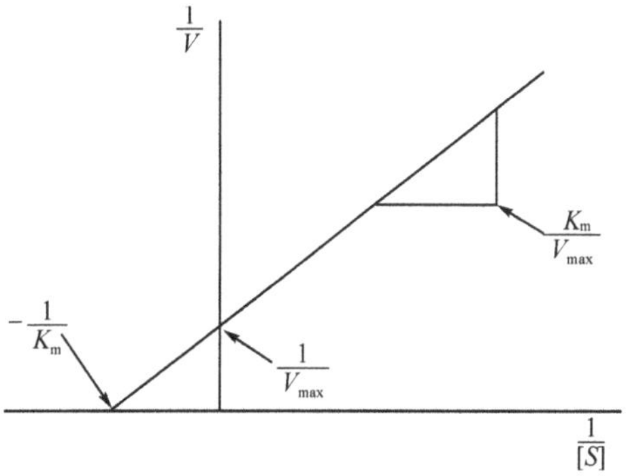

图 17-2　Lineweaver-Burk 作图法

在 pH=10，37℃条件下，碱性磷酸酶能分解磷酸苯二钠产生酚和磷酸，酚在碱性溶液中与 4-氨基安替比林（AAP）作用，经铁氰化钾氧化生成红色的醌衍生物，根据红色深浅可用分光光度法对其进行测定。将标准酚经同样的上述反应处理，则可测出碱性磷酸酶生成的酚的含量。在本实验中，磷酸苯二钠的含量在反应前后的差异即为反应速度（V）。具体反应过程如下：

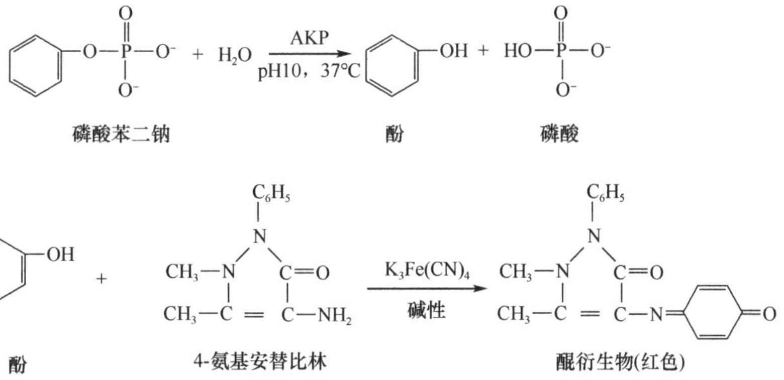

【器材与试剂】

1. 器材

（1）水浴锅。

（2）试管。

（3）刻度移液管。

（4）721A 型分光光度计。

2. 试剂

（1）0.04mol/L 底物溶液：称取 10.16g 磷酸苯二钠（$C_6H_5PO_4Na_2 \cdot 2H_2O$），用煮沸后冷却的蒸馏水溶解并稀释至 1000mL，加 4mL 氯仿防腐，贮于棕色瓶内，置 4℃保存，于 7 日内可用。

（2）0.1mol/L pH10 碳酸盐缓冲液：称取无水碳酸钠 6.36g 及 $NaHCO_3$ 3.36g，溶解于蒸馏水并稀释至 1000mL。

（3）碱性磷酸酶液：取纯化的碱性磷酸酶 5mg，用 pH10 缓冲液配制成 100mL 溶液，4℃保存。或用自己提取的碱性磷酸酶液，用 pH10 缓冲液稀释至 5～7 倍。

（4）0.5mol/L NaOH 溶液：称取 2g NaOH，溶于蒸馏水中，定容至 100mL。

（5）0.3% 4-氨基安替比林：称取 3g 4-氨基安替比林及 $NaHCO_3$ 42g，用蒸馏水溶解，并稀释至 1000mL，贮于棕色瓶中，4℃保存。

（6）0.5%铁氰化钾：称取 5g 铁氰化钾及 15g 硼酸各溶于 400mL 蒸馏水中，溶解后两液混合加水至 1000mL。置棕色瓶中，4℃保存。

【实验操作】

1. **加样** 取干净试管 8 支，按表 17-1 操作。

表 17-1 碱性磷酸酶 K_m 值的测定 （单位：mL）

试剂	管号							
	1	2	3	4	5	6	7	0
0.04mol/L 底物溶液	0.15	0.20	0.25	0.30	0.40	0.60	0.80	0
pH10 碳酸盐缓冲溶液	0.90	0.90	0.90	0.90	0.90	0.90	0.90	0.90
蒸馏水	0.85	0.80	0.75	0.70	0.60	0.40	0.20	0.10
混匀，于 37℃预热 5min								
酶液	0.10	0.10	0.10	0.10	0.10	0.10	0.10	0.10

各管加入酶液，混匀之后立即计时，在 37℃水浴中准确保温 15min 后，立即加入 0.5mol/L NaOH 溶液 1mL 以终止反应。

2. **显色** 各管中加入 0.3% 4-氨基安替比林 1mL 和 0.5%铁氰化钾 2mL，充分混匀，放置 10min，以“0”管为对照，在波长 510nm 下比色，测量各管的吸光度。

3. **作图** 所测各管的吸光度代表各管中反应速度 V，以之为纵轴，以底物浓度$[S]$为横轴，在坐标纸上连接各点作图，观察曲线的形状。再以 $\frac{1}{V}$ 为纵坐标，以 $\frac{1}{[S]}$ 为横坐标，Lineweaver-Burk 作图法求此酶的 K_m 值。

【注意事项】

K_m 应该用提纯的酶进行测定，本实验如果采用初步自提纯的酶液测定，可能与纯化的酶的 K_m 值有偏差。

【思考题】

1. K_m 值有何意义？
2. 用双倒数作图法和米氏曲线法求 K_m 值有何不同？

（杨映雪 易 芳）

Experiment 17 Isolating Alkaline Phosphatase and Determining It's K_m

【Purposes】

1. To master isolating alkaline phosphatase (AKP) and determining the K_m.
2. To learn the clinical significance behind determining AKP specific activity.

Ⅰ. Isolating alkaline phosphatase

【Principles】

The methods used to isolate and purify enzymes are the same as used for proteins. Generally, isolation and purification methods for proteins include salting-out by neutral salts [e. g. $(NH_4)_2SO_4$ or Na_2SO_4], electrophoresis (e. g. PAGE) , chromatography (e. g. polydextran gel column chromatography) and precipitation by organic solvents (e. g. ethanol, acetone, ethyl ether or n-butanol). Usually, these methods should be used in combination to obtain a higher amount of purified enzymes.

In this experiment, the method of precipitation using organic solvents is mainly used to isolate alkaline phosphatase from the liver. This is based on the fact that proteins have different solubilities in varying concentrations of organic solvents, which is termed as "organic-solvent segmented precipitation method". Ethanol and acetone are the most frequently used organic solvents. During the process, first, liver homogenate is prepared using a low concentration of sodium acetate solution that is protected with magnesium acetate to stabilize alkaline phosphatase activity. Second, to remove miscellaneous proteins, n-butyl alcohol is added to 20% final concentration to ensure that miscellaneous proteins are kept in the liver homogenate filtrate. Alkaline phosphatase is soluble in 30% and 33% acetic acid solutions and after removing centrifugal sedimentation, it remains in the supernatant fluid. On the other hand, alkaline phosphatase is not soluble in 50% and 60% acetic acid solutions and after removing the centrifugal supernatant, alkaline phosphatase exists in precipitation. Treated with different concentrations of acetic acid solutions, primary purification products of alkaline phosphatase are obtained by dissolution/precipitation while most miscellaneous proteins can be removed.

It is important to keep proper temperature during extraction of alkaline phosphatase using organic solvents. High temperature can cause denaturation and inactivation of enzymes. Preparation of liver homogenate by organic solvents would produce a large amount of heat, indicating that it should be prepared using an ice bath. To avoid production of a large amount of heat, grinding should be performed slowly as well.

【Apparatus and Reagents】

1. Apparatus

(1) Balance.
(2) Scissors.
(3) Mortar, grinding pestle and quartz sand.
(4) Measuring pipet and test tube.
(5) Centrifuge and centrifugal tube.
(6) Ice machine and refrigerator.
(7) Glass rod, filter paper and funnel.

2. Reagents

(1) 0.5mol/L $Mg(Ac)_2$ solution: Dissolve 107.23g of $Mg(Ac)_2$ in distilled water and make a final volume of 1,000mL.

(2) 0.1mol/L NaAc solution: Dissolve 8.2g of NaAc in distilled water and make a final volume of 1,000mL.

(3) 0.01mol/L $Mg(Ac)_2$-0.01mol/L NaAc mixture: Mix 20mL of 0.5mol/L $Mg(Ac)_2$ with 100mL of 0.1mol/L NaAc, and add distilled water up to 1,000mL.

(4) n-butyl alcohol (A.R.) .

(5) Acetone (A.R.) .

(6) 96% ethanol (A.R.) .

(7) 0.01mol/L pH8.8 Tris buffer: Dissolve 12.1g of Tris in a small volume of distilled water and dilute it to 1,000mL. The concentration should be 0.1mol/L. Add 790mL of distilled water and 100mL of 0.1mol/L NaAc to 100mL of 0.1mol/L Tris solution, mix and adjust the pH to 8.8 with 1% acetic acid. Dilute it to 1,000mL with distilled water.

【Procedures】

1. The procedure of AKP isolation and purification is shown in Fig. 17-1(perform all procedures at 0-4°C) .

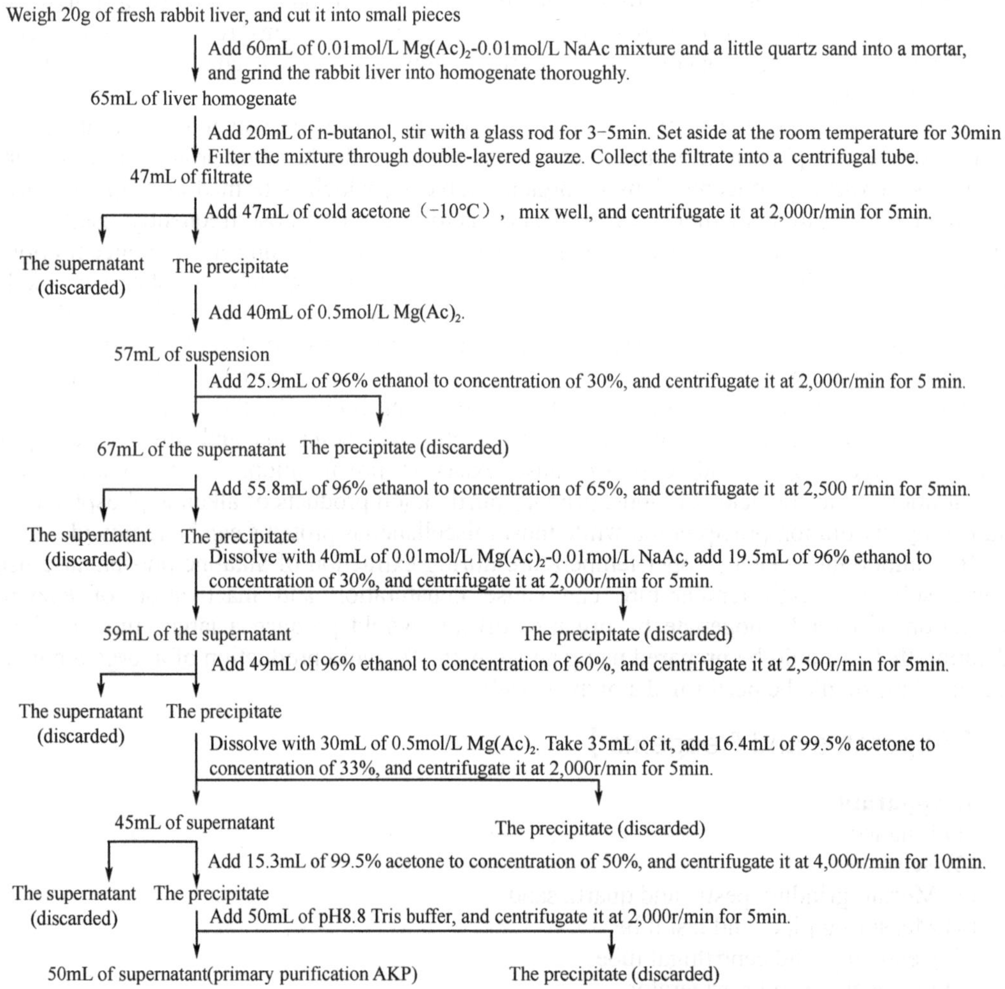

Fig. 17-1 Isolation and purification of AKP

2. The extracted AKP was separated and packed into 2mL/bottle. Freeze dry or use liquid preservation and store at −60°C. Dilute 5–7 times when measuring its K_m.

【 Notes 】

1. The formula for adding organic solvent volume is as follows.

$$X=V_o\times(C_s'-C_s'')/C_s-C_s'$$

where X represents the volume of the organic solvent to be added; V_o represents the original volume of the solution; C_s represents the percentage concentration of the organic solvent; C_s' represents the final percentage concentration of the organic solvent in the mixture; C_s'' represents the initial percentage concentration of the organic solvent in the mixture.

2. Proteins are denatured in high concentration of organic solvents. Therefore, it is necessary to perform the isolation and purification process at low temperatures.

Ⅱ. Determining the K_m of alkaline phosphatase

【 Principles 】

K_m is an important kinetic parameter of an enzymatic reaction. To determine an accurate K_m value, several linear equations can be obtained through the rearrangements of the Michaelis-Menten equation. Among them, the best known equation is the Lineweaver-Burk plot (Fig. 17-2). If $1/V$ is plotted against $1/[S]$, a straight line is obtained where the *horizontal axis* is equal to $-1/K_m$. According to this intercept the K_m could be determined.

$$\frac{1}{V}=\frac{K_m+[S]}{V_{max}[S]}=\frac{K_m}{V_{max}}\frac{1}{[S]}+\frac{1}{V_{max}}$$

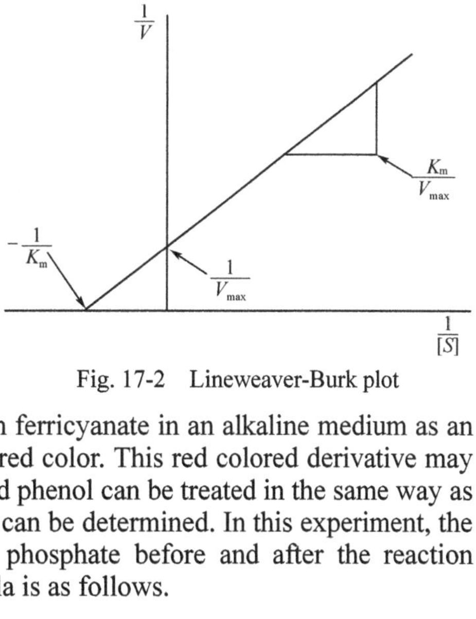

Fig. 17-2 Lineweaver-Burk plot

AKP catalyzes the hydrolysis of disodium phenyl phosphate releasing phenol in a medium with a pH of 10 at 37°C. Phenol will react with 4-aminoantipyrine (AAP) in the presence of potassium ferricyanate in an alkaline medium as an oxidizing agent and form a quinone derivative with a red color. This red colored derivative may be used for spectrophotometric determination. Standard phenol can be treated in the same way as above. Thus, the quantity of phenol produced by AKP can be determined. In this experiment, the difference in the concentration of disodium phenyl phosphate before and after the reaction equals to the reaction velocity (V). The reaction formula is as follows.

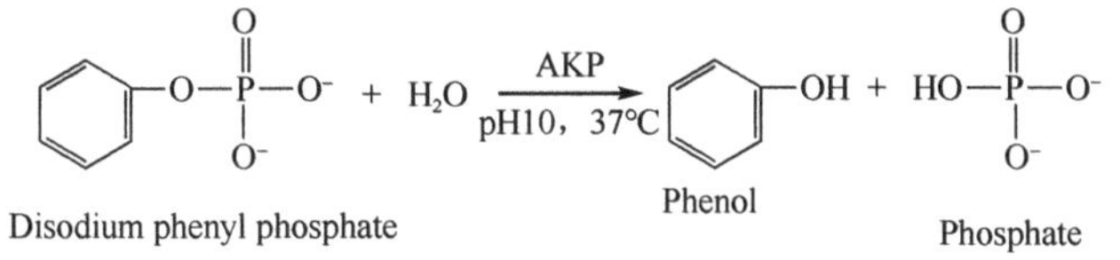

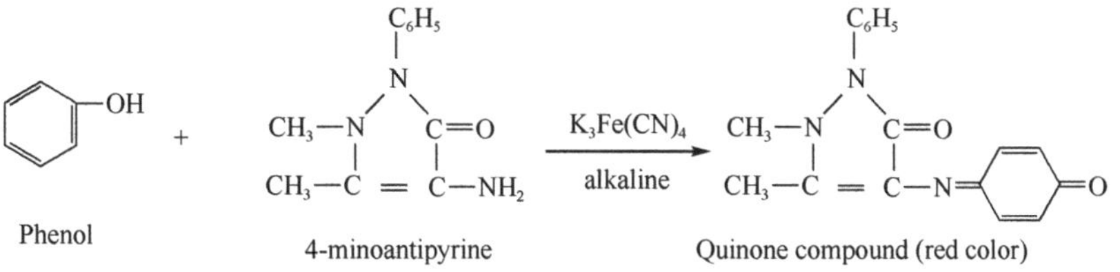

【Apparatus and Reagents】

1. Apparatus

(1) Water bath cauldron.

(2) Test tube.

(3) Measuring pipet.

(4) Type 721A spectrophotometer.

2. Reagents

(1) 0.04mol/L substrate solution: Dissolve 10.16g of disodium phenyl phosphate ($C_6H_5PO_4Na_2 \cdot 2H_2O$) in chilled distilled water and dilute it to 1,000mL. Add 4mL of chloroform as preservative and store it in a dark bottle at 4°C. This solution should be used within 7 days.

(2) 0.1mol/L pH10 carbonate buffer: Dissolve 6.36g of anhydrous sodium carbonate and 3.36g of sodium bicarbonate in distilled water and dilute it to 1,000 mL.

(3) AKP solution: Dissolve 5mg of purified alkaline phosphatase in the pH10 buffer, make a final volume of 100mL and store it at 4°C, or dilute the partially purified AKP extraction 5-7 times using the pH10 buffer.

(4) 0.5mol/L NaOH: Dissolve 2g NaOH in distilled water, and dilute it to 100mL.

(5) 0.3% 4-aminoantipyrine: Dissolve 3g of 4-aminoantipyrine and 42g of sodium bicarbonate in distilled water, and dilute it to 1,000mL. Store it in a dark bottle at 4°C.

(6) 0.5% potassium ferricyanate: Dissolve 5g of potassium ferricyanate and 15g of boric acid separately in 400mL of distilled water. Mix the two solutions, add distilled water up to 1,000 mL, and store it in a dark bottle at 4°C.

【Procedures】

1. Add samples Take 8 test tubes and add reagents based on Table 17-1.

Table 17-1 K_m determination for AKP (Unit: mL)

Reagents	Tube numbers							
	1	2	3	4	5	6	7	0
0.04mol/L substrate solution	0.15	0.20	0.25	0.30	0.40	0.60	0.80	0
pH10 carbonate buffer	0.90	0.90	0.90	0.90	0.90	0.90	0.90	0.90
Distilled water	0.85	0.80	0.75	0.70	0.60	0.40	0.20	0.10
Mix well, and preheat at 37°C for 5min								
Enzyme solution	0.10	0.10	0.10	0.10	0.10	0.10	0.10	0.10

Start timing immediately after adding the enzyme solution to each tube and mixing. Add immediately 1mL of 0.5mol/L NaOH to stop the reaction after accurately incubating the tubes at 37°C water bath for 15min.

2. Color rendering Add 1mL of 0.3% 4-aminoantipyrine and 2mL of 0.5% potassium ferricyanate into each tube, mix well and set aside for 10min. Measure the absorbance of each tube at 510nm using tube 0 as the blank.

3. Plotting The absorbance of each tube represents the reaction rate V, using this as the vertical axis and the substrate concentration as the horizontal axis. Connect the points on graph paper and observe the shape of the curve. Draw a Lineweaver-Burk plot of $1/V$ against $1/[S]$ and calculate the K_m value.

【Notes】

K_m should be measured using pure enzyme. In this experiment, if partially purified enzyme is used, the obtained K_m may deviate from the K_m of pure enzyme.

【Questions】

1. What is the significance of K_m?
2. What is the difference between the Lineweaver-Burk plot and the Michaelis-Menten plot when it comes to determine the K_m?

(Yang Yingxue, Yi Fang)

实验 18　质粒 DNA 的分离纯化与鉴定

【实验目的】

1. 掌握碱裂解法提取质粒 DNA 的原理。
2. 熟悉分光光度计测定 DNA 含量的方法。
3. 了解质粒的基本特性。

【实验原理】

质粒是独立存在于染色体外、能自主复制并能稳定遗传的一种环状双链 DNA 小分子（1～200kb），在 DNA 重组技术中主要起转移基因的作用。

DNA 遇加热、极端 pH、有机溶剂等条件会变性，去除变性条件又可复性。质粒 DNA 可用十二烷基磺酸钠（SDS）配制的碱裂解法制备。SDS 是一种阴离子表面活性剂，能使细菌蛋白质变性，导致细菌细胞壁破裂，释放出基因组 DNA 及质粒 DNA，释放出的 DNA 在强碱性条件下会变性。乙酸钾中和后溶液呈中性，质粒 DNA 分子量小，复性迅速，而染色体 DNA 由于分子巨大在短时间内难以复性。因此离心后，质粒 DNA 留在上清液中，染色体 DNA 则与细胞碎片一起沉淀到离心管的底部。通过这种方法即可将质粒 DNA 从细菌中提取出来。

测定 DNA 浓度的方法有两种。第一种是紫外光吸收法，通过测定 260nm 和 280nm 处的吸光度即可对 DNA 进行定量。根据 OD_{260}（光密度）计算 DNA 浓度。另一种是用琼脂糖凝胶电泳测定质粒 DNA 的产量（和质量）。GoldView（参见实验 15）能与 DNA 结合并嵌入双链中。当受紫外光照射时会激发产生荧光，且荧光的强度与 DNA 含量呈正比。

【器材与试剂】

1. 器材

（1）离心机。

（2）1.5mL 或 2mL 的离心管。

（3）电泳仪。

（4）紫外分光光度计。

（5）凝胶图像分析系统。

（6）手套。

2. 试剂

（1）质粒小提试剂盒（Omega 公司 Plasmid Mini Kit 试剂盒）。

（2）100mg/mL RNase A。

（3）6×上样缓冲液（参见实验 15）。

（4）5×TBE（参见实验 15）。

（5）大肠杆菌 DH5α。

（6）琼脂糖。

（7）无水乙醇。

（8）LB液体培养基：约800mL蒸馏水中溶入胰蛋白胨10g、酵母提取物5g、NaCl 10g，用NaOH溶液调pH至7.0，蒸馏水定容至1000mL。121℃高压蒸汽灭菌20min。

【实验操作】

1. 质粒DNA的提取

（1）将带有质粒的单克隆大肠杆菌接种到含适当抗生素的1～5mL LB液体培养基中，37℃振荡培养（300r/min）12～16h，到细菌对数生长期即可收获（OD_{600}<3.0）。

（2）取1mL细菌培养液于离心管中，6000r/min离心5min，弃上清液。

（3）质粒提取具体步骤详见供应商试剂盒操作说明书。

2. 质粒DNA含量和质量的测定

（1）取2μL提取的质粒DNA，加入98μL蒸馏水稀释。

（2）蒸馏水作为空白，分别在波长260nm和280nm处调节紫外分光光度计读数至零。

（3）加入DNA稀释液，测定260nm及280nm的吸光度。

（4）计算确定DNA浓度或纯度，公式如下：

$$\text{DNA浓度（μg/mL）}=OD_{260}\times 50\times \text{稀释倍数}$$

OD_{260}/OD_{280}用于估计核酸的纯度。一般DNA的纯品，比值为1.8表示约90%的纯度，低于此比值说明有蛋白质污染。

3. 质粒DNA的琼脂糖电泳

琼脂糖电泳鉴定的具体操作见实验15。

【思考题】

1. 质粒的特点是什么？
2. 细菌收获的最佳时期是什么时期？
3. 请解释你的质粒DNA电泳图谱。

（陈瑾歆　易　芳）

Experiment 18　Isolation, Purification and Identification of Plasmid DNA

【Purposes】

1. To master the principle of alkaline lysis method for the extraction and purification of plasmid DNA.
2. To learn how to measure DNA concentration by spectrophotometry.
3. To learn the characteristics of plasmid DNA.

【Principles】

Plasmids are small (1–200kb) , circular and double-stranded units of DNA that replicate within a cell independent from chromosomal DNA and are often found in bacteria. Plasmids are used in recombinant DNA research to transfer genes between cells.

Heat, extreme pH and organic solvents have the ability to denature DNA. DNA is renatured in an environment where these denaturing conditions are eliminated. Plasmid DNA can be prepared by alkaline lysis using sodium dodecyl sulfate(SDS). SDS is an anionic detergent that breaks bacterial cells and denatures proteins. When the bacterial cells are lysed, plasmid DNA and genomic DNA are released and will be denatured in an alkali environment. When the solution is neutralized by acidic reagents (such as KAc) , plasmid DNA will be rapidly renatured due to its small size. However, genomic DNA cannot be easily renatured because of its large size. After centrifugation, plasmid DNA will be present in the supernatant, while genomic DNA will stay in the sediment at the bottom of the tube along with other cellular debris. Plasmid DNA can be extracted from bacteria in this way.

There are two methods used to measure the concentration of plasmid DNA. One method includes ultraviolet light absorption. Determine the UV absorbance at 260nm and 280nm. DNA concentration is calculated based on OD_{260}. Alternatively, plasmid DNA yield (as well as quality) can be determined by agarose gel electrophoresis. GoldView (Refer to Exp.15) can bind with DNA by inserting into the base pairs of DNA molecules. Excited by UV, the DNA band in agarose gel electrophoresis will emit a red fluorescence that can be detected. Fluorescence intensity is proportional to DNA content.

【Apparatus and Reagents】

1. Apparatus
(1) Centrifuge.
(2) 1.5mL or 2mL centrifugal tube.
(3) Electrophoresis apparatus.
(4) Ultraviolet spectrophotometer.
(5) Gel image analysis system.
(6) Glove.
2. Reagents
(1) Plasmid miniprep kit(Omega Plasmid Mini Kit).
(2) 100mg/mL RNase A.
(3) 6×loading buffer (Refer to Exp. 15).
(4) 5×TBE buffer (Refer to Exp. 15).
(5) *E. coli* DH5α.
(6) Agarose.

(7) 100% ethanol.

(8) Lysogeny broth (LB) liquid medium: Dissolve 10g tryptone, 5g yeast extract and 10g NaCl in about 800mL distilled water, adjust it to pH7.0 using the NaOH solution, and dilute it to 1,000mL. Autoclaving at 121℃ for 20min.

【Procedures】

1. Extraction of plasmid DNA

(1) Inoculate monoclonal *E. coli* with plasmids into 1–5mL of LB liquid medium containing appropriate antibiotics. Incubate for 12–16h at 37℃ with vigorous shaking at 300r/min until the bacteria grow to the logarithmic phase(Note: do not exceed an OD_{600} of 3.0) .

(2) Add 1mL of bacterial culture into a centrifugal tube, then harvest the bacteria by centrifugation at 6,000r/min for 5min. Discard the supernatant completely to remove the residue medium.

(3) Please refer to the plasmid purification handbook of the supplier for a detailed protocol purifying plasmid DNA.

2. Determining the yield and quality of plasmid DNA

(1) Dilute 2μL plasmid DNA in 98μL distilled water.

(2) Using distilled water in a cuvette, set OD_{260} and OD_{280} in the UV spectrophotometer to 0.

(3) Remove distilled water, add samples to cuvettes and record the absorbance at 260nm and 280nm.

(4) The DNA concentration or purification is calculated as follows:

$$\text{DNA concentration } (\mu g/mL)=OD_{260}\times 50\times N \text{ (Diluted times)}$$

The value of OD_{260}/OD_{280} is an indication of nucleic acid purity. A value of about 1.8 indicates 90% nucleic acid purity. The value less than 1.8 indicates protein contaminant.

3. Identification of plasmid DNA

Identification of plasmid DNA on an agarose gel, please refer to Exp. 15.

【Questions】

1. What are the characteristics of plasmid DNA?
2. What is the optimal harvesting time for the bacterial culture?
3. Please explain your plasmid DNA electropherogram.

(Chen Jinxin, Yi Fang)

实验 19　动物肝脏中 DNA 的提取和检测

【实验目的】

1. 掌握动物组织总 DNA 的提取方法及其原理。
2. 了解测定 DNA 含量的原理和操作方法。

【实验原理】

天然状态的 DNA 以脱氧核糖核蛋白（DNP） 形式存在于细胞核中。从细胞核中提取 DNA 时，要先把 DNP 抽提出来，再把蛋白质除去，再除去细胞中的糖、RNA 及无机离子等，从中分离 DNA。DNP 和核糖核蛋白（RNP）在盐溶液中的溶解度受盐浓度的影响而不同。在 0.14mol/L 的氯化钠溶液中，RNP 溶解度大，而 DNP 溶解度小，相反在 1mol/L 的氯化钠溶液中，DNP 的溶解度大，而 RNP 的溶解度小，从而使 DNP 和 RNP 分开。然后用蛋白质变性沉淀剂去除蛋白，使核酸释放出来，再利用核酸不溶于乙醇的性质将核酸析出，达到分离 DNA 和 RNA 的目的。

分离出来的 DNA 在 260nm 具有最大吸收峰。1μg/mL DNA 溶液在 260nm 的吸光度为 0.020。故测定未知浓度的 DNA 溶液在 260nm 的吸光度即可计算出其中 DNA 的含量。

【器材与试剂】

1. 器材

（1）离心机。

（2）高压灭菌器。

（3）研钵。

（4）摇床。

（5）微量移液器。

（6）分光光度计。

2. 试剂

（1）0.14mol/L NaCl-0.15mol/L 乙二胺四乙酸（ethylenediaminetetraacetic acid disodium salt，EDTA）溶液：称取 8.18g NaCl 及 37.2g $EDTANa_2$ 溶解于蒸馏水，定容至 1000mL。

（2）20%SDS 溶液：称取 20g SDS 溶于 100mL 水。

（3）氯仿-异戊醇（V∶V=24∶1）混合液。

（4）95%乙醇溶液。

（5）80%乙醇溶液。

（6） TE （Tris-EDTA）缓冲液：①溶液 A（1mol/L Tris-HCl，pH8.0）：称取 Tris 碱 6.06g，加蒸馏水 40mL 溶解，以浓 HCl pH 至 8.0，定容至 50mL；②溶液 B（0.5mol/L EDTA，pH8.0）：称取 $EDTANa_2 \cdot 2H_2O$ 9.306g，加蒸馏水 35mL，搅拌并用 NaOH 颗粒调 pH 至 8.0，溶解后加蒸馏水定容至 50mL。取溶液 A 1mL 和溶液 B 0.2mL，加蒸馏水定容至 100mL。121℃高压蒸汽灭菌 20min。

【实验操作】

1. DNA 分离

（1）称取2g新鲜动物肝脏，切成小块，加入4mL 0.14mol/L NaCl -0.15mol/L EDTA溶液，于研钵中研磨至匀浆，转入离心管中，以4000r/min的转速离心 10min。

（2）在上述沉淀物中加入0.14mol/L NaCl -0.15mol/L EDTA溶液，使总体积为 4mL，然后在60℃下，滴加20%SDS溶液2～3滴，摇动10min，使核酸与蛋白质分离。

（3）加固体氯化钠0.4g混匀，60℃水浴30min。

（4）加等体积的氯仿-异戊醇，混匀，摇动5min以4000r/min的转速离心10min。离心管内的物质分为三层，上层为含DNA的水相层，下层为氯仿-异戊醇混合物，中间层为变性蛋白凝胶。

（5）吸出上清液，加入2倍体积95%乙醇溶液（预冷），产生沉淀。

（6）再以4000r/min 的转速离心溶液10min，弃去上清液，沉淀用80%乙醇溶液离心洗涤。

（7）将沉淀置于滤纸上，除尽乙醇，室温自然干燥后，加入200μL TE缓冲液，使DNA充分溶解。

2. DNA 浓度测定

（1）取2μL提取的DNA溶液，加入98μL蒸馏水将待测DNA样品进行稀释（1∶50或更高倍数）。

（2）蒸馏水作为空白对照，测定DNA稀释液在260nm及280nm的吸光度。

（3）计算确定DNA浓度，公式如下：

$$\text{DNA浓度}(\mu g/mL)=50\times OD_{260}\times\text{稀释倍数}$$

【思考题】

1. 核酸提取、鉴定的原理是什么？
2. 在本实验的操作过程中应注意什么问题？

（汤建才　易　芳）

Experiment 19 DNA Extraction and Detection from Animal Liver

【Purposes】

1. To master the principles and procedures extracting total DNA from animal tissue.
2. To learn the principle and method to quantify DNA.

【Principles】

Native DNA is a deoxyribonucleoprotein (DNP) located in the nucleus of the cell. To separate DNA from its nuclear compartment, DNPs are extracted followed by the removal of proteins and then sugar, RNA and inorganic ions. The solubility of DNPs and ribonucleoproteins (RNPs) are influenced by salt concentration. In 0.14mol/L NaCl solution, the solubility of RNP is higher than that of DNP. In contrast, the solubility of DNP is higher than that of RNP in 1mol/L NaCl solution. DNPs and RNPs can be separated based on solubility and binding proteins are removed by denaturing protein precipitates to release nucleic acid. Nucleic acid is insoluble in ethanol and can be precipitated.

Isolated DNA has the maximum absorption peak at the wavelength of 260nm. The absorbance at 260nm is 0.020 of 1μg/mL DNA solution. Therefore the absorbance at 260nm is commonly used to determine DNA concentration.

【Apparatus and Reagents】

1. Apparatus

(1) Centrifuge.
(2) Autoclave.
(3) Mortar.
(4) Shaker.
(5) Micropipette.
(6) Spectrophotometer.

2. Reagents

(1) 0.14mol/L NaCl-0.15mol/L EDTA solution: Dissolve 8.18g NaCl and 37.2g $EDTANa_2$ in 100mL distilled water and dilute it to 1,000mL.

(2) 20% SDS solution: Dissolve 20g SDS in 100mL distilled water.

(3) Chloroform-isoamyl alcohol (V : V=24 : 1) mixture.

(4) 95% ethanol.

(5) 80% ethanol.

(6) TE(Tris-EDTA) buffer. ①Solution A(1mol/L Tris-HCl, pH 8.0): Dissolve Tris base 6.06g in 40mL distilled water, bring it to pH8.0 using HCl, and dilute it to 50mL. ②Solution B(0.5mol/L EDTA, pH8.0): Dissolve $EDTANa_2 \cdot 2H_2O$ 9.306g in 35mL distilled water, stir and bring it to pH8.0 with NaOH powder, and dilute it to 50mL. Mix 1mL solution A and 0.2mL solution B, and dilute it with distilled water to 100mL. Autoclaving at 121°C for 20min.

【Procedures】

1. DNA extraction

(1) Using 2g of fresh animal liver, cut it into small pieces and add 4mL of 0.14mol/L NaCl-0.15mol/L EDTA solution, grind it using a mortar, transfer it to a centrifugal tube and

centrifugate it at 4,000r/min for 10min.

(2) Add 0.14mol/L NaCl-0.15mol/L EDTA solution to the above precipitate to yield a total volume of 4mL, and then add 2–3 drops of 20% SDS solution at 60°C. Separate nucleic acid and proteins by shaking for 10min.

(3) Add 0.4g NaCl and place it into a 60°C water bath for 30min.

(4) Add an equal volume of chloroform-isoamyl alcohol, mix and shake for 5min, and then centrifugate it at 4,000r/min for 10min. Substances will be divided into three layers in the centrifugal tube. The upper aqueous layer contains DNA, the lower layer contains a mixture of chloroform-isoamyl alcohol and the middle layer contains the denatured protein gel.

(5) Transfer the supernatant to another tube and add 95% ethanol solution (precooled, twice of the supernatant volume) to precipitate DNA molecules.

(6) Centrifugate it at 4,000r/min for 10min, discard the supernatant and wash the precipitate using the 80% ethanol solution.

(7) Place the precipitate on filter paper to dry precipitated DNA at the room temperature. Add 200μL TE buffer to dissolve DNA.

2. Determining DNA concentration

(1) Add 2μL of extracted DNA and add 98μL distilled water (1∶50 or higher fold).

(2) Use distilled water as a blank control and determine the absorbance of DNA at the wavelengths of 260nm and 280nm.

(3) The concentration of DNA is determined using the following formula:

$$\text{DNA concentration } (\mu g/mL) = 50 \times OD_{260} \times N(\text{Diluted times})$$

【Questions】

1. What are the principles of extraction and identification of nucleic acid?
2. What should be paid attention to when purifying DNA?

(Tang Jiancai, Yi Fang)

实验 20　血清 IgG 的 SDS-PAGE 鉴定

【实验目的】

1. 掌握 SDS-PAGE 的工作原理。
2. 熟悉 SDS-PAGE 的基本过程。
3. 了解 SDS-PAGE 系统中各个试剂、成分的主要作用。

【实验原理】

IgG 是血清免疫球蛋白的主要成分之一，共包括 IgG1～4 四个亚型，在体液免疫中起着“主力军”的作用。分子量为（150～160）kDa，沉降系数约为 7S，约占血清蛋白总量的 17%。

分离纯化 IgG 的主要方法有饱和硫酸铵盐析法、聚乙二醇（PEG）置换法、Protein A 亲和膜色谱法等。饱和硫酸铵盐析法由于不需特殊设备，是最常用的生化分离纯化手段之一（具体步骤参见实验 16）。饱和硫酸铵盐析法分离 IgG 主要经过二次盐析，即根据 IgG 的理化性质使用不同浓度的硫酸铵分段盐析，以去除白蛋白、纤维蛋白原、IgM 等其他杂蛋白质，后续脱盐、层析步骤一致。

十二烷基磺酸钠-聚丙烯酰胺凝胶电泳（SDS-PAGE） 是以聚丙烯酰胺凝胶为支持介质的电泳。聚丙烯酰胺凝胶是由单体丙烯酰胺（Acr）和交联剂 *N*，*N*′-亚甲基双丙烯酰胺（Bis），在催化剂过硫酸铵（AP）和加速剂四甲基乙二胺（TEMED）的催化下聚合交联形成的三维网状结构凝胶，其聚合物化学结构式如图 20-1 所示。聚丙烯酰胺具有多方面的优点，包括稳定的亲水性、无电渗作用、灵敏度高及分离样品范围广等，是广泛使用的电泳支持介质。

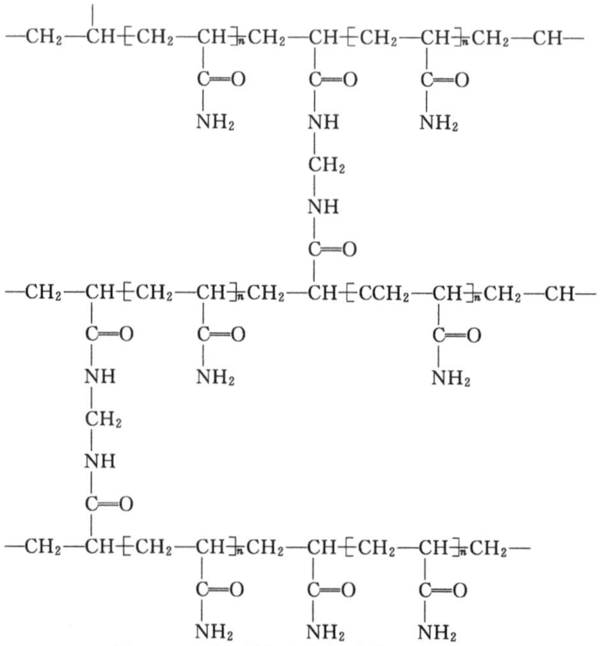

图 20-1　聚丙烯酰胺凝胶化学结构图

SDS 能与蛋白质特异结合并破坏蛋白质中的氢键和疏水键，并使蛋白质携带大量负电荷以消除不同种类蛋白质间原有电荷的差异，使蛋白质均带有相同密度的负电荷。蛋白质-SDS 复合物在凝胶电泳中的迁移率不再受蛋白质原有电荷的影响，而仅与蛋白质分子量相关。此外，试剂中的巯基乙醇可还原蛋白质分子中的二硫键，使多肽链解聚成单个亚单位。

在 SDS-PAGE 不连续电泳系统中，浓缩胶的浓度为 3%，缓冲液是 Tris-HCl（pH6.8），主要作用是使样品在进入分离胶前，被浓缩成一条狭窄的区带，以此提高电泳的分离效果。分离胶浓度为 10%左右，缓冲液是 Tris-HCl（pH8.9），电泳缓冲液是 Tris-甘氨酸（pH8.3），此时蛋白质仅以其分子量的差异进行泳动，最终达到分离出不同分子量蛋白质的目的。

上样缓冲液中含有溴酚蓝等离子型示踪染料和甘油。其中，前者可以指示电泳的分离位置；后者可以增大样品缓冲液的密度，有利于样品沉积在上样孔中。

运用 SDS-PAGE 分离血清蛋白可分离得到 12～30 个组分，由于具有高度的灵敏性，其被广泛用于蛋白质混合物的分离、定性分析、纯度检测及半定量分析等方面。

【器材与试剂】

1. 器材

（1）垂直板型电泳槽和直流稳压电源。

（2）水浴锅。

（3）50μL 或 100μL 微量移液器。

（4）染色槽。

（5）摇床。

（6）分离、纯化器材（参考实验 16）。

2. 试剂

（1）10×SDS-电泳缓冲液（pH8.3）：称取甘氨酸 28.8g、Tris 6.0g，加入 10%SDS 溶液 1mL，加蒸馏水定容到 100mL。

（2）10%SDS 溶液：SDS 在低温易析出结晶，用前微热，使其完全溶解。

（3）4×浓缩胶缓冲液（pH6.8）：将 1mol/L HCl 48.0mL 与 Tris 5.98g 加蒸馏水溶解，调至 pH6.8，加蒸馏水定容到 100mL。

（4）30%Acr-Bis：称取丙烯酰胺 29.2g、*N*，*N'*-亚甲基双丙烯酰胺 0.8g，加蒸馏水定容到 100mL。置于棕色试剂瓶中，4℃保存。

（5）10% AP 催化剂：质量体积比，现配现用。

（6）TEMED 加速剂：10%TEMED，体积比，配制 10mL 备用。

（7）4×分离胶缓冲液（pH 8.9）：取 1mol/L HCl 24.0mL 与 Tris 18.2g 加蒸馏水溶解，调节 pH 至 8.9，加蒸馏水定容到 100mL。

（8）上样缓冲液：SDS 100mg、巯基乙醇 0.1mL、甘油 1mL、溴酚蓝 2mg、0.2mol/L pH 7.2 磷酸缓冲液 0.5mL，加水溶解至 10mL。

（9）考马斯亮蓝 R250 染色液：取考马斯亮蓝 R250 0.25g，溶解于 454mL 甲醇中，加冰醋酸 46mL，滤纸过滤备用。

（10）脱色液：75mL 冰醋酸，875mL 蒸馏水与 50mL 甲醇混匀。

【实验操作】

1. 饱和硫酸铵盐析法分离、纯化 IgG 使用盐析法分离 IgG 的步骤请参考实验 16。血清蛋白首先经 50%饱和硫酸铵沉淀球蛋白，再经 33%硫酸铵沉淀 IgG，后续脱盐、DEAE-Sephadex A50 层析（0.005mol/L，pH 7.4，磷酸盐洗脱缓冲液）、浓缩均一致。

2. 样品处理 将待测样品与上样缓冲液按比例混合均匀，使浓度为 0.5～1mg/mL，于沸水中煮沸 5min 备用。

3. 安装垂直板电泳仪 垂直板电泳仪有很多型号，根据具体不同型号的要求进行操作。注意：安装前，胶条、玻板、槽子都要洁净干燥，勿用手接触灌胶面的玻璃。

4. 配胶 根据所测蛋白质分子量范围，选择适宜的胶浓度，按表 20-1 配制分离胶和浓缩胶。

（1）分离胶的配制：按照表 20-1 的配方配制分离胶溶液。将配制好的溶液沿玻璃壁缓缓注入两块玻璃板之间，液面高度距梳子齿沿约 1cm。灌完凝胶后，将蒸馏水沿玻璃壁缓缓加注在分离胶的液面上以水封。约 30min 后，待聚合充分完成，凝胶与水层之间形成清晰可辨的界面，方可进行下一步操作。

表 20-1 SDS-PAGE 浓缩胶和分离胶配方 （单位：mL）

试剂名称	分离胶（浓度 9%）所需试剂用量	浓缩胶（浓度 3%）所需试剂用量
单体溶液	3.00	1.00
浓缩胶缓冲液	—	2.50
分离胶缓冲液	2.50	—
10% SDS	0.10	0.10
10% AP	0.05	0.05
1% TEMED	0.10	0.10
蒸馏水	4.25	6.25
总体积	10	10

（2）浓缩胶的配制：按表 20-1 配制浓缩胶溶液。轻轻倒出上层水封液，并用滤纸吸去残余液体，注意不能触碰或划伤分离胶。将配制好的溶液沿玻璃壁缓缓注入，灌完后即将梳子插入浓缩胶溶液中。注意动作应轻柔，不能产生气泡。静置等待，待浓缩胶完全聚合后，小心拔出梳子，注意不要破坏样品槽。将配制好的凝胶安装到电泳槽中，在上槽、下槽中均注入电泳缓冲液，应没过短板约 0.5cm。

5. 加样 一般加样体积为 10～15μL（即 2～10μg 蛋白质）。如样品较稀，可增加加样体积。用微量移液器小心将样品通过缓冲液加到凝胶凹形样品槽底部，待所有凹形样品槽内都加了样品，即可开始电泳。

6. 电泳 正确连接电泳仪的正、负极，在浓缩胶范围内电泳时，以 5V/cm 的电压恒压电泳。当溴酚蓝进入分离胶后，将电压增加到 8V/cm 继续电泳。当溴酚蓝迁移至胶底部时，关闭电源，停止电泳。

7. 剥胶 用小铲轻轻将一块玻璃板撬开去掉，在胶底部切除一角以标记，然后将胶板移至大培养皿中染色与漂洗。

8. 染色与脱色 将凝胶浸入染色液中 10min，然后用清水冲洗掉多余的染料，放脱色液中脱色，多次更换脱色液，直到背景几乎无色时停止。凝胶可在 7%乙酸溶液中长期保存。

9. 拍照 用凝胶图像分析系统拍摄实验结果，保存备用。

【注意事项】

（1）根据目标蛋白的大小选择合适的凝胶浓度。一般为 50～100kDa 选用 10%胶，30～50kDa 选用 12%胶，10～30kDa 选用 15%胶。

（2）制备聚丙烯酰胺凝胶时，如果两个玻璃板密封不严，凝胶在凝固前往往发生泄漏。所以这步要特别注意。

（3）电泳染色液注意进行回收再利用，一般可重复使用 2～3 次。

（4）AP 是催化剂，TEMED 是加速剂，过少则凝胶聚合很慢甚至不聚合，过多则聚合过快，影响倒胶。

【思考题】

1. SDS-PAGE 的几个不连续性分别是指什么？
2. 上样缓冲液中加入甘油的作用是什么？
3. SDS-PAGE 系统中，哪些成分中含有 SDS，作用是什么？巯基乙醇的作用是什么？
4. 在变性 PAGE 系统中，除了 SDS 之外，还有哪些试剂可作为变性剂，各自的优缺点是什么？
5. 运用 SDS-PAGE 测定蛋白质的分子量，是不是所有蛋白质测定出来都是准确的？请说明原因。

（蒋　振　郭冬梅）

Experiment 20 Identifying Serum IgG Using SDS-PAGE

【Purposes】

1. To master the principles of SDS-PAGE.
2. To learn the basic process of SDS-PAGE.
3. To understand the main functions of reagents and components used in SDS-PAGE.

【Principles】

IgG is the main components of human serum immunoglobulin and include IgG1, IgG2, IgG3 and IgG4 that are the main components of humoral immunity in humans. The molecular weight of IgG is 150-160 kDa, and the sedimentation coefficient is about 7S and accounts for 17% of total serum proteins.

Methods to isolate IgG include ammonium sulfate salting-out, polyethylene glycol (PEG) replacement and protein A affinity chromatography. Ammonium sulfate salting-out is the most common method used to isolate IgG because there is no need for special equipment (see Exp. 16). Ammonium sulfate salting-out requires two salt-precipitation steps, where different concentrations of ammonium sulfate are used to deposit albumin, fibrinogen, IgM and other proteins based on the physicochemical properties of IgG. The remaining steps are similar to salt-precipitation and ion exchange chromatography with DEAE cellulose.

SDS-PAGE is electrophoresis with polyacrylamide gel as a supporting medium. Polyacrylamide gel (PAG) originates from the chemical co-polymerization of acrylamide (Acr) monomers with a cross-linking reagent *N*, *N'*-methylene bis-acrylamide (Bis) , which is catalyzed by the catalyst ammonium persulfate (AP) and an accelerating agent tetramethylethylenediamine (TEMED). The structure of PAG is shown in Fig. 20-1. PAG is a widely used supporting medium for electrophoresis since it exhibits stable hydrophilicity, almost no electro-osmosis, high sensitivity and can be used for a large variety of samples.

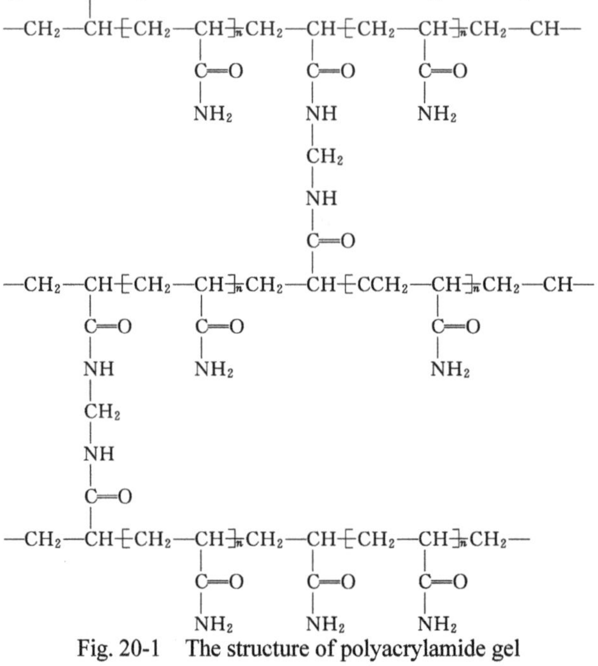

Fig. 20-1 The structure of polyacrylamide gel

SDS can specifically bind to proteins and destroy their hydrogen and hydrophobic bonds. Since SDS is negatively charged, it promotes more negative charges on proteins and masks differences in charges among proteins. As a result, proteins have the same negative charge density. The migration rate of the protein-SDS complex in the PAG mainly depends on differences in molecular weights rather than their original charges. In addition, mercaptoethanol is added to protein samples to reduce disulfide bonds within proteins and cause depolymerization of polymers.

In discontinuous SDS-PAGE systems, the concentration of the stacking gel is 3%, and Tris-HCl (pH6.8) buffer is used. The purpose of using the stacking gel is to concentrate proteins into a narrow zone before the resolving gel to increase separating efficiency. The concentration of the resolving gel is 10%, and the resolving and electrophoresis buffers used are Tris-HCl(pH8.9) and Tris-glycine (pH8.3), respectively. Protein mobility mainly depends on the differences in protein molecular weight. In this way, SDS-PAGE can separate proteins with different molecular weights.

The loading buffer contains bromophenol blue isotonic tracer dye and glycerol. The former indicates the protein location during electrophoresis, and the latter increases sample solution density, allowing the sample to easily settle to the bottom of loading wells.

For SDS-PAGE, 12–30 ingredients of serum proteins can be obtained. Because of its high sensitivity, it is widely used in the separation, qualitative analysis, purity detection and semi-quantitative analysis of protein mixture.

【Apparatus and Reagents】

1. Apparatus

(1) Vertical plate electrophoresis tank and DC regulated power supply.

(2) Water bath cauldron.

(3) A 50μL or 100μL micropipette.

(4) Staining jar.

(5) Shaker.

(6) For apparatus used in the isolation and purification of proteins, please see Exp. 16.

2. Reagents

(1) 10×SDS electrophoresis buffer (pH8.3): Add 28.8g glycine and 6.0g Tris to 1mL 10% SDS solution and make the final volume of 100mL.

(2) 10% SDS solution: SDS in low temperature is easy to crystallize, and it should be heated before using to make it completely dissolved.

(3) 4×stacking gel buffer (pH6.8): Dissolve 48.0mL 1mol/L HCl and 5.98g Tris with distilled water, adjust pH to 6.8 and make the final volume of 100mL.

(4) 30% Acr-Bis: Add 29.2g Acr and 0.8g Bis and make the final volume of 100mL. Store it in a dark bottle at 4°C.

(5) 10% AP catalyst: *W* : *V*, and is freshly prepared.

(6) TEMED accelerator: 10% TEMED, *V* : *V*, and prepare 10mL standby.

(7) 4×resolving gel buffer (pH 8.9): Dissolve 24.0mL 1mol/L HCl and 18.2g Tris in distilled water. Adjust pH to 8.9 and make the final volume of 100mL.

(8) Loading buffer: Add 100mg SDS, 0.1mL mercaptoethanol, 1mL glycerol, 2mg bromophenol blue, 0.5mL 0.2mol/L pH7.2 phosphoric acid buffer, and make the final volume of 10mL.

(9) Coomassie brilliant blue R250 staining solution: Dissolve R250 0.25g in 454mL methanol, add 46mL glacial acetic acid. Filter the solution through filter paper.

(10) Decolorization solution: Mix 75mL acetic acid, 875mL distilled water and 50mL methanol well.

【Procedures】

1. Isolation and purification of IgG using saturated ammonium sulfate Steps to separate IgG by salting-out are seen in Exp 16. At first, globulin is deposited using 50% saturated ammonium sulfate. Second, IgG is precipitated using 33% saturated ammonium sulfate. Third, the remaining procedures for dialysis, DEAE-Sephadex A50 chromatography (0.005mol/L, pH7.4, phosphoric acid buffer) and concentrating are the same as listed in Exp. 16.

2. Sample preparation Dissolve the sample and loading buffer based on the proportion, make the concentration be 0.5–1mg/mL and boil it for 5min.

3. Assemble the vertical plate electrophoresis apparatus There are different types of vertical plate electrophoresis apparatus. Assemble the apparatus of your choices based on instructions provided by the manufacturer. Note: clean and dry the rubber strip, glass plate and electrophoresis tanks before assembling. Do not touch the side of the glass plate that will be in contact with the gel.

4. Gel preparation Choose the proper gel concentration based on the molecular weight range of the measured protein. Prepare the resolving gel and stacking gel according to Table 20-1.

(1) Preparing the resolving gel: Prepare the resolving gel based on Table 20-1. Carefully pour the gel solution into the gap between the glass plates. Leave about 1cm height from the gel top to the teeth of the well-forming comb. After pouring, add distilled water to carefully overlay the gel solution. After about 30min, the next step can not be performed until a clear interface between the gel and aqueous layer can be seen after gel polymerization.

Table 20-1 Solution for the stacking and resolving gel (Unit: mL)

Reagents	9% resolving gel	3% stacking gel
Acr-Bis	3.00	1.00
Stacking gel buffer	—	2.50
Resolving gel buffer	2.50	—
10% SDS	0.10	0.10
10% AP	0.05	0.05
1% TEMED	0.10	0.10
Distilled water	4.25	6.25
Total volume	10	10

(2) Preparing the stacking gel: Prepare the stacking gel based on Table 20-1. Carefully pour off the overlay and remove remaining water with filter paper. Do not touch or cut the gel. Pour the stacking gel solution directly onto the surface of the resolving gel and immediately insert the comb into the stacking gel solution. This should be performed carefully and no bubbles should be generated during the process. After completing polymerization, carefully remove the comb without destroying sample wells. Install the gel plate in the electrophoresis tanks and add the electrophoresis buffer to the top and bottom tanks. The buffer should be above the short plate about 0.5cm.

5. Loading samples Generally, the volume of each sample loaded should be 10-15μL (2-10μg proteins). The volume can be increased if the concentration of the sample is low. Load the sample into the bottom of the sample wells using a micropipette. After all sample wells are loaded, the electrophoresis process can be started.

6. Electrophoresis Properly connect the electrophoresis apparatus to an electric power supply. In the stacking gel, a voltage of 5V/cm can be used. Increase the voltage to 8V/cm when the bromophenol blue moves into the resolving gel. When the bromophenol blue moves to the bottom of the resolving gel, turn the power off to stop electrophoresis.

7. Stripping the gel Gently pry glass plates apart with a spatula, remove the gel and mark the gel orientation by cutting a corner of the gel. Transfer the gel into a staining jar for staining and destaining.

8. Staining and decolorization Immerse the gel into the staining solution for 10min, then remove the solution and rinse the gel with distilled water. Put the gel into the decolorization solution to destain the gel. The decolorization solution should be replaced multiple times until the gel background is almost colorless. The gel can be stored in 7% acetic acid solution for a long time.

9. Photographing Scan the gel using the gel image analysis system and store the gel for analysis.

【Notes】

(1) Choose the proper concentration of the gel based on the molecular weight of the sample. Generally, 10% gel is used for 50–100 kDa, 12% gel is used for 30–50 kDa and 15% gel is used for 10–30 kDa.

(2) When preparing the polyacrylamide gel, the gel often leaks before solidifying if the two glass plates are not properly sealed. Therefore, pay attention to whether the gel leaks in this step.

(3) Electrophoresis staining solution should be recycled and reused 2–3 times.

(4) AP is a catalyst and TEMED is an accelerator. Gel polymerization may be slow or even not polymerized if the volume of these two reagents is too low. Otherwise, the polymerization is too fast if the volume of these two reagents is too high.

【Questions】

1. What are discontinuities of SDS-PAGE?
2. What is the function of glycerol in the loading buffer?
3. Which components of the SDS-PAGE system contain SDS and what are its functions? What is the function of mercaptoethanol?
4. In the denaturing PAGE system, which reagents can be used as denaturants besides SDS? What are the advantages and disadvantages of these reagents?
5. Is it accurate to determine the molecular weight of each protein when using SDS-PAGE? Please explain.

(Jiang Zhen, Guo Dongmei)

实验 21　人肝癌细胞株 HepG2 中内参 GAPDH 的免疫印迹检测

【实验目的】

1. 掌握免疫印迹的原理和实验操作过程。
2. 熟悉细胞蛋白样品的制备方法。
3. 了解蛋白质含量测定的基本方法。

【实验原理】

免疫印迹（WB）是一种免疫化学方法。如图 21-1 所示，它利用 SDS-PAGE 技术将生物样品中的蛋白质分子按分子量的大小在凝胶上分离开，然后用电转移的方法将蛋白转移到固相膜（硝酸纤维素膜或 PVDF 膜）上，膜上的目的蛋白或多肽（本实验为 GAPDH）与对应的抗体（第一抗体，本实验为 GAPDH 兔抗人多抗） 起免疫反应，以此作为探针来检测目标蛋白的表达。为了避免非特异性结合，在与一抗结合前先用奶粉或牛血清白蛋白（BSA） 封闭固相膜，封闭结合一抗后，再与酶或同位素标记的第二抗体起反应，最后经过底物显色或放射自显影以检测电泳分离的特异性目的蛋白。目前第二抗体通常耦联辣根过氧化物酶（HRP）。HRP 可催化超敏增强化学发光（ECL） 反应。通过二抗产生的荧光可识别一抗。

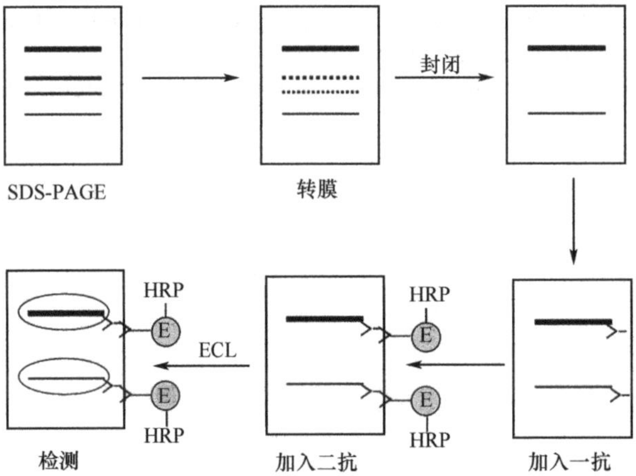

图 21-1　免疫印迹程序

【器材与试剂】

1. 器材

（1）电泳仪。

（2）SDS-PAGE 电泳仪和电染仪。

（3）摇床。

（4）细胞超声破碎仪。

（5）高速离心机。

（6）各种量程的加样枪。

（7）吸头、离心管、PVDF 膜、滤纸、海绵、乳胶手套、X 线片细胞刮。

（8）玻璃器材：各种规格的烧杯、量筒、平皿。

（9）白浅盘（>20cm×20cm）、剪刀、镊子、暗盒。

2. 细胞株 人肝癌细胞株 HepG2。

3. 试剂

（1）细胞裂解液。

（2）二喹啉甲酸（bicinchoninic acid，BCA）蛋白浓度测定试剂盒。

（3）30% Acr-Bis（29∶1）。

（4）1mol/L pH 6.8 Tris-HCl。

（5）10% SDS 溶液。

（6）10×电泳缓冲液（pH8.3）：Tris 30.3g、甘氨酸 144g、SDS 10g，加蒸馏水溶解，定容至 1000mL。

（7）过硫酸铵。

（8）1mol/L pH8.8 Tris-HCl。

（9）2×上样缓冲液。

（10）10×转膜缓冲液：Tris 30.3g、甘氨酸 144g，加蒸馏水溶解，定容至 1000mL。

（11）10×TBS 缓冲液：24.23g 三羟甲基氨基甲烷盐酸盐（Trizma HCl）、80.06g NaCl，加 800mL 蒸馏水溶解，HCl 调节 pH 至 7.6，定容至 1000mL。

（12）含吐温 20 的 Tris 缓冲液(TBST 缓冲液)：量取 100mL 10×TBS、900mL 蒸馏水和 1mL Tween20，混匀。

（13）显影定影试剂盒。

（14）超敏增强化学发光（Enhanced Chemiluminescence，ECL）试剂盒。

（15）奶粉。

（16）PBS（0.01mol/L，pH7.2～7.3）：称取 NaCl 8.0g、KCl 0.2g、KH_2PO_4 0.24g、$Na_2HPO_4 \cdot 12H_2O$ 3.628g，溶于 800mL 蒸馏水中，用盐酸调 pH 为 7.4，蒸馏水定容至 1000mL。

（17）100mmol/L 苯甲基磺酰氟溶液（PMSF）。

（18）蛋白质分子量标准。

4. 抗体 GAPDH 兔抗人多抗、二抗（羊抗兔）。

【实验操作】

1. 蛋白样品制备

（1）让细胞长至 80%～90%融合度后倒掉培养液，用冰预冷的 PBS 洗两次。

（2）每瓶细胞（$25cm^2$）加入 500μL 裂解液（100mmol/L PMSF），于冰上裂解 10min，经常来回摇动培养瓶使细胞充分裂解，用干净的细胞刮将细胞刮下，将细胞悬浮液移至 1.5mL 离心管中。

（3）冰上进行超声破碎（3W，3s，间歇 20s，15 次）。

（4）4℃ 12 000r/min 离心 5min。

（5）取少量上清液进行定量，加入等体积的 2×SDS 电泳上样缓冲液后煮沸 5min，−20℃保存。

2. 蛋白含量的测定　取出25mg/mL BSA稀释至终浓度为0.5mg/mL，将标准品按0μL、1μL、2μL、4μL、8μL、12μL、16μL、20μL 加到 96 孔板的标准品孔中，加标准品稀释液补足到 20μL，其余孔加入待测样品各 20μL（每个样品设三个复孔），然后每孔各加入 200μL BCA 试剂 A 和 BCA 试剂 B 的混合物（A∶B 为 50∶1），摇床室温孵育 30min，酶标仪测定 562nm 处吸光度（A_{562}），根据标准品的 A_{562} 做出标准曲线，计算样品的蛋白浓度。

3. SDS-PAGE

（1）10%凝胶的配制：参见实验 20，装好制胶架，加入适量 10%分离胶，蒸馏水封胶，待分离胶凝固，倒掉蒸馏水，5%的浓缩胶加满，放好梳子，待浓缩胶凝固，放入电泳槽，加入 1×电泳缓冲液。

（2）电泳：拔掉梳子，用电泳缓冲液冲洗每个梳孔使其没有气泡，每加样孔加入 20mL（约 50μg）样品，留一孔（第一或最后一孔）加入 5μL 预染的蛋白质分子量标准品（10～170kDa）作蛋白大小的对照。接通电源，电压 80V 至样品浓缩成一条直线，调电压 120V，电泳直到上样缓冲液中的溴酚蓝行至电泳槽下端停止。

4. 膜电转移

（1）膜处理：预先裁好与胶条同样大小的 PVDF 膜，将膜放入甲醇里激活约 1min，随后倒掉甲醇，转入转膜缓冲液中浸泡平衡 5min。

（2）制作胶-膜三明治：在浅盘里加少量的转移液，电泳结束后从盒中剥出胶，将浓缩胶切去，用转膜缓冲液平衡 5min。将转移盒打开使黑的一面保持水平，按下面的顺序制作转膜三明治：黑面（阴极）、一块海绵、3 层滤纸、待转移凝胶、PVDF 膜、3 层滤纸、另一块海绵、白面（阳极）。以上所有组件需浸泡在转移缓冲液中。每一步均需用干净玻棒轻轻地擀去气泡。锁上盒子，将膜三明治放入转移槽，在转移电泳槽加入预冷的转膜缓冲液，使夹子的黑面对转印装置的黑面。

（3）电转移：电转移时会产热，在槽的一边放一冰盒来降温，并将转移槽置于冰浴中转膜。连接电极一般用 100V 转移 90min。

5. 免疫检测

（1）取出 PVDF 膜（在膜正面做好标记），用蒸馏水洗膜，洗 3 次，每次 5min。

（2）封闭：加封闭液（含 5%奶粉或 3% BSA 的 TBST 缓冲液），室温下轻轻振荡 1h。

（3）倒掉封闭液，用 TBST 缓冲液洗膜，洗 4 次，每次 5min。

（4）加入内参 GAPDH 抗体（一抗），用含 0.5%奶粉的 TBST 缓冲液按 1∶2000 稀释，4℃下摇膜过夜。

（5）将膜取出，用 TBST 缓冲液洗膜，剧烈振荡清洗，洗 4 次，每次 5min。

（6）加入二抗（用含 0.5%奶粉的 TBST 缓冲液按 1∶5000 稀释），室温下轻轻振荡 1h。

（7）将膜取出，用 TBST 缓冲液洗膜，剧烈振荡清洗，洗 4 次，每次 5min。

（8）检测：按说明书 A 液+B 液（1∶1）配制 ECL 发光液，吸去膜上的 TBST 缓冲液，在膜的正面加配好的发光液，孵育 2min（避光），吸去多余的发光液，用干净塑料袋装好防止干膜，放入暗盒，在暗室用 X 线片曝光。

（9）结果：X 线片可见目的蛋白质的条带。扫描胶片，用图像处理系统分析目的带的光密度值。

【思考题】

1. 简述免疫印迹的基本步骤。
2. 要一次分离不同分子量（如 21kDa、66 kDa、170 kDa） 的蛋白质，该怎么操作?
3. 为什么 X 线片有时会出现非特异性条带?

（陈瑾歆　王含彦）

Experiment 21 Detecting GAPDH in the Human Hepatoma Cell Line HepG2 Using a Western Blotting

【Purposes】

1. To master the principle and procedures of Western blotting assay.
2. To understand how to prepare cell extract for Western blotting.
3. To understand how to determine protein concentration.

【Principles】

Western blotting (WB) is an immunochemical technique. As shown in Fig. 21-1, protein molecules can be separated using SDS-PAGE based on their molecular weights. After separation, proteins are transferred from the gel to a solid phase membrane (nitrocellulose or PVDF membrane). The target protein or polypeptide (GAPDH in this experiment) is specifically bound by an antibody (primary antibody, GAPDH rabbit anti-human polyclonal antibody in this experiment) which is used as a probe for detecting target protein expression. To prevent non-specific binding, membranes are "blocked" using milk or bovine serum albumin (BSA) before adding the primary antibody. After blocking, a secondary antibody is used to recognize and bind to the primary antibody. Usually, in order to catalyze the enhanced chemiluminescent (ECL) reaction, the secondary antibody is conjugated to a labeling enzyme such as the horseradish peroxidase (HRP). Through the reaction, fluorescence allows visualization of the product and identification of the target protein.

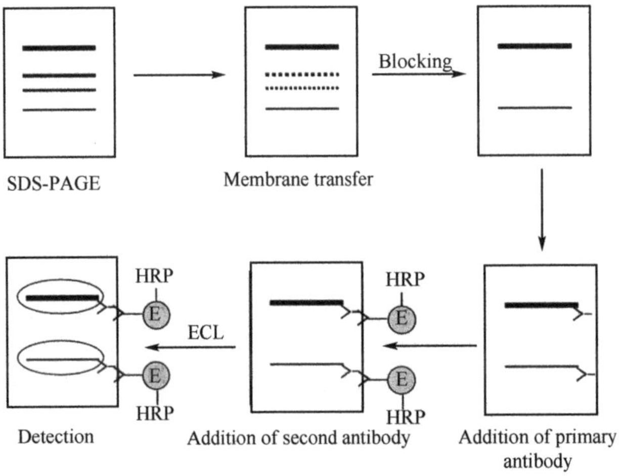

Fig. 21-1 The procedure of Western blotting

【Apparatus and Reagents】

1. Apparatus

(1) Electrophoresis apparatus.

(2) SDS-PAGE electrophoresis apparatus and electroblotting apparatus.

(3) Shaker.

(4) Cell ultrasonication instrument.

(5) High-speed centrifuge.

(6) Various pipettes.

(7) Tip, centrifugal tube, PVDF membrane, filter paper, sponge, latex gloves, X-ray film, and cell scraper.

(8) Glass equipment: various beaker, cylindrical glass and flat plate.

(9) White shallow tray (>20cm×20cm) , scissors, tweezers and film cassette.

2. Cell lines Human hepatoma cell lines HepG2.

3. Reagents

(1) Cell lysis buffer.

(2) BCA protein assay kit.

(3) 30% Acr-Bis (29：1).

(4) 1mol/L pH 6.8 Tris-HCl.

(5) 10% SDS buffer.

(6) 10 × electrophoresis buffer (pH 8.3): Dissolve 30.3g Tris, 144g glycine and 10g SDS in distilled water, and bring it to a total volume of 1,000 mL.

(7) Ammonium persulphate (AP).

(8) 1mol/L pH 8.8 Tris-HCl.

(9) 2×sample buffer.

(10) 10×transfer buffer: Dissolve 30.3g Tris and 144g glycine in distilled water, and bring it to a total volume of 1,000 mL.

(11) 10×TBS buffer: Dissolve 24.23g Tri(hydroxymethyl) aminomethane hydrochloride (Trizma HCl) and 80.06g NaCl in 800 mL distilled water. Adjust pH to 7.6 with HCl. Add it to 1,000 mL with distilled water.

(12) Tris-buffered saline with Tween 20 (TBST) buffer: Measure out 100 mL of 10×TBS, 900 mL distilled water and 1mL Tween 20, and mix well.

(13) Developing and fixing kit.

(14) Hypersensitive ECL kit.

(15) Milk powder.

(16) PBS (0.01mol/L, pH7.2–7.3): Dissolve 8.0g NaCl, 0.2g KCl, 0.24g KH_2PO_4, 3.628g $Na_2HPO_4 \cdot 12H_2O$ in 800mL distilled water. Adjust pH to 7.4 with HCl. Add it to 1,000mL with distilled water.

(17) 100mmol/L PMSF.

(18) Protein marker.

4. Antibodies GAPDH rabbit anti-human polyclonal antibody, second antibody (goat anti-rabbit IgG).

【Procedures】

1. Protein preparation

(1) Allow cells to grow to 80%–90% confluency. Pour out all the growth medium and wash cells twice using cold sterile PBS.

(2) Add 500μL of lysis buffer (PMSF, 100mmol/L) to each culture flask(25cm^2). Place flasks on an ice tray for 10min coupled with shaking the flask to lyse the cells completely, after which all cells are scraped off using a clean cell scraper. Transfer the cell suspension into 1.5mL centrifugal tubes.

(3) Sonicate on ice (3W, 3s, 15 times, wait 20s before each time) .

(4) Centrifugate the pellet debris at 12,000r/min for 5min at 4°C.

(5) Take a small quantity of supernatant for quantitation. Add equal volumes of 2×SDS sample buffer and heat at 100°C for 5min. Store it at −20°C.

2. Protein concentration determination Dilute the 25mg/mL BSA to 0.5mg/mL. Using a 96-well plate, add 0, 1, 2, 4, 8, 12, 16 and 20μL standards into separate wells, use the standard diluent to make up for 20μL, and then pipette 20μL of each unknown sample (every sample repeated three times) into separate wells. Add 200μL of mixed solution of BCA reagent A plus

BCA reagent B (A and B are mixed in a ratio of 50∶1) to each well. Place the well plate on the shaker at the room temperature for 30min. Read the absorbance at 562nm (A_{562}) using a plate-reading spectrophotometer. Construct a protein standard curve by the linear regression of the A_{562} readings of the standards. Using this standard curve and the A_{562} of each sample, the corresponding protein concentration can be calculated.

3. SDS-PAGE

(1) 10% gel preparation: Prepare the gel by referencing Exp. 20. After setting up the casting frame, add the freshly made 10% separating gel into the glass sandwich, cover the gel with distilled water and allow it to solidify. Once the gel solidifies, discard the water, and add the 5% stacking gel to the top. A comb is inserted into the stacking gel, which should be allowed to solidify. After the stacking gel solidifies, the gel is then placed into the electrophoresis apparatus, which is then filled with 1× electrophoresis buffer.

(2) Electrophoresis: Remove the comb, rinse the wells of the gel with the electrophoresis buffer and make sure there are no bubbles. Load each well with an appropriate amount of 20μL sample (about 50μg). Load the pre-stained protein marker (about 5μL) , which ranges from 10–170kDa, in the first or last well in order to monitor the separation during electrophoresis, and subsequently verify the protein size during analysis. Connect the electrophoresis equipment to the electricity supply, run the gel at 80V until the sample forms a line and then run the gel at 120V until bromophenol blue of the loading buffer reaches the bottom.

4. Membrane electro transfer

(1) Membrane preparation: Cut a piece of membrane based on the gel size. A PVDF membrane first needs to be activated in methanol for 1min at the room temperature. Remove methanol and equilibrate the membrane in 1× transfer buffer for 5min.

(2) Arrange the gel-membrane sandwich: After electrophoresis, use a shallow tray with some transfer buffer, remove the gel from the cassette, discard the stacking gel, and then equilibrate the gel in the transfer buffer for 5min. Open the transfer cassette and create a sandwich stack by placing components as follows: black side (the cathode) , a sponge, 3 pieces of filter paper, the gel to be transferred, the PVDF membrane, 3 additional pieces of filter paper, another sponge, white side (the anode). All of the above components must be immersed in the buffer liquid. For each step, use a clean glass rod to gently remove air bubbles. Lock the cassette and mount the sandwich in the transfer tank containing cold transfer buffer. Place the black side near the black side of the transfer device.

(3) Electro transfer: It is necessary to transfer with a cold pack in the apparatus in order to prevent heat build-up. Attach the electrodes. Set the power supply to 100V for 90min.

5. Immunodetection

(1) Remove the PVDF membrane from the cassette (make a mark on the right side of the membrane). Wash it using distilled water three times for 5min each time.

(2) Blocking: Incubate the membrane with the blocking solution (TBST buffer, containing 5% milk powder or 3% BSA) by gently shaking for 1h at the room temperature.

(3) Pour the blocking solution and wash the membrane with the TBST buffer 4 times for 5 min each time.

(4) Add GAPDH (the primary antibody) , and dilute it with the TBST buffer containing 0.5% milk powder at the concentration of 1∶2,000. Shake the membrane overnight at 4℃.

(5) Take out the membrane, wash it using the TBST buffer while shaking vigorously, and repeat 4 times for 5 min each time.

(6) Dilute the secondary antibody with the TBST buffer containing 0.5% milk powder at a concentration of 1∶5,000 and shake the membrane for 1h at the room temperature.

(7) Take out the membrane, wash it using the TBST buffer, shake vigorously, and repeat 4 times for 5 min each time.

(8) Detection: Mix equal parts of ECL reagents A and B (1∶1) according to instructions provided by the manufacturer. Remove the TBST buffer from the membrane and add ECL reagent to the right side. Incubate the membrane for 2min while avoiding light. Remove the

excess solution from the membrane. Place the membrane in clear plastic wrap to avoid drying. Expose the membrane using the X-ray film in the cassette.

(9) Results: Bands should be present on the developed X-ray film corresponding to the target protein. Relative band densities can be analyzed using image processing software.

【Questions】

1. Describe the Western blotting procedure.

2. How can one separate proteins that have different molecular weights such as 21kDa, 66kDa or 170kDa by Western blotting?

3. Why are non-specific bands sometimes present in X-ray films?

(Chen Jinxin, Wang Hanyan)

实验 22　运动对骨骼肌糖代谢的影响

【实验目的】

1. 熟悉运动时肌肉组织糖代谢的变化。
2. 掌握检测乳酸的原理和方法。

【实验原理】

糖为多羟基醛类或多羟基酮类化合物，在人体内的代谢十分活跃，无论是在有氧或无氧条件下，都可以为人体提供能量。

在有氧条件下，葡萄糖被彻底氧化成二氧化碳和水，同时释放出大量能量，1 分子葡萄糖经有氧氧化可生成 30 或 32 分子的 ATP，是糖分解代谢的最主要方式，绝大多数细胞都通过此途径获得能量。在缺氧或氧供应不足的情况下，葡萄糖生成乳酸和少量能量，此称为糖酵解。1 分子葡萄糖经糖酵解可生成 2 分子 ATP（图 22-1）。

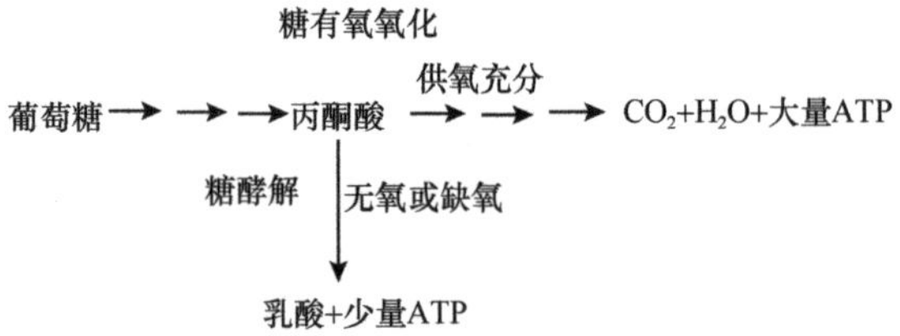

图 22-1　乳酸生成途径

所以，在正常生理情况下，糖通过有氧氧化为机体提供大量能量，很少进行酵解过程，糖的有氧氧化对糖酵解的抑制作用称为巴斯德效应。但在特殊情况下，如剧烈运动时，机体耗氧量增加，且消耗大量能量，有氧氧化加剧。尽管呼吸和循环也加速，但仍不能满足机体的需氧量。此时肌肉组织增强酵解作用以补充能量。血液和尿液中乳酸浓度便升高。

乳酸又称 2-羟基丙酸，是一种含羟基的羧酸。乳酸在铜离子的催化下，与浓硫酸作用生成乙醛，乙醛能与对羟基联苯作用生成紫红色物质（图 22-2）。采集运动前后尿液，可以检测乳酸浓度差异以及糖酵解强度。

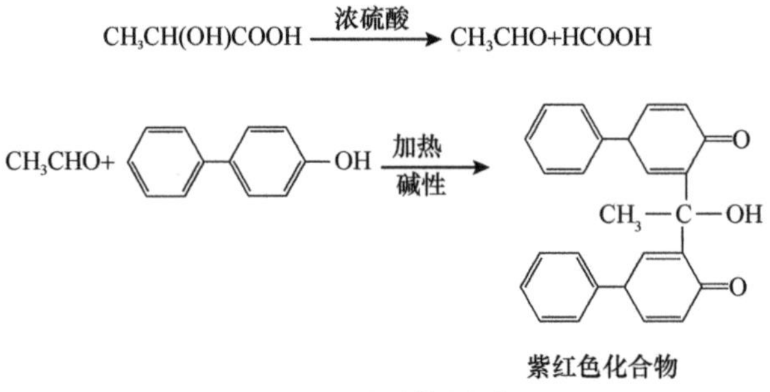

图 22-2　乳酸检测原理

【器材与试剂】

1. 器材

（1）离心机。

（2）试管及试管架。

（3）恒温水浴锅。

（4）容量瓶及烧杯。

（5）滴管及移液器。

2. 试剂

（1）尿液（运动前后各一份）。

（2）20% $CuSO_4$溶液：称取硫酸铜 20g，溶解于蒸馏水，加蒸馏水定容至 100mL。

（3）对羟基联苯溶液：称取对羟基联苯 1.5g，溶于 50mL 的 1% NaOH 溶液，加蒸馏水定容至 100mL。配制时加热助溶，溶解后为澄清液体，储存于棕色瓶中。

（4）$Ca(OH)_2$粉末。

（5）浓硫酸。

【实验操作】

（1）收集尿液标本：受试实验前排尿一次，以排除饮食、运动及尿液浓缩等影响因素。30min 后收集全部尿液，此为运动前尿，立即剧烈运动 5min，自运动开始后 30min 内再收集全部尿液，此为运动后尿。

（2）分别取两尿样标本各 5mL 于试管中，再分别加 20% $CuSO_4$溶液 1mL、$Ca(OH)_2$ 0.5g，至溶液呈纯蓝色，搅拌均匀，静置 10min，3000r/min 离心 10min。

（3）取试管 2 支，编号后按表 22-1 加入各种试剂。

表 22-1　运动对骨骼肌糖代谢的影响

试剂	管号	
	1	2
运动前尿上清液/滴	10	—
运动后尿上清液/滴	—	10
先将 2 支试管冷水浴 1min，再加浓硫酸		
浓硫酸/mL	3	3
混匀，放沸水浴 5min，再取出放冷水浴 3min		
对羟基联苯溶液/滴	3	3

（4）观察 2 支试管的颜色反应，并说明不同现象产生的原因。

【注意事项】

（1）$CuSO_4$和 $Ca(OH)_2$可以去除尿液中的蛋白质和糖类。加 $Ca(OH)_2$时要使溶液呈碱性（纯蓝色），并且注意加尿液上清液时不要有沉淀。

（2）运动的剧烈程度直接决定结果的颜色差异是否明显，所以要剧烈运动。身体素质好的运动健将由于耐氧能力较好，运动前后产生的乳酸量差异可能不明显。

（3）某些无机离子如铁离子、铬离子、锌离子等干扰乙醛与对羟基联苯的颜色反应。
（4）对羟基联苯难溶于浓硫酸，必须充分振摇均匀。
（5）浓硫酸具有强腐蚀性，使用时要注意安全。

【思考题】

1. 为什么运动剧烈程度会影响到实验结果的颜色？
2. 为什么要加 $Ca(OH)_2$ 使溶液呈纯蓝色后才能进行下面的乳酸氧化过程？
3. 剧烈运动是否会引起酸中毒？

（任勇刚　杨映雪）

Experiment 22 Effects of Exercise on Glycometabolism in Skeletal Muscle

【Purposes】

1. To learn about how glycometabolism changes during exercise in muscle tissue.
2. To master the principles and methods used for the detection of lactic acid.

【Principles】

Carbohydrates, hydroxy aldehyde or hydroxy ketone compounds, are very active in human metabolism. In both aerobic and anaerobic conditions, carbohydrates can provide energy for the human body.

In aerobic conditions, glucose is completely oxidized to carbon dioxide and water and releases a lot of energy. A molecule of glucose can produce 30 or 32 molecules of ATP by aerobic oxidation, which is the most important method used to metabolize carbohydrates. Most cells obtain energy through this way. In anaerobic or hypoxic conditions, glucose produces lactic acid and a small amount of energy. This process is termed as glycolysis and 2 molecular ATPs can be produced per glucose molecule (Fig. 22-1) .

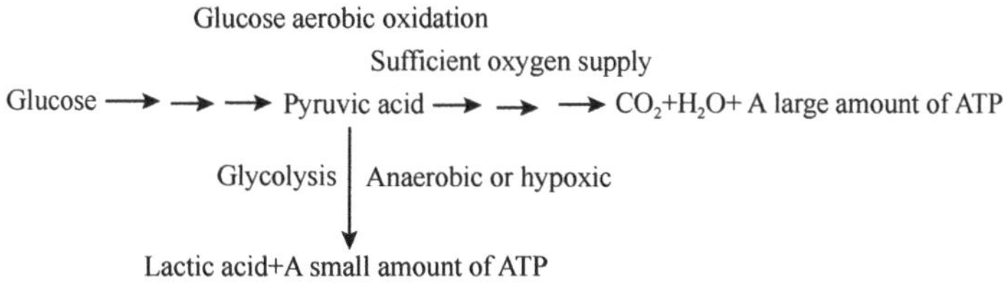

Fig. 22-1 The pathway of lactic acid generation

In normal circumstances, the body's energy supply relies on aerobic oxidation and rarely on anaerobic oxidation. Inhibition of glycolysis by aerobic oxidation is termed as the Pasteur effect. Under special circumstances, strenuous exercise increases oxygen and energy consumption and aerobic oxidation increases. Even though breathing and circulation accelerates, the body's oxygen demand cannot be met. In hypoxic muscle tissue, glycolysis increases to supplement energy and lactic acid concentration will be elevated in the blood and urine.

Lactic acid is also known as 2-hydroxy acrylic acid, which is a type of hydroxy carboxylic acid. In the presence of copper ions, lactic acid reacts with concentrated sulfuric acid to generate acetaldehyde. An additional reaction between acetaldehyde and hydroxyl diphenyl yields a purple red product (Fig. 22-2). Collecting urine before and after exercise allows one to detect lactic acid concentration differences as well as the extent of glycolysis.

【Apparatus and Reagents】

1. Apparatus

(1) Centrifuge.
(2) Test tube and test tube rack.
(3) Thermostatic water bath cauldron.
(4) Volumetric flask and beaker.
(5) Dropper and pipette.

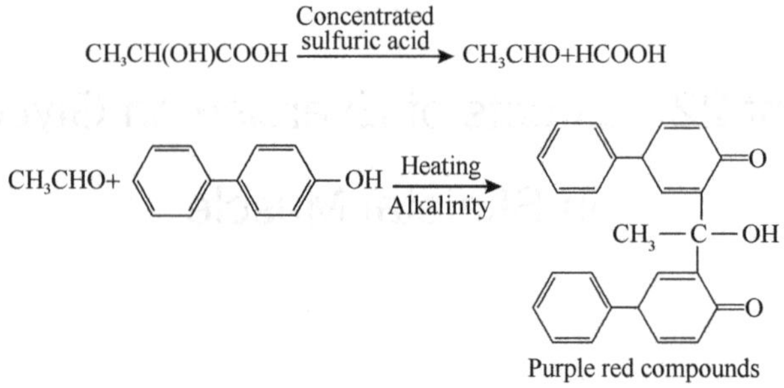

Fig. 22-2　The principle of lactic acid detection

2. Reagents

(1) Urine (before and after exercise).

(2) 20% $CuSO_4$ solution: Dissolve 20g of copper sulfate into distilled water to 100mL.

(3) Hydroxybenzyl diphenyl solution: Dissolve 1.5g of hydroxyl diphenyl into 50mL 1% NaOH solution, add distilled water to 100mL, heat until dissolved completely and store in a dark bottle.

(4) $Ca(OH)_2$ powder.

(5) Concentrated sulfuric acid.

【Procedures】

(1) Urine sample collection: The subject should urinate 30min before sample collection to eliminate factors that can influence the data such as diet, exercise and urine concentration. After 30min, urine should be collected as pre-exercise urine. Strenuous exercise should be performed immediately for 5min. Urine should be collected within 30min after the start of exercise and labeled as post-exercise urine.

(2) 5mL of each sample should be added into the test tubes, 1mL of 20% $CuSO_4$ solution should be added along with 0.5g $Ca(OH)_2$ until it turns a pure blue, and the solution should be evenly stirred. The solution should stand for 10min and be centrifugated at 3,000 r/min for 10min.

(3) Two test tubes should be prepared as described in Table 22-1.

Table 22-1　Effects of exercise on glycometabolism in skeletal muscle

Reagents	Tube numbers	
	1	2
The supernatant of pre-exercise urine/drops	10	—
The supernatant of post-exercise urine/drops	—	10
Put two test tubes in the cold water for 1min, and then add concentrated sulfuric acid		
Concentrated sulfuric acid/mL	3	3
Mix well, put it in boiling water for 5min, and then put it in the cold water for 3min		
The hydroxyl diphenyl solution/drops	3	3

(4) Observe color changes of the two test tubes. Explain reasons for different results.

【Notes】

(1) Add $CuSO_4$ and $Ca(OH)_2$ to remove proteins and carbohydrates from urine. When adding $Ca(OH)_2$, the solution should be alkaline (pure blue) and the added urine sample should be free of precipitate.

(2) The intensity of exercise directly determines whether the color difference of the results is obvious, so it is necessary to exercise vigorously. There would be no obvious difference in

samples obtained from people with good aerobic capacity.

(3) Some inorganic ions, such as iron ions, chromium ions and zinc ions, interfere with the color reaction of acetaldehyde and hydroxyl diphenyl.

(4) Hydroxyl diphenyl is difficult to dissolve in concentrated sulfuric acid and must be shaken both carefully and vigorously.

(5) Concentrated sulfuric acid is highly corrosive, so please handle with care.

【Questions】

1. Why does exercise intensity affect the color of experimental results?
2. Why do we need to add $Ca(OH)_2$ until the solution turns pure blue before the lactic acid oxidation process?
3. Does strenuous exercise cause acidosis?

(Ren Yonggang, Yang Yingxue)

实验 23　水果中维生素 C 的含量测定及温度、碱和重金属对样品中维生素 C 影响的动态观察

【实验目的】

1. 掌握维生素 C 含量测定的基本原理。
2. 了解维生素 C 的理化性质、生理功能。
3. 动态观察重金属、碱、温度等因素对维生素 C 的破坏作用。

【实验原理】

维生素 C 又称抗坏血酸，包括氧化型和还原型两种。它易溶于水，在空气中不稳定，遇碱、热和重金属离子易被氧化破坏，故常用无氧化作用的稀酸溶液来提取。

还原型维生素 C 能还原某些氧化型的物质，如氧化型 2,6-二氯酚靛酚（图 23-1）。氧化型的 2,6-二氯酚靛酚在酸性环境中呈红色，被还原后褪色。因此利用氧化还原滴定反应，比照 2,6-二氯酚靛酚的颜色变化，确定反应中 2,6-二氯酚靛酚的消耗量，便可算出样品中维生素 C 的含量。通过分别测定不同温度、不同浓度碱或重金属盐处理后的样品中剩余维生素 C 含量，可以评估温度、碱和重金属盐的破坏作用。

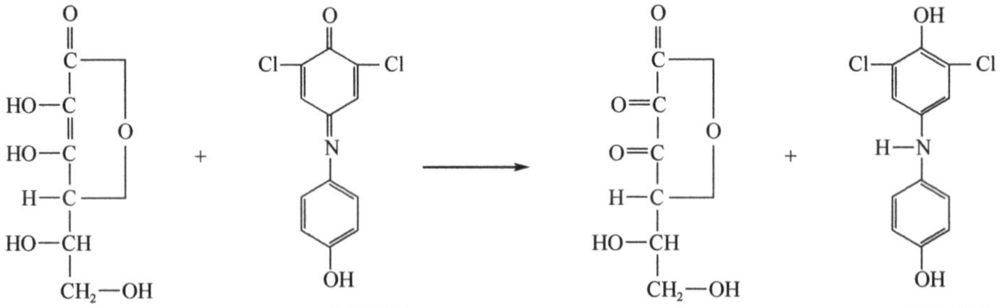

维生素C（还原型）　2,6二氯酚靛酚（氧化型）红色　维生素C（氧化型）　2,6二氯酚靛酚（还原型）无色

图 23-1　2,6-二氯酚靛酚与维生素 C 的氧化还原反应

【器材与试剂】

1. 器材

（1）50mL 容量瓶、50mL 锥形瓶。

（2）研钵、漏斗、纱布（双层）。

（3）碱式滴定管（10mL）、刻度移液管。

（4）天平。

（5）水浴锅。

2. 试剂

（1）2%草酸溶液：称取草酸 2g，用蒸馏水溶解并定容至 100mL。

（2）白陶土。

（3）标准维生素 C 液（0.5mg/mL）：称取纯维生素 C 25mg，溶于 25mL 2%草酸溶液中，并用 2%草酸溶液定容至 50mL。

（4）0.1% 2,6-二氯酚靛酚溶液：称取氧化型 2,6-二氯酚靛酚 0.5g，溶于约 300mL 热水中，加 $NaHCO_3$ 104mg 充分振摇，定容至 500mL，装入棕色瓶内。置 4℃冰箱内保存过夜。临用前过滤，用标准维生素 C 标定其浓度。

吸取标准维生素 C 溶液 5mL，置 50mL 锥形瓶中，加 5mL 2%草酸溶液，用配制的 2,6-二氯酚靛酚滴定，然后将 2,6-二氯酚靛酚稀释为 1mL 消耗维生素 C 0.088mg，贮于棕色瓶中，置冰箱中可保存一周。

（5）含维生素 C 的样品：广柑、苹果或者青椒等。

（6）5%$CuSO_4$溶液：5g $CuSO_4$溶解并定容至 100mL 蒸馏水。

（7）1mol/L、3mol/L、5mol/L、7mol/L NaOH 溶液：分别称取 NaOH 40g、120g、200g、280g，溶解定容至 1000mL。

（8）1mol/L、3mol/L、5mol/L、7mol/L HCl 溶液：分别取浓度为 12mol/L 浓盐酸 83.3mL、250.0mL、416.7mL、583.3mL，用蒸馏水稀释至 1000mL。

【实验操作】

1. 提取　用天平准确称取新鲜样品 50g，置研钵中加入少量 2%草酸溶液（5～10mL），充分研磨提取 3～4 次（勿溅出溶液），几次提取液通过两层纱布漏斗滤入 50mL 的容量瓶中（勿使提取液由纱布滴在瓶外）。最后用 2%草酸溶液定容至刻度并混匀。

2. 脱色　若有色样品提取液的颜色妨碍滴定终点的观察，可以将提取液倒入干燥锥形瓶中，加白陶土（1g/20mL 样品液），充分振摇约 5min，过滤。

3. 破坏因素处理维生素 C 提取液

（1）NaOH 对维生素 C 的影响：用不同浓度 NaOH 处理维生素 C 提取液（表 23-1）。

表 23-1　碱对维生素 C 的影响

试剂和处理	管号				
	1	2	3	4	5
维生素 C 提取液/mL	4.0	4.0	4.0	4.0	4.0
NaOH 溶液/mL	—	0.5	0.5	0.5	0.5
NaOH 溶液浓度/(mol/L)	—	1	3	5	7
蒸馏水/mL	0.5	—	—	—	—
处理时间/min	20	20	20	20	20

处理 20min 后，加入等浓度 HCl 中和 NaOH（表 23-2）。

表 23-2 HCl 中和 NaOH 及维生素 C 含量测定

试剂	管号				
	1	2	3	4	5
HCl/mL	—	0.5	0.5	0.5	0.5
盐酸溶液浓度/（mol/L）	—	1	3	5	7
蒸馏水/mL	0.5	—	—	—	—
2,6-二氯酚靛酚/mL					
维生素 C 含量/（mg/100g）					

用 2,6-二氯酚靛酚溶液滴定（滴定宜迅速以减少还原型维生素 C 的氧化），直至出现红色 30s 不褪为止。每管重复三次，记录消耗的 2,6-二氯酚靛酚的体积（mL）平均值，按下式计算维生素 C 浓度。

$$\text{维生素 C 含量（mg/100g）}=\text{2,6-二氯酚靛酚体积平均值} \times 0.088\times\frac{50}{4}\times\frac{100}{50}$$

（2）铜离子对维生素 C 的影响：用不同浓度铜离子处理维生素 C 提取液（表 23-3）。

表 23-3 $CuSO_4$ 处理维生素 C 提取液

试剂和处理	管号				
	1	2	3	4	5
维生素 C 提取液/mL	4.5	4.5	4.5	4.5	4.5
$CuSO_4$ 溶液/mL	—	0.1	0.2	0.3	0.4
蒸馏水/mL	0.5	—	—	—	—
处理时间/min	20	20	20	20	20
2, 6-二氯酚靛酚/mL					
维生素 C 含量/(mg/100g)					

处理 20min 后，用 2,6-二氯酚靛酚溶液滴定直到出现红色 30s 不褪为止。每管重复三次，记录消耗的 2,6-二氯酚靛酚的体积（mL） 平均值，按下式计算维生素 C 浓度。

$$\text{维生素 C 含量（mg/100g）}=\text{2,6-二氯酚靛酚体积平均值}\times 0.088\times\frac{50}{4.5}\times\frac{100}{50}$$

（3）温度对维生素 C 的影响：用不同温度处理维生素 C 提取液（表 23-4）。

表 23-4 不同温度处理维生素 C 提取液

试剂和处理	管号				
	1	2	3	4	5
维生素 C 提取液/mL	5	5	5	5	5
温度/℃	室温	37	60	80	100
处理时间/min	20	20	20	20	20
2,6-二氯酚靛酚/mL					
维生素 C 含量/（mg/100g）					

处理 20min 后，用 2,6-二氯酚靛酚溶液滴定直到出现红色 30s 不褪为止。每管重复三次，记录消耗的 2,6-二氯酚靛酚的体积（mL）平均值，按下式计算维生素 C 浓度。

$$维生素C含量（mg/100g）=2,6\text{-}二氯酚靛酚体积平均值 \times 0.088 \times \frac{50}{5} \times \frac{100}{50}$$

【注意事项】

（1）样品研磨应充分，水果要去皮。
（2）实验过程应迅速，以减少维生素 C 的氧化。
（3）滴定时每次均应从 0.00 刻度开始，以减少误差。

【思考题】

1. 维生素 C 为何具有易氧化的特性，提取维生素 C 时为何要加 2%草酸溶液？
2. 维生素 C 有何生理功能，人体缺乏维生素 C 时有何临床症状？

（唐　珍　王含彦）

Experiment 23 Determination of Vitamin C in Fruits and Dynamic Observation of the Effects of Temperature, Alkali and Heavy Metals on Vitamin C in Samples

【Purposes】

1. To master the basic principle of vitamin C content determination.
2. To learn the physicochemical properties and physiological functions of vitamin C.
3. Dynamic observation of the destructive effect of heavy metal, alkali, temperature and other factors on vitamin C.

【Principles】

Vitamin C, also known as ascorbic acid, exists in an oxidized or reduced form. It is easily soluble in water, unstable in air, and easily destroyed by oxidation in the presence of alkali, heat and heavy metal ions. Diluted acid is often used to extract vitamin C to protect it from oxidation.

Vitamin C can reduce some oxidized substances (e.g. oxidized 2,6-dichlorophenol-indophenol, DCPIP, Fig. 23-1). Oxidized DCPIP is red in an acid environment and will turn colorless when reduced. Vitamin C content in samples can be calculated based on the consumption of DCPIP, which is determined by the oxidation-reduction titration referring to the color change of DCPIP. The destructive effects of temperature, alkali and heavy metal salt can be evaluated by determining the residual vitamin C content in samples treated with different temperatures and different concentrations of alkali or heavy metal salts, respectively.

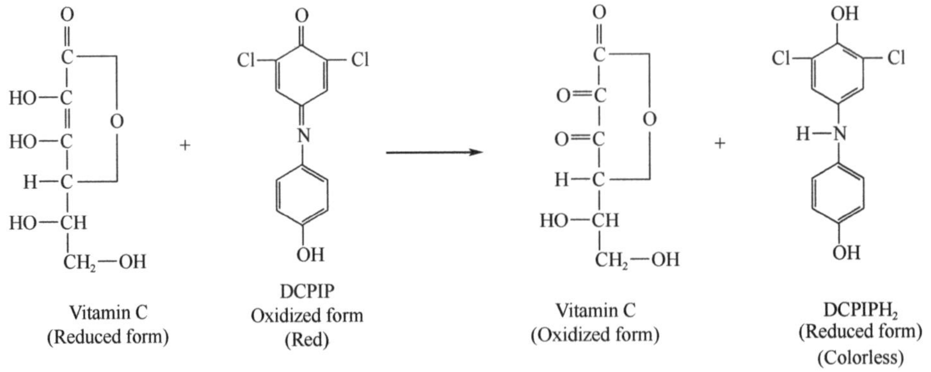

Fig. 23-1 Redox reaction between DCPIP and vitamin C

【Apparatus and Reagents】

1. Apparatus

(1) 50mL volumetric flask and 50mL erlenmeyer flask.
(2) Mortar, funnel and gauze (double layer) .
(3) Basic burette (10mL) and measuring pipet.
(4) Balance.
(5) Water bath cauldron.

2. Reagents

(1) 2% oxalic acid solution: Dissolve 2g oxalic acid and dilute it to 100mL with distilled water.

(2) Kaolin.

(3) Standard vitamin C solution (0.5mg/mL): Weigh 25mg pure vitamin C, dissolve it in 25mL 2% oxalic acid solution and dilute it with 2% oxalic acid solution to 50mL.

(4) 0.1% DCPIP solution: Weigh 0.5g oxidized DCPIP, dissolve it in 300mL hot water containing 104mg $NaHCO_3$, shake sufficiently and dilute it to 500mL with distilled water. Store the solution in a dark bottle at 4°C overnight. Filtrate the solution before use and determine its concentration using the standard vitamin C solution.

Place 5mL standard vitamin C solution into a 50mL erlenmeyer flask, add 5mL 2% oxalic acid solution and titrate it with prepared DCPIP to calibrate its concentration. Adjust the content of DCPIP until 1mL DCPIP can consume 0.088mg vitamin C. DCPIP solution can be stored in a dark bottle at 4°C up to one week.

(5) Samples containing vitamin C: oranges, apples or green peppers and so on.

(6) 5%$CuSO_4$ solution: Weigh 5g $CuSO_4$, dissolve it in distilled water, and dilute the solution to 100mL.

(7) 1mol/L, 3mol/L, 5mol/L, 7mol/L NaOH solution: Dissolve 40g, 120g, 200g and 350g NaOH, and dilute them to 1,000mL using distilled water respectively.

(8) 1mol/L, 3mol/L, 5mol/L, 7mol/L HCl solution: Place 83.3mL, 250.0mL, 416.7mL and 583.3mL concentrated HCl (12mol/L) and dilute them to 1,000mL using distilled water respectively.

【Procedures】

1. Extraction Weigh 50g fresh sample accurately with the balance, put it into a mortar, add a small amount of 2% oxalic acid solution (5–10mL) and grind well (keep the solution from spilling out) to extract vitamin C for 3–4 times. Filtrate all the extract solution into a 50mL volumetric flask using double-layer gauze (keep the extract solution from dropping out of the bottle along the gauze). Finally, use 2% oxalic acid solution to dilute to 500mL and mix well.

2. Decoloring If the color of extract solution affects the observation of the end point of titration, the extract solution can be poured into a dry erlenmeyer flask, add Kaolin (1g/20mL) , shake well for 5min, and then filtrate again.

3. Destructive factor treatment of vitamin C extracts

(1) The effect of alkali treatment on vitamin C : Treat vitamin C extracts with different concentrations of NaOH (Table 23-1) .

Table 23-1 The effects of alkali on vitamin C

Reagents and treatments	Tube numbers				
	1	2	3	4	5
The vitamin C solution/mL	4.0	4.0	4.0	4.0	4.0
NaOH solution/mL	—	0.5	0.5	0.5	0.5
NaOH concentration/(mol/L)	—	1	3	5	7
distilled water /mL	0.5	—	—	—	—
Disposing time/min	20	20	20	20	20

After 20min, HCl solution of equal concentration is added to neutralize NaOH in each conical flask (Table 23-2) .

Table 23-2　HCl neutralization of NaOH and determination of vitamin C

Reagents and Treatments	Tube numbers				
	1	2	3	4	5
HCl/mL	—	0.5	0.5	0.5	0.5
HCl concentration/(mol/L)	—	1	3	5	7
Distilled water /mL	0.5	—	—	—	—
DCPIP/mL					
The content of vitamin C/(mg/100g)					

Titrate each flask with DCPIP until the red color does not fade for 30s. Have three replicates for each test tube, and record average volume values of DCPIP consumed (V_{DCPIP}) . Calculate the vitamin C content using the following equation:

$$\text{The content of vitamin C (mg/100g)}=V_{DCPIP}\times 0.088\times\frac{50}{4}\times\frac{100}{50}$$

(2) Effect of copper ions on vitamin C : Treat vitamin C extracts with different concentrations of copper ions (Table 23-3).

Table 23-3　Effect of copper ions on vitamin C

Reagents and treatments	Tube numbers				
	1	2	3	4	5
The vitamin C solution/mL	4.5	4.5	4.5	4.5	4.5
$CuSO_4$ solution/mL	—	0.1	0.2	0.3	0.4
Distilled water /mL	0.5	—	—	—	—
Disposing time/min	20	20	20	20	20
DCPIP/mL					
The content of vitamin C/(mg/100g)					

After 20min, titrate each flask with DCPIP until the red color does not fade for 30s. Have three replicates for each test tube, and record average volume values of DCPIP consumed (V_{DCPIP}). Calculate the vitamin C content using the following equation:

$$\text{The content of vitamin C (mg/100g)}=V_{DCPIP}\times 0.088\times\frac{50}{4.5}\times\frac{100}{50}$$

(3) Effect of different temperatures on vitamin C : Treat vitamin C extracts with different temperatures (Table 23-4).

Table 23-4　Effect of different temperatures on vitamin C

Regents and treatments	Tube numbers				
	1	2	3	4	5
The vitamin C solution/mL	5	5	5	5	5
Temperatures/°C	Room temperature	37	60	80	100
Disposing time/min	20	20	20	20	20
DCPIP/mL					
The content of vitamin C/(mg/100g)					

After 20min, titrate each flask with DCPIP until the red color does not fade for 30s. Have three replicates for each test tube, and record average volume values of DCPIP consumed (V_{DCPIP}). Calculate the vitamin C content using the following equation:

$$\text{The content of vitamin C (mg/100g)} = V_{\text{DCPIP}} \times 0.088 \times \frac{50}{5} \times \frac{100}{50}$$

【Notes】

(1) The experimental sample should be well ground. Fruits should be peeled before use.
(2) The experiment should be conducted rapidly to decrease the oxidation of vitamin C.
(3) Titration should begin from a 0.00 scale each time to decrease error.

【Questions】

1. Why does vitamin C tend to be oxidized? Why is 2% oxalic acid used during the vitamin C extraction process?

2. What are the physiological functions of vitamin C and the clinical symptoms of vitamin C deficiency?

(Tang Zhen, Wang Hanyan)

第四章　设计性实验

实验 24　基因克隆技术：人髓鞘碱性蛋白基因重组质粒的构建与鉴定

【实验目的】

1. 掌握基因克隆的基本原理和实验技术方法。
2. 了解基因克隆技术的各种应用。

【实验原理】

构建重组 DNA 分子的主要步骤包括：分离基因或目标 DNA 片段，目标 DNA 和载体的酶切和连接，将重组载体转化到宿主细胞中，筛选和鉴定正确的重组载体。

限制性核酸内切酶可识别特定位点并切割 DNA 产生黏性末端或平端的外源片段，酶切后的目标 DNA 和载体经纯化处理可用于连接反应，形成重组 DNA 分子。

本实验的目标序列为人髓鞘碱性蛋白基因，由学生自行挑选一个常用原核表达质粒（如 pET-30），设计引物，并进行 PCR 扩增。在 PCR 所使用引物中，配合所选质粒，设计两种不同的限制性核酸内切酶的酶切位点。设计的酶切位点应同时符合以下要求，选择的质粒载体的多克隆位点（MCS）区段应含有这两个位点，但目的基因当中没有便于 PCR 产物的后继酶切的相应序列。设计好的引物可交给商业公司合成。PCR 扩增步骤参见实验 14。

【器材与试剂】

1. 器材

（1）水平电泳仪。
（2）电泳仪电源。
（3）凝胶图像分析系统。
（4）微量移液器。
（5）PCR 仪。
（6）恒温水浴锅。
（7）超净工作台。
（8）已灭菌的多种型号的离心管和移液器枪头。
（9）离心机。

2. 试剂

（1）快速 DNA 连接试剂盒。
（2）限制性核酸内切酶（如 *Hind* Ⅲ、*Sal* Ⅰ）。
（3）PCR 试剂盒。

（4）质粒提取试剂盒。

（5）DNA 凝胶回收试剂盒。

（6）0.1mol/L $CaCl_2$ 溶液：称取 $CaCl_2 \cdot 2H_2O$ 1.47g，蒸馏水定容至 100 mL。

（7）6×电泳上样缓冲液（参见实验 15）。

（8）*E. coli* DH5α。

（9）LB 培养基（参见实验 18）。

（10）15%甘油。

（11）氨苄青霉素：在 9mL 蒸馏水中溶解氨苄青霉素 1g 粉末并定容至 10mL，然后将氨苄青霉素溶液通过 0.22μm 的无菌过滤器。分装成小份存于−20℃。

【实验操作】

1. PCR 扩增（参见实验 14） 待扩增基因片段为人髓鞘碱性蛋白基因，请挑选一个常用原核表达质粒（如 pET-30），确定两个不同的限制性内切酶的消化位点，设计引物，并进行 PCR 扩增。

设计引物的常用软件有 Primer Premier 5.0、Oligo 6.22 等，以及在线设计程序如 http：//www. yeastgenome. org/cgi-bin/web-primer 及 NCBI 上的 Primer Blast 等。这些软件能根据引物设计基本原则及需求，设计并推荐最优引物。引物设计后交由商业公司合成。

2. 质粒提取，酶切及鉴定

1）质粒提取（参见实验 18）

2）质粒 DNA 限制性双酶切及回收

（1）用微量移液枪在 1.5mL 离心管中配制酶切反应体系如下：

质粒	4μL
10×酶切缓冲液	3μL
两种限制性核酸内切酶	各 1μL
蒸馏水	11μL

轻轻地混匀溶液。

（2）合适温度水浴（通常为 37℃） 2～4h。

（3）1%琼脂糖凝胶电泳检测及回收 DNA（参见实验 15）：1～3 泳道分别加入 DNA 标记、提取质粒样品、酶切后质粒样品（电泳后比较提取质粒及双酶切质粒的迁移速率判断酶切是否成功）。切胶回收 DNA，回收步骤参见 DNA 回收试剂盒。

3. 目的 DNA 酶切及回收 准备 1 个 1.5mL 离心管，配制 20μL 反应体系如下：

目的 DNA	4μL
10×酶切缓冲液	3μL
两种限制性核酸内切酶	各 1μL
蒸馏水	11μL

轻轻吹打混匀，37℃水浴 3h。反应后 1%琼脂糖凝胶电泳，紫外灯下观察电泳结果，切胶回收目的 DNA 片段（回收步骤参见 DNA 回收试剂盒） 。

4. 连接 准备 1 个 1.5mL 离心管，配制 20μL 连接反应体系如下：

双酶切回收目的基因	2μL

双酶切回收载体	6μL
10×T4 DNA 连接酶缓冲液	2μL
T4 DNA 连接酶	1μL
蒸馏水	9μL

轻轻吹打混匀，16℃水浴连接过夜。同时设置一个无插入目的 DNA 片段的连接对照，以检查形成非重组子背景的可能性（可选做）。

5. 转化 需超净台无菌操作。

1）感受态细胞的制备

（1）从 LB 平板上挑取新活化的 *E. coli* DH5α 单菌落，接种于 3～5mL LB 液体培养基中，37℃下振荡培养过夜。

（2）取 1mL 该菌液接种于 100mL LB 液体培养基中，37℃振荡培养 3～4h 至 OD_{600} 为 0.4。

（3）将培养液转入离心管中，冰上放置 10min，然后于 4℃下 3000r/min 离心 10min。

（4）弃去上清液，后续步骤都应在低温下操作。用预冷的 0.05mol/L 的 $CaCl_2$ 溶液 10mL 轻轻悬浮细胞，冰上放置 15～30min 后，4℃下 3000r/min 离心 10min。

（5）弃去上清液，加入 4mL 预冷含 15%甘油的 0.05mol/L 的 $CaCl_2$ 溶液，轻柔振摇或吹打悬浮细胞，每 200μL 分装至 1.5mL 离心管中，即成感受态细胞悬浮液。感受态细胞保存于−80℃可保持转化效率长达 6 个月。

2）转化

（1）取 10μL 连接产物，与 100～200μL 感受态细胞悬浮液轻柔混匀，冰上孵育 30min（超净台，冰上操作）。

（2）42℃水浴中热击 90s，不可振荡。热击后迅速置于冰上冷却 3～5min。

（3）向管中加入 1mL LB 液体培养基（不含抗生素 Amp），混匀后 37℃振荡培养 60min，使细菌恢复正常生长状态，并表达抗生素抗性基因。

（4）将上述菌液摇匀后取 100μL 涂布于含抗生素 Amp 的 LB 平板上，正面向上放置 30min，待菌液完全被培养基吸收后倒置培养皿，37℃培养过夜。

同时做三个对照：

对照组 1：以同体积的蒸馏水代替连接产物，其他操作与上面相同。此组正常情况下在含抗生素的 LB 平板上应没有菌落出现。

对照组 2：以同体积的蒸馏水代替连接产物，但在转化的第（4）步涂板时只取 100μL 菌液涂布于不含抗生素 Amp 的 LB 平板上，此组正常情况下应产生大量菌落。

对照组 3：以 1μL 质粒提取液代替连接产物，其他操作与上面相同。此组正常情况下在含抗生素 Amp 的 LB 平板上应有大量菌落出现。

6. 重组质粒的鉴定

（1）以灭菌枪头从 LB 平板上挑取数个菌落于含抗生素 Amp 的 LB 培养液中，37℃培养过夜。

（2）提取质粒，进行限制性酶切分析。

【思考题】

1. 为什么在转化前制备大肠杆菌感受态细胞很重要？

2. 为什么要设置对照组？如果一个同学的转化结果如下，应如何解释实验结果？
连接产物：无菌落。
对照组 1：无菌落。
对照组 2：大量菌落。
对照组 3：大量菌落。

（易　芳　王含彦）

Chapter Ⅳ Design Experiments

Experiment 24 Gene Cloning—Construction and Identification of the Recombinant Plasmid of the Human Myelin Basic Protein Gene

【Purposes】

1. To master the basic principles and experimental techniques of DNA cloning.
2. To learn the applications of DNA cloning.

【Principles】

The main steps to create a recombinant DNA molecule include separating a gene or target DNA fragment, enzyme digestion and ligation of the target DNA and vector, transforming the recombinant vector into the host cell and screening and identification for the correct recombinant vectors.

A restriction endonuclease is able to identify and digests specifics DNA sequences and produces sticky ends and blunt ends. After enzyme digestion, the target DNA and vector can be purified for ligation to form recombinant DNA molecules.

The target sequence here is the human myelin basic protein gene. Choose a commonly used prokaryotic expression vector (e.g. pET-30) , design PCR primers and perform PCR. PCR primers should be designed according to the interest vector, including two different digestive sites. The designed digestive sites should meet the following requirements simultaneously. The multiple cloning site (MCS) on segment of selected plasmid vectors should contain these two sites, but there is no corresponding sequence in the target genes, which is convenient for the subsequent digestion of PCR products. Designed primers can be synthesized by a commercial corporation. Please refer to Exp. 14 for the PCR procedure.

【Apparatus and Reagents】

1. Apparatus

(1) Horizontal electrophoresis apparatus.
(2) Power supply of electrophoresis apparatus.
(3) Gel image analysis system.
(4) Micropipette.
(5) PCR thermocycler instrument.
(6) Thermostatic water bath cauldron.
(7) Super clean bench.
(8) Various sterilized centrifugal tubes and pipette tips.
(9) Centrifuge.

2. Reagents

(1) Rapid DNA connection kit.
(2) Restriction endonuclease(e. g. *Hind* Ⅲ、*Sal* Ⅰ).
(3) PCR kit.
(4) Plasmid extraction kit.

(5) DNA gel extraction kit.

(6) 0.1mol/L $CaCl_2$ solution: Weigh $CaCl_2 \cdot 2H_2O$ 1.47g, and add distilled water to 100mL.

(7) 6× electrophoresis loading buffer (Please refer to Exp. 15).

(8) *E. coli* DH5α.

(9) LB medium (Please refer to Exp. 18).

(10) 15% glycerol.

(11) Sodium ampicillin: Dissolve 1g of sodium ampicillin in 9mL distilled water to make a final volume of 10mL. Pass the sodium ampicillin solution through a 0.22 μm sterile filter. Store the sodium ampicillin in aliquots at −20°C.

【Procedures】

1. PCR amplification (Please refer to Exp. 14) The target gene here is human myelin basic protein gene. Choose a commonly used prokaryotic expression vector such as pET-30, determine two different digestive sites of restriction enzyme and design primers for PCR, and perform PCR amplification.

Many common software tools for primer design are available, such as Primer Premier 5.0, Oligo 6.22, or online design program Primer Blast in NCBI and http://www. yeastgenome. org/cgi-bin/web-primer. These software have the ability to design and recommend optimal primers based on basic design principles. Designed primers are synthesized by commercial corporations.

2. Plasmid extraction, digestion and identification

1) Plasmid extraction (Please refer to Exp. 18).

2) Double enzymatic digestion and recovery of DNA plasmid.

(1) Assemble the following components in a new 1.5mL centrifugal tube with the micropipette:

Plasmid	4μL
10× digestion buffer	3μL
Two restriction endonucleases	1μL for each one
Distilled water	11μL

Gently mix the solution.

(2) Incubate at the appropriate temperature (usually 37°C) for 2–4h.

(3) Run a 1% agarose gel electrophoresis to determine the extent of digestion and prepare for recovering DNA from the gel (refer to Exp. 15). Load the DNA marker, plasmid sample and double enzyme-digested plasmid sample in lanes 1–3, respectively (after electrophoresis, compare the travel speed of the two samples to determine if the DNA has been digested). Recover the DNA from the gel based on the DNA gel extraction kit.

3. Enzyme digestion and recovery of the target DNA Assemble 20μL reaction system in a 1.5mL centrifugal tube:

Target DNA	4μL
10× digestion buffer	3μL
Two restriction endonucleases	1μL for each one
Distilled water	11μL

Gently mix the solution. Incubate at the appropriate temperature (usually 37°C) for 3h. Run a 1% agarose gel electrophoresis, and the results of electrophoresis are observed under an ultraviolet lamp. Recovery DNA from the gel based on the DNA gel extraction kit.

4. Ligation Assemble the 20μL reaction system in a 1.5mL centrifugal tube:

Double enzymatic recovery of target gene	2μL
Double enzymatic recovery of pET vector	6μL
10× T4 DNA ligase buffer	2μL
T4 DNA ligase	1μL
Distilled water	9μL

Gently mix the solution by stirring with a pipet tip. Incubate at 16°C overnight. Set up a control reaction where the insert is omitted to check for non-recombinant background (optional) .

5. Transformation Sterile operation at a super clean bench are required.

1) Preparation of competent cells

(1) A single colony of *E. coli* DH5α is transferred to a tube with 3–5mL LB medium and incubated overnight with shaking at 37°C.

(2) 1mL of bacterium solution is transferred to 100mL LB medium and incubated with shaking at 37°C for 3–4h till OD_{600} equals about 0.4.

(3) Transfer culture medium to centrifugal tubes and place cells on ice for 10min. Centrifugate cells at 4°C for 10min (3,000r/min) .

(4) Discard the supernatant. Cells must remain cold for the rest of the procedure. Resuspend cells (by pipetting) in 10mL pre-cooled 0.05mol/L $CaCl_2$ solution gently and incubate them on ice for 15–30min. Centrifugate cells at 4°C for 10min (3,000r/min) .

(5) Discard the supernatant. Resuspend cells by gently shaking or blowing in 4 mL pre-cooled 0.05mol/L $CaCl_2$ solution containing 15% glycerol. Transfer 200μL into 1.5mL centrifugal tubes and competent cell suspensions are obtained. Cells stored at −80°C can be used for transformation for up to 6 months.

2) Transformation

(1) Add 10μL of the ligation product into 100-200μL competent cells and mix gently. Incubate the tubes on ice for 30min.

(2) Place the tubes in a 42°C water bath for exactly 90s; do not shake. Place the tubes on ice for 3-5min.

(3) Add 1mL LB liquid medium without antibiotics Amp into each tube, mix well, and shake at 37°C for 60min to allow the cells to be reanimated and express the resistant gene for Amp.

(4) Shake well and spread 100μL of the above liquid on LB plates containing antibiotic Amp. Put the plates face up at 37°C for 30min to allow excess liquid to be absorbed, and then invert the plates and incubate overnight at 37°C.

Setting 3 controls for transformation:

Control 1: Replace the ligation product with the same volume of distilled water. The other operations are the same as above. There should be no colonies on the LB plate with Amp after incubation.

Control 2: Replace the ligation product with the same volume of distilled water. In step (4) of transformation, spread 100μL bacterium solution on LB plates without Amp. There should be a large number of colonies on the LB plate after incubation.

Control 3: Replace the ligation product with 1μL plasmid extracting solution. The other operations are the same as above. There should be a large number of colonies on the LB plate with Amp after incubation.

6. Identification of recombinant plasmids

(1) Pick several colonies from an LB plate using a sterile pipette tip into LB medium with Amp and incubate them at 37°C overnight.

(2) Extract the plasmids and perform restriction endonuclease analysis.

【Questions】

1. Why is it important to prepare *E. coli* competent cells before transformation?

2. Why are there 3 controls? How do you explain the following transformation results?
Ligation products: no colonies.
Control 1: no colonies.
Control 2: a large number of colonies.
Control 3: a large number of colonies.

(Yi Fang,Wang Hanyan)

实验 25　人基因多态性分析

【实验目的】

1. 了解基因多态性在阐明人体对疾病和毒物的易感性与耐受性、疾病临床表现的多样性以及对药物治疗的反应中的重要作用。

2. 了解分析基因多态性的基本原理和研究方法。

【实验原理】

基因多态性是指在一个生物群体中，同时存在两种及以上的变异型或基因型或等位基因，也称为遗传多态性。第一，人类基因多态性对阐明人体对疾病和毒物的易感性与耐受性、疾病临床表现的多样性以及对药物治疗的反应有重大意义；第二，与致病基因连锁的多态性位点可作为遗传病的诊断标记，并为分离克隆致病基因提供依据；第三，病因未知的疾病与候选基因多态性的相关性分析，可用于辅助筛选致病易感基因。

聚合酶链式反应-限制性片段长度多态性（PCR-RFLP）分析是一种常用的 DNA 分子标记。该技术基于以下原则。首先通过 PCR 扩增获得目的基因。若目的基因存在等位变异（多态性），且变异正好发生在某种限制性内切酶识别位点上，使酶切位点增加或者消失，则酶切结果就会产生大小不同的片段，即片段长度多态性，再利用琼脂糖凝胶电泳分离，可呈现出多态性电泳图谱。若将患者与正常的多态性图谱比较，可确定是否变异。应用 PCR-RFLP，研究者可检测某一感兴趣的致病基因已知的点突变，进行直接基因诊断，也可以此为遗传标记进行连锁分析作出间接基因诊断。

【器材与试剂】

1. 器材

（1）离心机。

（2）PCR 仪。

（3）电泳仪。

（4）电泳仪电源。

（5）紫外线探测器。

（6）微量移液器。

2. 试剂

（1）口腔拭子 DNA 抽提试剂盒（SwabGen DNA Kit）。

（2）琼脂糖。

（3）50×TAE 母液：向烧杯中加入 Tris 121g、0.5mol/L EDTA（pH8.0） 50mL、冰醋酸 28.55mL，搅拌，用蒸馏水定容至 500mL。

（4）1×TAE 电泳缓冲液：980mL 蒸馏水中加入 50×TAE 母液 20mL。

（5）6×上样缓冲液（参见实验 15）。

（6）GoldView（参见实验 15）。

（7）DNA 分子量标准。

【实验操作】

1. 基因组 DNA 抽提

（1）细胞采集：口腔拭子（消毒后的棉签） 擦拭两侧脸颊各 10 次，采集口腔黏膜脱落细胞，将拭子转置于 2mL 离心管中，用剪刀将棉签部分剪下，加入 DNA 抽提试剂盒中的 400μL 缓冲液 GA。

注意：为了保证样本不被食物或者饮料污染，取样前 30min 内请勿进食和饮水。

（2）DNA 提取：参照试剂盒说明书操作。

（3）样品保存：DNA 产物应保存在−20℃，以防 DNA 降解。

2. DNA 浓度及纯度检测

（1）琼脂糖凝胶电泳法检测 DNA 片段大小（参照实验 15）。

（2）紫外分光光度法检测 DNA 浓度及纯度（参照实验 19）。

测定浓度后，用蒸馏水稀释至 0.25μg/μL，−20℃保存备用。

3. PCR-RFLP 分析

（1）查找目标基因的核酸序列：选择你感兴趣的目的基因，首先查阅文献，如果已有报道并提供了该基因在 Genbank 中的 ID 号，可直接在美国国家生物技术信息中心（NCBI）中搜索其详细信息。登录 http：//www. ncbi. nlm. nih. gov，先选择核酸数据库，点击下拉框选择 Nucleotide，再把 Genbank ID 号输入搜索框，点击 Search，如图 25-1 所示。

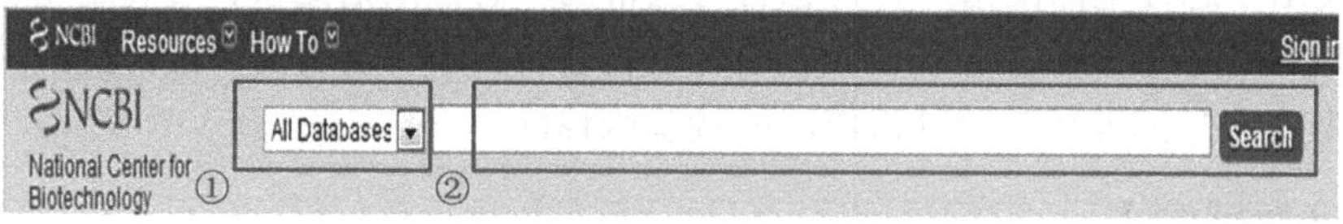

图 25-1 查找目的基因步骤 1

如果只是知道基因的名字，则搜索框中输入基因名称，点击 Search。通常会产生大量的搜索结果，例如搜索人乙醛脱氢酶-2 基因，点击 Search 后进入如下界面（图 25-2），共有 700 余条结果。

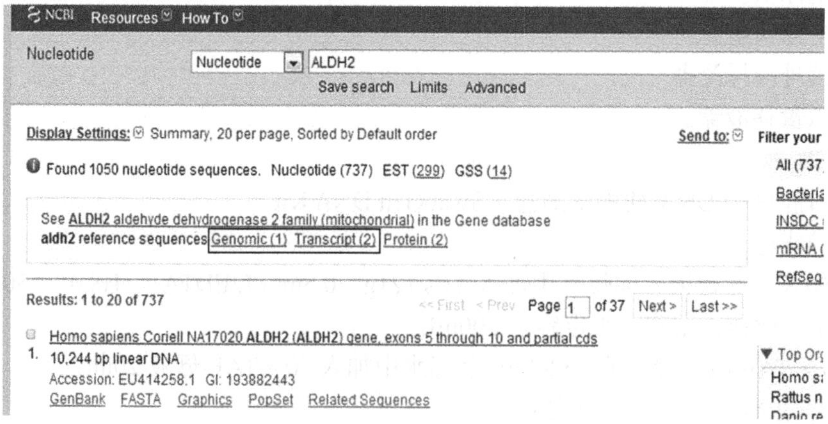

图 25-2 查找目的基因步骤 2

真核生物基因通常是断裂基因，含有大量内含子，序列庞大。若查看全基因序列，可点击 Genomic；如果只想获取转录区，点击 Transcript 查看转录本（图 25-2），点击后进入如下界面（图 25-3）。

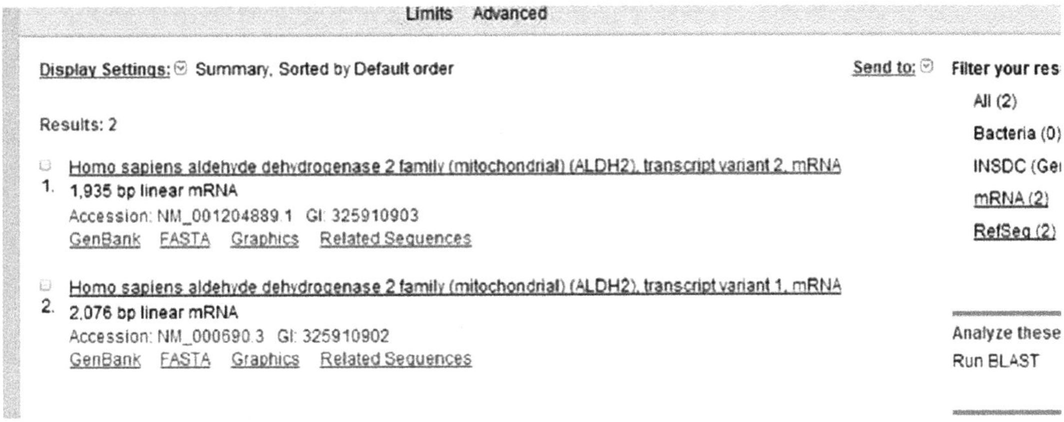

图 25-3　查找目的基因步骤 3

一些基因通过转录后加工，通常不止一个转录本，例如此处的 ALDH2。根据以往的报道和基因的说明选择所需要的序列。点击后进入图 25-4 所示的界面。

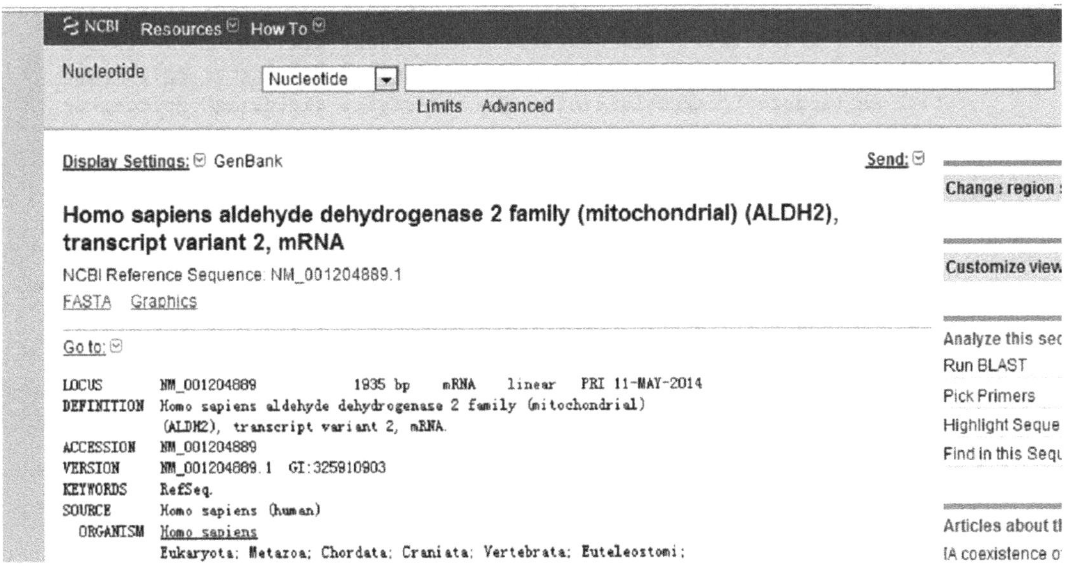

图 25-4　查找目的基因步骤 4

图 25-4 所示界面中有关于该基因信息的详尽描述，可直接到页面底部查看基因序列（图 25-5）。

（2）设计引物：参考实验 24。

```
ORIGIN
        1 attggctgcc gcgcggggcg gggagcgggg tcggctcagt ggccctgaga ccctagctct
       61 gctctcggtc cgctcgctgt ccgctagccc gctgcgatgt tgcgcgctgc cgcccgcttc
      121 gggccccgcc tgggccgccg cctcttgtca gccgccgcca cccaggccgt gcctgccccc
      181 aaccagcagc ccgaggtctt ctgcaaccag attttcataa acaatgaatg gcacgatgcc
      241 gtcagcagga aaacattccc caccgtcaat ccgtccactg gagaggtcat ctgtcaggta
      301 gctgaagggg acaaggcctt ggagaccctg gacaatggca agccctatgt catctcctac
      361 ctggtggatt tggacatggt cctcaaatgt ctccggtatt atgccggctg ggctgataag
      421 taccacggga aaaccatccc cattgacgga gacttcttca gctacacacg ccatgaacct
      481 gtgggggtgt gcgggcagat cattccgtgg aatttcccgc tcctgatgca agcatggaag
      541 ctgggcccag ccttggcaac tggaaacgtg gttgtgatga aggtagctga gcagacaccc
      601 ctcaccgccc tctatgtggc caacctgatc aaggaggctg gctttccccc tggtgtggtc
      661 aacattgtgc ctggatttgg ccccacggct ggggccgcca ttgcctccca tgaggatgtg
      721 gacaaagtgg cattcacagg ctccactgag attggccgcg taatccaggt tgctgctggg
      781 agcagcaacc tcaagagagt gaccttggag ctggggggga agagccccaa catcatcatg
      841 tcagatgccg atatggattg ggccgtggaa caggcccact tcgccctgtt cttcaaccag
      901 ggccagtgct gctgtgccgg ctcccggacc ttcgtgcagg aggacatcta tgatgagttt
      961 gtggagcgga gcgttgcccg ggccaagtct cgggtggtcg ggaacccctt tgatagcaag
     1021 accgagcagg ggccgcaggt ggatgaaact cagtttaaga agatcctcgg ctacatcaac
     1081 acggggaagc aagagggggc gaagctgctg tgtggtgggg gcattgctgc tgaccgtggt
     1141 tacttcatcc agcccactgt gtttggagat gtgcaggatg gcatgaccat cgccaaggag
     1201 gagatcttcg ggccagtgat gcagatcctg aagttcaaga ccatagagga ggttgttggg
     1261 agagccaaca attccacgta cgggctggcc gcagctgtct tcacaaagga tttggacaag
     1321 gccaattacc tgtcccaggc cctccaggcg ggcactgtgt gggtcaactg ctatgatgtg
     1381 tttggagccc agtcaccctt tggtggctac aagatgtcgg ggagtggccg ggagttgggc
     1441 gagtacgggc tgcaggcata cactgaagtg aaaactgtca cagtcaaagt gcctcagaag
     1501 aactcataag aatcatgcaa gcttcctccc tcagccattg atggaaagtt cagcaagatc
     1561 agcaacaaaa ccaagaaaaa tgatccttgc gtgctgaata tctgaaaaga gaaatttttc
     1621 ctacaaaatc tcttgggtca agaaagttct agaatttgaa ttgataaaca tggtgggttg
     1681 gctgagggta agagtatatg aggaaccttt taaacgacaa caatactgct agctttcagg
     1741 atgattttta aaaaatagat tcaaatgtgt tatcctctct ctgaaacgct tcctataact
     1801 cgagtttata ggggaagaaa aagctattgt ttacaattat atcaccatta aggcaactgc
     1861 tacaccctgc tttgtattct gggctaagat tcattaaaaa ctagctgctc ttaacttaca
     1921 aaaaaaaaaa aaaaa
```

图 25-5　查找目的基因步骤 5

（3）配制反应体系：在冰浴中，将以下成分依次加入无菌 PCR 管中：

10×PCR 缓冲液	2.5μL
dNTP 混合物（2mmol/L）	2μL
引物 1（10pmol）	1μL
引物 2（10pmol）	1μL
Taq 聚合酶（2U/μL）	0.2μL
DNA 模板（0.25μg/μL）	2μL

加蒸馏水至 25 μL，混匀后稍加离心。

（4）PCR 扩增：在 PCR 仪上运行以下程序：

预变性：	94℃，5min
变性：	94℃，30s
退火：	X℃，30s（X 通常比引物熔解温度（T_m）低 5℃）

延伸： 72℃，30s

39 次循环

末次循环后延伸：72℃，10min

（5）限制性酶切：利用软件 Primer Premier 5.0 寻找酶切位点，选择相应的限制性核酸内切酶，酶切体系及反应条件参照酶试剂说明书。

（6）电泳检测酶切产物：取酶切产物 5～10μL，用 3%琼脂糖凝胶电泳进行检测，同时加 DNA 分子量标准作对照，紫外检测仪下观察并分析结果。

4. 统计与分析 根据限制性内切酶位点的有无得到一个 1（酶切位点存在）、0（酶切位点不存在） 数据矩阵，统计所有样品的基因型，根据需要可用于遗传进化、疾病相关性、群体遗传学等多方面的分析。

【思考题】

1. 分析基因多态性还有什么方法，各自的优缺点是什么？
2. 试举一例说明通过检测患者的基因多态性研究如何指导个性化用药。

（王含彦）

Experiment 25 Gene Polymorphism Analysis of Humans

【Purposes】

1. To learn the important role of genetic polymorphisms in elucidating human susceptibility and tolerance to disease and toxicants, the diversity of clinical manifestations of disease, and the responsiveness to drug therapy.

2. To learn the principles and research methods of gene polymorphism.

【Principles】

Gene polymorphism, also known as genetic polymorphism, indicates two or more genotypes or alleles in a biological population. Human gene polymorphism helps clarify the important role of genetic polymorphisms in elucidating human susceptibility and tolerance to disease and toxicants, the diversity of clinical manifestations of disease, and the responsiveness to drug therapy. Second, polymorphism loci linked with the disease-causing gene can be used as diagnostic markers for genetic diseases and can provide basis for the separation and cloning of pathogenic gene. Third, the relativity analysis of diseases of unknown etiology and candidate gene polymorphism can be used for screening disease susceptibility genes.

Polymerase chain reaction-restriction fragment length polymorphism (PCR-RFLP) is a common DNA molecular marker. This technique is based on the following principle: First, the target gene is obtained by PCR amplification. If there are variations (polymorphism) existing in the target gene and the variations just exist in restriction enzyme recognition sites, which makes enzyme sites increase or disappear, the enzyme digestion produces different fragment sizes, which is termed fragment length polymorphism. Then the map of fragment length polymorphism is obtained by agarose gel electrophoresis to separate enzyme digestion production. Comparing the polymorphism map of the patient with a normal individual can determine whether variations exist. Therefore, PCR-RFLP can be applied to direct gene diagnosis by detecting point mutations in a known pathogenic gene and can also be used for indirect genetic diagnosis on linkage analysis as genetic markers.

【Apparatus and Reagents】

1. Apparatus

(1) Centrifuge.

(2) PCR thermocycle instrument.

(3) Electrophoresis apparatus.

(4) Power supply of electrophoresis apparatus.

(5) Ultraviolet detector.

(6) Micropipette.

2. Reagents

(1) Oral swab DNA extraction kit (SwabGen DNA Kit).

(2) Agarose.

(3) 50×TAE stock solution: Add Tris 121g, 0.5mol/L EDTA (pH8.0) 50mL and acetic acid 28.55mL into a beaker, stir and make the final volume of 500mL with distilled water.

(4) 1×TAE electrophoretic buffer solution: Add 20mL 50×TAE stock solution into 980mL distilled water.

(5) 6×loading buffer (please refer to Exp. 15).

(6) GoldView (please refer to Exp. 15).

(7) DNA marker.

【Procedures】

1. Genomic DNA extraction

(1) Collecting cells: Scrub both sides of your cheek 10 times using oral swabs to collect oral mucosal exfoliated cells. Transfer the swabs into a 2mL centrifugal tube, cut off the cotton and add 400μL buffer GA from the DNA extraction kit into the tube.

Note: do not eat or drink half an hour before sampling in case of food or drink contamination.

(2) DNA extraction: Operate according to the manual of kit.

(3) Sample retention: DNA production should be preserved at −20°C to keep DNA from degrading.

2. Detection of DNA concentration and purity

(1) Agarose gel electrophoresis for detecting the size of DNA fragment(please refer to Exp. 15).

(2) Ultraviolet spectroscopy for detecting the concentration and purity of DNA (please refer to Exp. 19)

After determining the DNA concentration, dilute the DNA samples to 0.25μg/μL using distilled water and store them at −20°C.

3. PCR-RFLP analysis

(1) Seeking the nucleotide sequence of the target gene: Choose a target gene of interest. First, research literature for the gene ID using Genbank. You can search for detailed information regarding a gene based on its ID in National Center for Biotechnology Information (NCBI). Log into http://www. ncbi. nlm. nih. gov, select the nucleic acid database, click on the drop-down box to select *Nucleotide*, input the Genbank ID into the search box,and then click on the *Search* button, as shown in Fig. 25-1.

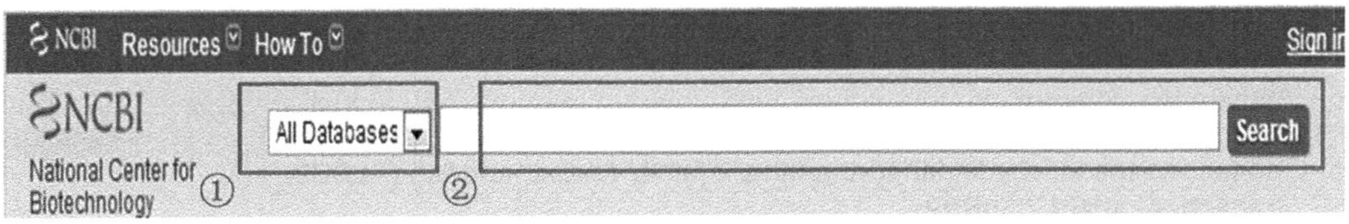

Fig. 25-1 Step 1 for seeking a gene of interest

If you only know the gene name, input the name into the search box, then click on the *Search* button. Generally, there will be a large number of search results. For example, searching human acetaldehyde dehydrogenase 2 (ALDH2) gene produces more than 700 results as shown in Fig. 25-2.

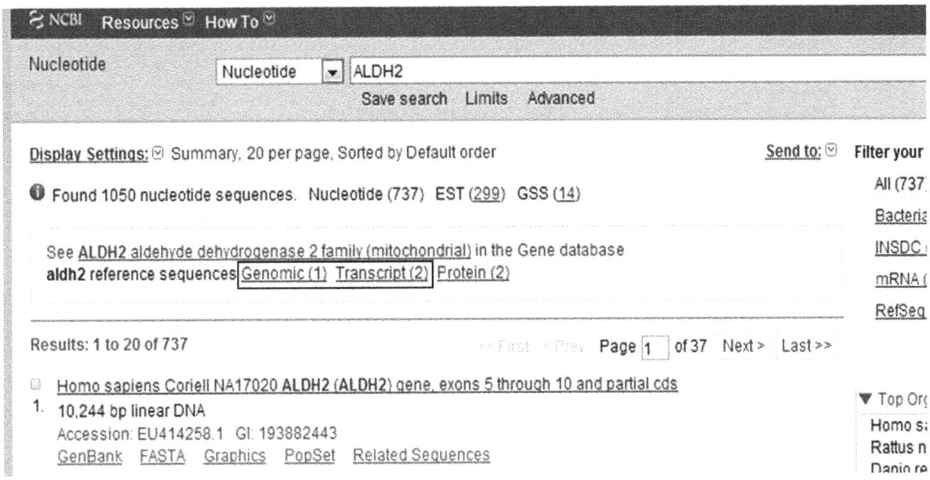

Fig. 25-2 Step 2 for seeking a gene of interest

An eukaryotic gene is usually a split gene, namely containing a lot of introns and has a large sequence. To determine the entire gene sequence, click on *Genomic*. Or click *Transcript* to check the transcription region (Fig. 25-2) , and enter the interface as Fig. 25-3.

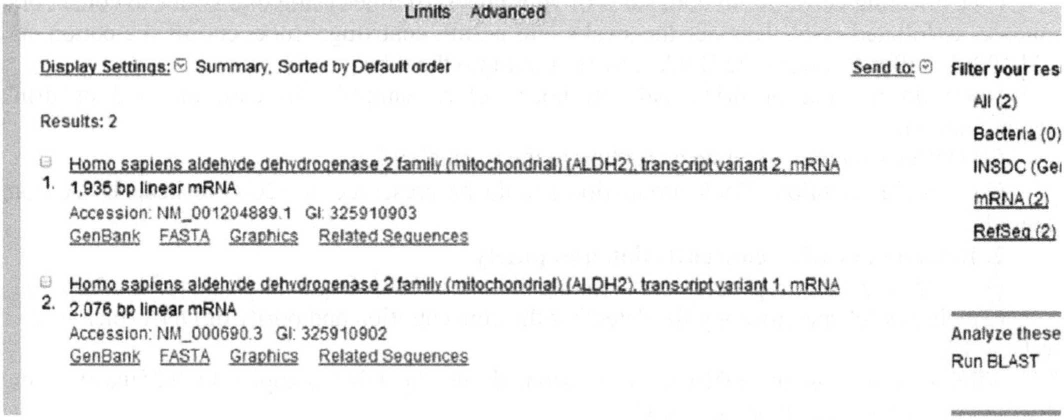

Fig. 25-3　Step 3 for seeking a gene of interest

Some genes produce more than one transcript by post-transcriptional processing, such as ALDH2. Choose the sequence that is needed based on previous reports and illustration of the gene. Then click what is selected and enter the interface as Fig. 25-4.

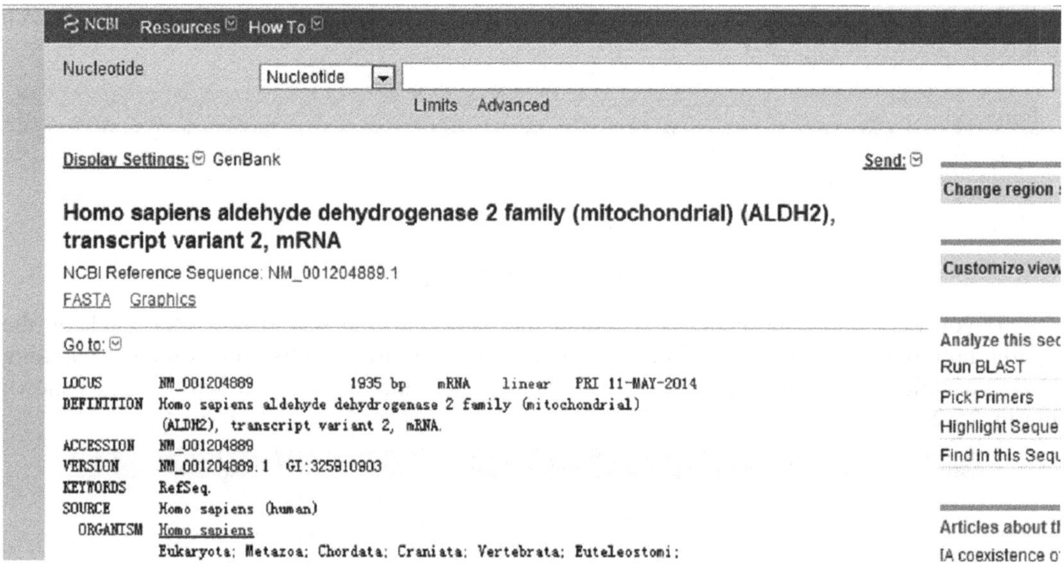

Fig. 25-4　Step 4 for seeking a gene of interest

This page has a detailed description of the gene, you can go directly to the bottom of the page to view the gene sequence (Fig. 25-5) .

(2) Designing primers: Please refer to Exp. 24.

```
ORIGIN
        1 attggctgcc gcgcggggcg gggagcgggg tcggctcagt ggccctgaga ccctagctct
       61 gctctcggtc cgctcgctgt ccgctagccc gctgcgatgt tgcgcgctgc cgcccgcttc
      121 gggccccgcc tgggccgccg cctcttgtca gccgccgcca cccaggccgt gcctgccccc
      181 aaccagcagc ccgaggtctt ctgcaaccag attttcataa acaatgaatg gcacgatgcc
      241 gtcagcagga aaacattccc caccgtcaat ccgtccactg gagaggtcat ctgtcaggta
      301 gctgaagggg acaaggcctt ggagaccctg gacaatggca agccctatgt catctcctac
      361 ctggtggatt tggacatggt cctcaaatgt ctccggtatt atgccggctg ggctgataag
      421 taccacggga aaaccatccc cattgacgga gacttcttca gctacacacg ccatgaacct
      481 gtgggggtgt gcgggcagat cattccgtgg aatttcccgc tcctgatgca agcatggaag
      541 ctgggcccag ccttggcaac tggaaacgtg gttgtgatga aggtagctga gcagacaccc
      601 ctcaccgccc tctatgtggc caacctgatc aaggaggctg gctttccccc tggtgtggtc
      661 aacattgtgc ctggatttgg ccccacggct ggggccgcca ttgcctccca tgaggatgtg
      721 gacaaagtgg cattcacagg ctccactgag attggccgcg taatccaggt tgctgctggg
      781 agcagcaacc tcaagagagt gaccttggag ctggggggga agagccccaa catcatcatg
      841 tcagatgccg atatggattg ggccgtggaa caggcccact tcgccctgtt cttcaaccag
      901 ggccagtgct gctgtgccgg ctcccggacc ttcgtgcagg aggacatcta tgatgagttt
      961 gtggagcgga gcgttgcccg ggccaagtct cgggtggtcg ggaacccctt tgatagcaag
     1021 accgagcagg ggccgcaggt ggatgaaact cagtttaaga agatcctcgg ctacatcaac
     1081 acggggaagc aagaggggc gaagctgctg tgtggtgggg gcattgctgc tgaccgtggt
     1141 tacttcatcc agcccactgt gtttggagat gtgcaggatg gcatgaccat cgccaaggag
     1201 gagatcttcg ggccagtgat gcagatcctg aagttcaaga ccatagagga ggttgttggg
     1261 agagccaaca attccacgta cgggctggcc gcagctgtct tcacaaagga tttggacaag
     1321 gccaattacc tgtcccaggc cctccaggcg ggcactgtgt gggtcaactg ctatgatgtg
     1381 tttggagccc agtcaccctt tggtggctac aagatgtcgg ggagtggccg ggagttgggc
     1441 gagtacgggc tgcaggcata cactgaagtg aaaactgtca cagtcaaagt gcctcagaag
     1501 aactcataag aatcatgcaa gcttcctccc tcagccattg atggaaagtt cagcaagatc
     1561 agcaacaaaa ccaagaaaaa tgatccttgc gtgctgaata tctgaaaaga gaaatttttc
     1621 ctacaaaatc tcttgggtca agaaagttct agaatttgaa ttgataaaca tggtgggttg
     1681 gctgagggta agagtatatg aggaaccttt taaacgacaa caatactgct agctttcagg
     1741 atgattttta aaaaatagat tcaaatgtgt tatcctctct ctgaaacgct tcctataact
     1801 cgagtttata ggggaagaaa aagctattgt ttacaattat atcaccatta aggcaactgc
     1861 tacaccctgc tttgtattct gggctaagat tcattaaaaa ctagctgctc ttaacttaca
     1921 aaaaaaaaaa aaaaa
```

Fig. 25-5 Step 5 for seeking a gene of interest

(3) Making a reaction system: In an ice bath, add the following components sequentially to a sterile PCR tube:

10×PCR buffer	2.5μL
dNTP mix (2mmol/L)	2μL
Primer 1 (10pmol)	1μL
Primer 2 (10pmol)	1μL
Taq polymerase (2U/μL)	0.2μL
DNA template (0.25μg/μL)	2μL

Add distilled water to make the final reaction volume of 25 μL and gently centrifuge after mixing well.

(4) PCR amplification: The following program should be followed using a PCR thermocycle instrument:

Initial denaturation:	94°C, 5min
Denaturation:	94°C, 30s
Annealing:	X°C, 30s (X is 5°C lower than T_m of primer)

Extension: 72°C, 30s

39 cycles

Final extension: 72°C, 10 min

(5) Restriction enzyme digestion: Enzyme digestive sites can be identified using software of Primer Premier 5.0 where appropriate restriction enzymes could be chosen. Please refer to the enzyme kit manual for the enzyme cutting system and reaction conditions.

(6) Detection of digestion production using electrophoresis: Detect 5–10μL digestion products by 3% agarose gel electrophoresis with a DNA marker control. Observe and analyze the gel using an ultraviolet detector.

4. Data analysis Set up a data matrix of 1 (presence of enzymatic cutting sites) and 0 (Absence of enzymatic cutting sites) based on restriction endonuclease sites. Collect all sample genotypes that can be analyzed for genetic evolution, correlation with disease and population genetics.

【Questions】

1. Are there alternative methods for gene polymorphism analysis? What are the advantages and disadvantages for each method?

2. Provide an example showing how a patient's gene polymorphism can guide personalized medicine.

(Wang Hanyan)

附录　实验室安全须知

1. 首次进入生物化学实验室需提前阅读实验室规则要求。

2. 实验室内禁止饮水、进食、抽烟及化妆。

3. 在实验室内需始终穿着实验服，禁止穿拖鞋进入。

4. 熟悉《工作场所健康与安全（危险物质）条例》。任何泄漏或溢出必须及时正确处理。

5. 在熟悉正确操作程序之前不可开始仪器操作。发现仪器异常情况及时报告给实验室指导教师。

6. 实验完毕及时清理实验台及通风橱等工作区域。

7. 实验完毕彻底清洗所有用过的玻璃器皿。

8. 所有人员需熟悉实验室紧急情况处理程序及相关设备的使用。

9. 不可用嘴吸取任何液体。正确使用移液管及洗耳球。

10. 出现意外情况及时报告。

Appendix　Laboratory Safety Procedures

1. Read the laboratory rules and requirements before you first enter a biochemistry lab.

2. Avoid drinking, eating, smoking or using cosmetics in the laboratory.

3. Laboratory coats must be worn all the time. Sandals are not acceptable.

4. Be familiar with the *Regulations of Health and Safety at Work (Hazardous Substances)*. All spills must be cleaned immediately and properly.

5. Do not use any instrument until you have read their respective instructions and consulted with instructors. Please immediately report any equipment malfunctions.

6.Working areas (benches, fume cupboards, etc.) should be properly cleaned once work is completed.

7. Thoroughly wash and rinse all used glassware.

8. All persons need to be familiar with laboratory emergency procedures and the use of related equipment.

9. Pipetting using your mouth is NOT acceptable. Use pipettes and ear wash bulb properly.

10. An instructor must be notified immediately in the case of an accident.

参考文献

陈牧, 2009. 生物化学实验讲义(南京大学自编讲义) .

何开跃, 李关荣, 2013. 生物化学实验(双语). 北京: 科学出版社.

Lee P Y, Costumbrado J, Hsu C Y, 2012. Agarose gel electrophoresis for the separation of DNA fragments. Journal of Visualized Experiments, 62: e3923.

Lucotte G, Baneyx F, 1993. Introduction to Molecular Cloning Techniques. Oxford: Wiley-Blackwell.

Lyklema J, 2005. Fundamentals of Interface and Colloid Science. Waltham: Academic Press.

Sambrook J, Russell D W, 2001. Molecular Cloning: A Laboratory Manual. 3rd ed. New York: Cold Spring Harbor Laboratory Press.

Schochetman G, Ou C-Y, Jones W K, 1988. Polymerase chain reaction. The Journal of Infectious Diseases, 158(6): 1154-1157.